A FRESH START

For A New Age Relationship

by

Charles D. Leviton & Stephanie Hill

Synergy House   1979   Costa Mesa, California

Printed in the United States of America.

Design and pre-press production by Padre Productions, San Luis Obispo CA

ISBN: 0-934962-00-6

Library of Congress Cataloging in Publication Data

Library of Congress Catalog Card No.: 79-66745

Leviton, Charles and Hill, Stephanie

    A fresh start
    1. Psychology   2. Personality Development

Costa Mesa, CA.: Synergy House

212 p.

7911   790720

Synergy House   P.O. Box 1827   Costa Mesa CA 92626

Dedication

We dedicate this book to our "miracle" child, Sean Christopher, who was literally born in the midst of our "labor" on this manuscript, and has helped to affect many of our own learnings and growth.

May Sean and the other "New Age" children of our world reap the benefits of being reared by "New Age" parents with "New Age" values and relationships.

Acknowledgements

Many people have played direct and indirect roles in the development and refinement of our ideas and writing skills. Our deepest thanks go to the hundreds of clients who have passed through our lives and shared with us their struggles and growth.

They will find themselves indelibly in these pages, though we have changed names and some facts to protect individual privacy.

Specially we are indebted to Lachlan and Karen MacDonald for the editing and packaging that has been invaluable. Their professional guidance has been an indispensable asset to presenting our work.

Photography: Front Cover—Steve Kaufman
                Back Cover—Mike Reidling
                Art Work—Bernard A. Brown
Printed By: Apple Graphics
                Stanton, CA

Contents

Introduction

Reading This Book May Be Dangerous . . . To Your Neurosis

Reading this book may be dangerous. . to your neurosis. Like many others you may be most interested in self-actualization and personal growth from a distance. Perhaps you would like to experience it vicariously through the writings and lecturings of others, but are hesitant to take the risks and feel the pain of the real thing.

This is not an uncommon feeling. Many times, when giving a public lecture, we recognize the same feeling in the audience. People flock to hear about "Open Marriage," "Self Actualization," and "Intimacy" as a fantasy daydream of "what might have been." This occurs much in the same way as children dream about slaying dragons or teenagers imagine inheriting a million dollars. ("It will never happen to me, but let me dream of what it would have been like.")

We ask, "Do people really want to be better?" For instance, the sexual revolution of morals and mores has produced reams of written and pictorial information in the areas of sex pleasure and performance, even jumping to the peak of the best-seller lists and financial profit-making. That trend has proven only one thing: people are interested in, and turned on by, voyeuristically sharing other people's sexual experiences and fantasies, even to the point of sometimes preferring them to the real thing or reading about them in order to "prepare" for the real thing. They do not necessarily plan to change. But we believe that there are many persons who sincerely want to change their lives.

This book is written for those who *do* want to experience life differently, who are willing to go out on a limb where they've never been before, who *will* choose to search their inner being for new truth . . . and finding this truth, will be strong enough to *act* on it . . . to discover a scary but exciting new way in which to live.

One of our major goals in facilitating therapeutic change, is to take major, life-changing truth and reduce it to more simple terms and easy-to-digest principles that anyone can use to be better tomorrow than they are today. We call this *A Fresh Start*.

From our experience, *A Fresh Start* is especially needed in the sector of society where stress is greatest, the relationships of marriage and family. That's why we call our process *A Fresh Start . . . for A New Age Relationship*.

Therapy is one of the few situations where people pay someone $25 to $100 per hour to prove the expert can't help them. As psychiatrist Eric Berne would say, "There is a payoff in there somewhere." Apparently such people get their money's worth.

We hear the insurance truism that "married people are healthier, live longer, and are better adjusted emotionally, than their unmarried counterparts"—and that scares the hell out of us.

That says less about marriage than it does about people. Psychologist Abraham Maslow estimated that less than two per cent of the American population is what he calls "self-actualizing"—really healthy people.

Using the bell-shaped statistical curve we could come up with only 2.28 per cent "A" people and approximately 16 per cent "A" and "B" people, those at least above average on a scale of emotional stability and happiness. We cannot assume that all of them are happily married, but we would hope that they would at least be less likely to remain in a damaging marriage and would instead go looking for a better one. Even though people are divorcing in increasing numbers today, (primarily to find happiness in a better marriage, not because they don't wish to be married), it is probably still safe to say there are more *unhappy* marriages than good ones. But the actuarial fact remains that "married people are healthier, live longer and are better adjusted emotionally."

Evidently the *illusion* of comfort that comes from the familiar status quo, even in a sick and destructive marriage, could account for the above results. Marriage for some is a preferred choice over the unknown and/or feared loneliness. Like the deprived child, some spouses would rather be beaten than ignored.

Recently at a health conference, a medical doctor stated emphatically, from personal research and experience, that all psychic surgeries in the Philippines were fakery, without exception, but that the healings were genuine and real. While we can't comment on the validity of this statement, it illustrates how we feel about many marriages and about many clients who seek counseling. The marriage is fakery and sick, but the person appears healthier than he or she would be alone. This is not to say it's good to stay in a bad marriage, but that it's time for more people to consider the alternatives.

A strong impetus in writing this book comes from our impatience and frustration at watching people revel in their unhappiness and cling to it with such religious passion, when so much better is available to them, *now*.

The thrust of this book is to encourage people to look at their disturbed relationships in hopes they'll change them. Healthy relationships don't just happen. They are products of relatively healthy and reasonably well-adjusted people, who are willing to take the calculated risks involved in the complicated process of loving and being loved.

A Fresh Start

Is there anyone burdened by the responsibilities of family, overwhelmed by the stresses of business, pressured by guilt and obligations, tormented by the fears of inadequacy and the doubts of his/her own humanness who has *not* cried out in despair and anguish for *A Fresh Start*, a new life, even a brand new identity?

No more children, spouse, parents, bills, responsibilities or obligations. Wipe the slate clean, start over, declare bankruptcy without the consequences of guilt and inner pain. Perhaps we've been driven to desperation and found ourselves praying that others, our boss, even our spouse or family members, would be wiped out by accident or calamity—an "act of God" that would relieve us of the decision and provide freedom without guilt and the risk of public exposure.

Occasionally we read about someone who mysteriously disappears and is accidently exposed years later, or we see a movie or TV story that catches our attention and focuses on this theme . . . *A Fresh Start.*

If parents, family, marriage, bills and work were all "doing it to me" as it feels, then why not start over; create a new and loving environment of caring people, purposeful work and financial success? We *all* want to believe we're the victims of life, who only need a little luck and a new chance to make it big.

Who hasn't felt like running away from home? The trouble is that the core of the problem comes along for the ride—ME! It's true that some people *do* change jobs and occupations, divorce and remarry, move across country and start over, declare bankruptcy and sometimes even change their names.

Others carry such a heavy weight of "responsibility" they go down with their ship of state and never recover; but most of us just resign ourselves to fate and plug along in cemetery-like ruts.

How many of us in the cold light of another day, might say to our-selves: "I married the wrong person, had kids at the wrong time, stuck myself in a deadend job, mired the budget in untenable debt and see absolutely no way to get out. I'm trapped in my own choices, mired in dependencies, rendered helpless by my own lack of understanding and insight. Are there no solutions? Are my mistakes unpardonable and beyond redemption? How did I ever get into this mess?"

How often do we wonder:

WHAT *IS* REALITY?

WHAT *IS* FAIR?

Why must my rights always YIELD to those of my loved ones?

This book offers you *A Fresh Start* . . .

Not permission to run away from home and life . . .

but permission to take a fresh look at the core of the problem . . . ME. . .

get a fresh perspective of HOW I did all this to me and WHY . . . plus . . .

Some fresh solutions to old situations, born out of fresh under-standing and awareness, supported by fresh self-confidence and re-newed self-image . . .

moved along by a fresh supply of courage and strength.

Can we say:

I CAN start over . . .

DEATH OF THE OLD . . .

BIRTH OF THE NEW . . .

within me . . .

by me . . .

for me!

Stripped of neurotic guilt and phony obligations I am free to expe-rience and express the true, authentic self that will draw new kinds of relationships and discover a different sense of success (perhaps with the same people, perhaps with others).

No longer bound to *act* responsible against my will, I can be free to express the deepest level of genuine responsibility that is me . . . true to my character and integrity, appropriate to my choices and relationships.

A Fresh Start entails moving from self-hate to self-love; from mar-rying my opposite to marrying myself; from defensive hostility to genuine exposure and vulnerability; from being a dependent child to being a mature and healthy adult.

Easy? No!

Possible? Yes!

One of the reasons many people do not accomplish this fresh start more readily is that our society tends to worship at the shrine of "tact" and "diplomacy," rather than "directness" and "honesty". We become overly concerned with protecting feelings with "peace at any cost," because confrontation of real feelings is scary to both the conveyor of truth and the receiver. So, we often go to great lengths to justify the avoidance of this anxiety. As a matter of fact, directness and honesty can be tactful and diplomatic or can be a club on the head, depending on whether we want to improve the relationship or "distance" it.

Emotional Divorce

You can't start in a easterly direction without turning away from the west. You can't start a new type of relating without releasing the old. You can't have a new marriage until you divorce the old one, and *all* bad marriages need an *emotional* divorce, whether or not they lead to a legal one. In fact, what we call "emotional divorce" may be just what your marriage needs!

An emotional divorce is the willingness to be real with one's feelings, taking whatever risks are necessary to improve the communication and the relationship—even though you realize that you have no control over your spouse's reaction and they *might* just turn tail and run. When your own integrity and happiness become more important than the "security" of a bad marriage, you become willing to risk divorce in order to improve the marriage.

Therapists know that the biggest problem in therapy is not getting people to reach out for something better, but to let go of what's bad. The drowning man clings desperately to the seaweed at the bottom of the ocean (the bad part of the relationship) and won't let you pull him to the top and air (something better) because the trip might be too painful or scary (or, too fast) and he really doesn't know if he can make it to the top anyway. (If you are going to drown, at least you have the seaweed to comfort you.)

There is no guarantee you'll make it to the top, but the world needs people who'd rather drown half-way and know they tried, then cling to the old familiar seaweed and die in comfortable surroundings (taking a few loved ones and children with them for company). Some people find exhilaration in the trip, stretching their muscles, testing their strength, reaching out to the unknown adventure, passing through cloudy and uncharted, even dangerous waters, so that the effort itself makes life worth-while and worth living. Success is not always found in achieving a pre-set goal; sometimes it's the glory of the race itself—the challenge of the test.

Part I
How To Break The Stranglehold Of The Past

This book is for people who want to experience the challenge in the unknown, rather than to live in fear of it; whose goal is to grow, rather than to remain sedentary; who'd rather stretch out expectantly than pull back.

I. A New Age Relationship

A new age relationship is not just between people but also consists of a new way of relating to oneself as a human being. There can be no viable change in a relationship without a preceding change in the way one perceives and relates to oneself. It takes healthy people to create healthy relationships with others. The problems *between* us always start *within* us and luckily so do the solutions.

A new age relationship provides a safe environment for concurrent learning and growth.

In order to have a fresh start toward this new age relationship, a *new language* must be developed and learned. It is a language not inherent in human beings nor is it preached or taught in most schools, churches or homes.

Actually, good communication is very self-centered and self-serving, as well as other-centered and other-serving. It requires between two people a strong desire to create a language *they* understand and can apply practically to their lives.

The golden thread of all religions touches on this language slightly with the admonition to "Do unto others as you would have them do unto you" and "Love thy neighbor as thyself". We would interpret that to mean "*Be* unto others as you would have them *be* unto you." . . . with the emphasis on *my* responsibility for *my* beingness. While treatment of the others is important and necessary, we can't lose track of ourselves through making the *others* more important than *I* am in the transaction. How can one "love another as thyself" until that love is experienced by the self?

"Love thy neighbor as thyself" pre-supposes that it is OK to love myself first and use that for a model of how to love others. Somewhere that notion got turned around so that we are taught to believe love for others is good and self-love is bad!

Individuals can create together, a way or language in which their innermost beings—experienced as individual personalities—can function undisturbed and unmanipulated, on a basis of mutual respect and mutual self-love.

This type of life-giving change is available to anyone who wants it. It is sad to see people turn away short when success, happiness and fulfillment are close enough for them to touch, if only they knew how to reach out.

The purpose of learning a new language is to enable you to communicate facts, feelings and needs more accurately and more easily and to be understood by one another. It *is not* the other person's primary responsibility to sort through the muck and mire and try to figure out what the !!!! you're saying, and *it is* your responsibility to be clear. Hopefully, the other will care enough about you to ask questions and make it easier to clarify your thoughts, but the primary responsibility for clarity rests with you.

Too often, we try to predict the response of the other in advance and *that* determines what we say. Usually, that involves our telling them what we think they *want* to hear, rather than the truth of *how we feel*. The real need of a "new language" is to *express* how we really feel and who we really are in a non-defensive, non-attacking, straight forward and informative way. And to encourage and expect a similar response! While we cannot control the response of others, this direct approach has by far the best "track record" in any sort of relationship exchange.

A Closer Look

So many of us are not at all happy with ourselves, with what we are or what we feel, think or do. We have a deepseated inner fear saying, "If you really knew me, you wouldn't like me." In spite of statements to the contrary, inwardly we think, "I know me and I don't like me." This seems to be the basis of many relationships. Often we find ourselves attracted to our opposites, because another person's traits are those we admire and desire for our own. Does he or she have qualities that can fill in the gaps for us and help us live with those faults in ourselves that we can least stomach? Is that the hidden agenda in most marriages?

Marriage is a powerful institution. It tends to bring out the closet craziness in us, to reveal weakness and faults we had even hidden from ourselves.

Differences between us become exaggerated and intense. The very essense of attraction may surprisingly become the irritant of discontent. "Why don't you think, feel and act like I do?" we wonder, or as the esteemed Professor Henry Higgins bitterly complained, "Why isn't a woman more like a man?"

There is a solution to this dilemma, but it requires some effort. In simple terms, we have to learn to like ourselves, accept all aspects of our personalities—both good and bad—and integrate them into a well-rounded, rather whole person. That process can lead to choosing and loving the only kind of person who qualifies to share this new, integrated and happily successful human being. In other words, someone equal to this self I now love. If this sounds terribly egotistical, read on, your values are about to be explored.

We don't necessarily have to be identical twins but we should be sufficiently similar to share values, goals and interests, able to talk the same language and enjoy the same "turn ons."

That's what *A Fresh Start* is all about.

We are presently in a transitional age of blurred relativity and varying degrees of gray with regard to man-woman gender roles and relationships in particular. While our culture seems to be grinding slowly away from the easily structured black and white concepts of chauvinism, there has been no direction to a clearly defined substitute which can allay our fears and quiet our anxieties.

A Fresh Start points a new direction for men and women, one that combines the best elements of self-loving, self-determination *and* responsibility along with meaningful dialogue and the sharing of oneself in nurturing interdependence.

A Fresh Start is not just another book on communication skills. Neither is it a Dale Carnegie-like course on getting people to like you, or a power-drive formula showing you how to manipulate others to get what you want.

In removing the barriers to true intimacy we have found there are four basic areas that must be confronted and dealt with in each of our lives—not only at the level of the intellect but also on a feeling level of experience.

First, all of us need to contact, be comfortable with, understand and nourish the deprived, needy child within us. One must become the caring, tender disciplined parent who is in tune with the child's pain or need and respond with true nourishment and proper guidance, with plenty of room for freedom of expression.

Too often a judgmental, authoritarian parent arises within us to dominate and control the spontaneity of the natural child within. The loving parent is neither rigidly authoritarian nor fearfully overindulgent when relating to the child within.

The *second* step is to resolve the negative parent relationships most of us experience and tend to carry over into our marriages, to contaminate them. We believe that healing and correcting the parental relationships will benefit all concerned. Where the parent refuses to cooperate or is unavailable, we offer concrete steps for overcoming this negative influence even without parental help.

The *third* step is in learning how to be in touch with, aware of and comfortable in experiencing the full range of human feelings at any one time and thereby being able to act on those feelings appropriately. A part of this process is simply to share this new awareness with the important others in our lives, and finding out that this sharing is more important than getting others or yourself to *change* and of itself promotes intimacy, love and tenderness.

One of the handicaps of this third step is the trauma of anger. So, *fourth*, we learn to deal with angry emotions and expressions, whether our own or someone else's. We offer many suggestions of ways to explore the uses and abuses of anger and to discover its real value in the healing process.

As we accomplish these four essential steps, we discover how our inner struggles for self-identification often relate to our choice of a mate. Understanding this interrelation will give us insight into our struggles to improve external relationships.

These relationships are a product of the parent-child growth pattern and carry over into mate attraction, either in a negative or positive manner. Our basic need is to fully integrate the various subpersonalities (semi-autonomous personalities) within us into one integrated, comfortable whole. Unfortunately, this is where the problem arises. How often do we seek the outside help of a mate who fits the mold of our sub-personalities. We pick mates who are our opposites or who have undesirable traits. How much more satisfactory it would be to recognize and come to grips with some part of that "negative" trait within ourselves. This book will help you to discover the correlation between these inner and outer struggles and use each aspect to assist in the growth of the other.

A Fresh Start defines the barriers and roadblocks to change. It shows the correlations between one's external marital conflicts and internalized personal struggles. There are concrete insights, and self-help techniques for achieving both inner peace and relational satisfaction.

By relieving the reader from the pressures caused by the extremes of cultural and religous shock, it places him or her into a more realistic and truly loving atmosphere which is both supportive of the other person and nurturing to the self. In this atmosphere communication can then be at its best.

A Fresh Start can be used as a theoretical supplement and guide to assist in one's therapy if the reader is now seeking professional help. In addition, this book is written for those who have not sought the luxury of therapy or have been dissatisfied with it and are looking for a meaningful method of self-help.

Because our society is currently in a transition period, it is very difficult to define "what is" for the general population. We are in a flux of extremes and constant changes. In the next chapters we will attempt an overview of male/female cultural stereotypes and more recent reactions and counter-reactions to these.

Looking at these extremes and how they affect relationships will hopefully give us a springboard to the rest of the book: understanding how man/woman relationships correspond to our own internal struggle and growth and learning how to integrate both to bring the highest satisfaction.

II. The Old Language Of Love

There's (A Lot?) To Be Said For Male Chauvinism

Just a few years ago an article in the *Los Angeles Times* described a national survey of men and women to determine the effect of the Feminist Movement in their lives; 95% of the women and 97% of the men said it had not or did not touch their lives in any way. This makes two rather strong points: 1) people in general are not particularly aware of the many direct and indirect influences in their lives, and 2) while the 90% seems unnaturally biased and high, it is safe to say the majority of people prefer the old tried and true roles: passiveness, dependent women, jealousy and forced fidelity, controlling through fear and guilt, obligation over choice. Roles that continue in spite of the popularity of such concepts as "freedom to be me," new social mores, reversal of roles, equality for all and "open marriage."

A sad truth is, that when one's culture has taught for years the virtures of subservience and being taken care of, it is difficult to break out of the trap. We have to look no further than the welfare system to have plenty of evidence that both men and women find it appealing *not* to work when they don't have to in order to survive.

The nicest thing to say for male chauvinism is that it eliminates the need to think and make decisions, has the comfortable support of the gospel according to they ("they say") and thereby provides roles and rules by the majority vote. It is safe, secure, and predictable. It may not be the best potential, but it minimizes the gamble and also the pain. After all, it was good enough for mom and dad.

How can we properly define a chauvinistic approach to relationships?

In talking about Open and Closed Marriage contracts the O'Neils, in their book *Open Marriage*, quote the "Old" or "Closed" contract demands as follows (the parenthesis are ours):

1. *ownership of the mate* (if I own you and you own me, that spells security.)
2. *denial of self* (small price to pay for someone to be there when you need them.)
3. *playing the couples' game* (if we're together, neither one has to worry about the other being in a threatening place with someone else.)
4. *rigid role behavior* (predictable, comfortable and easy to respond to.)
5. *absolute fidelity* (who wants to worry about that subject?)
6. *total exclusivity* (why risk loneliness or loss for a little variety?)

The unrealistic expectations such as "it will last forever," "it means total commitment," "it will bring happiness, comfort and security," sound pretty damn good. Wouldn't we all like to be guaranteed a total commitment, lasting forever that brings happiness, comfort, and security? Why not?

The fact that there is no guarantee and that we are clinging to an *illusion* of security, seems to be for most people, beside the point. Better to kid yourself with illusions than face the reality of anxiety.

Why does change scare us? Why do we cling to the old, even when we have proof it has not brought us the desired results we say we want? Perhaps Margaret Mead said it most succinctly in her autobiography, *Blackberry Winter*, "The need to define who you are by the place in which you live remains intact, even when that place is defined by a single object." "The place in which you live" can be more psychological in context and powerful in motive than the house or apartment which is our address.

One asks: "Who am I?" The deep emotional response might be: "I am a person with very established and predictable ways of perceiving events, interpreting life, and relating to situations. I have an internalized picture or image of myself developed over the years and it's difficult to give it up . . . even if circumstances and my own desires tell me it is time to move on."

The cliche tells us "familiarity breeds contempt;" but (even more powerfully) it can also breed expectancy, comfort, calmness, and security. Some people are excited and turned on by the expectancy of the new experience; especially those whose self-image carries an expectancy of consistent and successful experiences—while others are immediately fearful of the possibility of failure and pain. Not even the most predictable person among us is immune to change.

The more these changes are connected to our deep inner self-identity, the greater the trauma involved. A raising or even lowering of salary may not be nearly so important as a change in job title or of assigned responsibility. The more important the life-change or transition, the deeper the result: child to adult, single to married, non-parent to parent.

We realize that truly for every gain there is a loss. Becoming independent means giving up primary dependency; the benefits of marriage must be weighed against the loss of single-ness; the freedom of not having to be responsible for the life of another is surrendered for the excitement and responsibility of parenthood. It is no coincidence that post-partum depression is one of life's most predictable and traumatic occurrences; giving birth is one of the few decisions in life we can't reverse, with consequences we find difficult to escape.

One of life's most secure absolutes has been the "divine right" of men to rule over women and her "divine right" to be taken care of and protected. For centuries she serviced his needs for sex, homemaker, mother of his children, and emotional support. He in turn cared for her material comforts and provided life-long security. Each promised eternal "parenting" till death do us part. Both men and women have found a comfortable happiness in this arrangement, and in our time giving it up has brought on a tremendous wave of anxiety and fear.

It is fairly easy to understand and even justify this arrangement in terms of a marriage where the woman has remained a "housewife-mother" for her husband and several children and therefore felt after 15-20 years of dependent subservience that she literally did not have the capabilities to survive financially or emotionally in a world where she had been so completely shut off from independence in most forms.

But emotional dependency and reality do not necessarily coincide. Alice was an 18-year-old unwed mother of a two-year old child when she came to therapy. She was on welfare, received no child support, and lived with a dominant mother who paid for her therapy. In a few months she had started training for a job as a beautician, confronted and broken the ties with her dominant mother, who subsequently threw her out, and even continued the therapy on her own. She found a source of inner strength and toughness that carried her through emotional jungles and environmental pitfalls with very little outside support.

More commonly we see people like Helen, 41 years old, with a teen-age daughter, a doctorate in School Administration and a $35,000 a year income from her position as an educator. She has been married 20 years to a man who never professed to love her and constantly threatened to leave if not given his way. They managed to share good sexual feelings but all his other interests involved competing in sports with his male friends. For years she denied the reality of this non-relationship and slowly buried herself in food, gaining about 50 extra pounds. One day her husband, Bob, found another woman and moved out. Helen came to therapy devastated, frightened, isolated and afraid to be alone. She described herself as without self-love, self-worth or pride, and had come seeking help in getting her husband back, preferring the relationship she had endured for 20 years to the prospect of "being alone." Even though she held no hope he would change, for her being married is "forever for better or worse." (How many use this empty rationalization to cover for a lack of courage to seek something better in life!)

Men are also not immune to this dependency pull. For example, Gordon, is a professional who is extremely successful, worth well in excess of a million dollars, deeply in love with a woman with whom he has had a three-year relationship. Unhappily married for over 20 years, Gordon came to therapy to discover why he can't get a divorce. There is enough income to support everyone's life style, Gordon's marriage love has been dead and buried, far longer than his affair has been alive and now he has found "true love" and everything he looks for in a partner and mate. But he can't leave. Is it security need, fear of the unknown, guilt, obligation, admitting failure, habit, public criticism? In therapy he meets Al, another professional in virtually identical circumstances. "What's wrong?" they ask. "Why can't we make a break.?"

While there is little doubt the old way has been jarred loose from its moorings, we have certainly not relinquished our hold on it. Furthermore, we not only have yet to achieve a new sense of man-woman relationship, we have yet to fully perceive what the final product is to become.

And Along Came Women's Lib

With all that has been said about change and its subsequent fear components, one of the most remarkable breakthroughs in history has to be the advent of Feminism. Somewhat confused and embittered, men might complain that "the female eunuch outmacho'd men," but she would reply with a certain pride that "I have no need to compete with or draw potency from men; I have my own source of energy potential and draw on that." Just when men were beginning to believe their own press clippings and had finally sold their wives on the double standard, along came the female chauvinists.

Suddenly there is a group of women who want equal pay, equal credit, equal opportunity, and a reversal of the double standard. Like any militant group trying to break the chains of slavery, some of them are tempted to try their hand with the whip.

The woman of today is competing in the market place, for equal dominance in the bedroom, for freedom from children and the mundane. The man who has been screaming for his wife to "get with it sexually" suddenly encounters a sexually demanding woman with even greater needs than his own. Instead of being turned-on and thrilled by this new emancipation, the man discovers fear and impotence . . . the cover of his God-like supremacy gone, he now finds it necessary to prove his masculinity in direct conflict rather than by pre-ordained authority.

What's more, they've even attempted to create their own law to make sure it's true with ERA—Equal Rights Amendment. "Equality of rights under law shall not be denied or abridged by the United States or by any State on account of sex." A simple and direct statement with complex and intangible ramifications.

What about the emotional impact of the woman's movement? It is relatively easy to see that the "macho" approach to life is often a cover-up for internalized and well- hidden insecurities and hostilities. It is an over-compensation for an inner fear of weakness. So the bully is often a coward, picking on a "safe" person. To an extent that has been true in the man-woman relationship; the emotional impact has been tremendous. A man who already fears women, who has seen them as capable of destroying or controlling him and, therefore, had to play "king of the mountain" in his home to keep that from happening, is suddenly stripped of his protection. Now he is forced to relate on "real" terms.

Impotence Replaces Frigidity—
Penis Envy Becomes Vagina Fear

A man whose wife was non-orgasmic and not a particularly good bed partner, complained bitterly about his needs not being met, but in many cases had some good advantages, too. Since it was "all her fault" that sex wasn't satisfactory, no one was judging his sexual performance, so why bother to try when she didn't like it anyway? Then he could further measure himself by indulging in casual affairs with a series of liberated, "good" sex partners. Since they were casual and not intimate, it didn't matter much to him if he satisfied them and so his performance is still not under judgment. Yet he stayed married. If they were so good and his wife so bad, why didn't he marry one of them? Because then he'd be on the spot and have to produce expected results as an equal partner rather than a consumer of the merchandise. When wives began to take their needs seriously, that's exactly what happened; they demanded equal partnership.

When sex therapists Masters and Johnson first started, they would treat the dysfunctional partner only. "Send your wife to St. Louis to become functional and orgasmic." She'd come home turned-on and orgasmic and the husband would become immediately impotent. "Now that she has needs, can I meet them?" Fear of inadequacy is the major cause of impotence. When men lose their rigid backbone of male supremacy, they go limp in other places as well. Masters and Johnson corrected this by treating both partners together, seeing it as a problem of the relationship, not the person.

We think it is only fair to point out, however, that the well known (by women at least)fragile male ego was pretty bitterly attacked by a hostility difficult to believe.

There was now a new breed of cat—the Female Chauvinist, resplendent in all her glory. Where many men are actually *unaware* of their hostility toward women (or feelings of superiority over women) and *very aware* of their desire for sexual involvement, often including feelings of love, desire and need, the Female Chauvinist is openly angry, hostile, and vindictive. Many of them are so deeply involved in this struggle against men that they find it impossible to experience a warm, loving relationship with one. This presents an even more scary picture for men, that some women really do hate and are out to "get" them. In middle-of-the road America, the cutting edge of any movement has to be pretty far out in order to nudge the great majority of "average" folks even a few inches, and that's our frustration with both sides. One is too far out and the other too hard to move. Let's face it folks, it's pretty difficult for most men to relate to someone who looks like Gloria Steinhem and hits like Muhammed Ali. Female chauvinism was a direct reaction to male chauvinism. Hopefully, these women are moving from this extreme toward the middle ground of true integration.

To show how deeply ingrained chauvinism is in our culture, even some therapists—who are supposed to be aware of such biases—are not immune to its lure. The Broverman study, a recent survey of clinical psychologists, asked this question: "What do you consider the qualities of a mentally healthy person?" The study asked them to identify the desirable qualities of male and female. Going directly to Webster's Dictionary, the professionals equated healthy males with qualities defined as masculine and healthy females with those defined as feminine. Healthy males were considered aggressive, assertive, non-emotional, and objective. Healthy females were agreed to be non-aggressive, passive, dependent, and very emotional. *But the traits of the male and the human being were almost identical.* Evidently a woman could either be a healthy female or a healthy human being.

She could not be both. Under these definitions neither male or female could qualify as healthy. We contend that *all* of us are both masculine and feminine and possess all the qualities of both. To the extent we are unable to experience and express these qualities in appropriate ways at appropriate times, we are *not* mentally sound or functioning well.

A healthy man would be aggressive and assertive as the need requires, and *so* would a healthy female. Moreover, it is foolish to believe that a healthy man is non-emotional and only objective. People are a combination of the intellectual, emotional and spiritual. To be a truly self-actualized, fully functioning human being requires an integration and synthesis of the full range of these qualities. One's emotions and intellect must work in harmony with each other for the fullest benefit. A non-aggressive, passive, dependent, and very emotional woman would not be treated in a therapeutic setting as having reached an ideal psychological state, but as a woman with a deeply serious problem who was a drain on her husband and family and a handicap to herself.

There is an appropriate time and place for the experiencing and expressing of all these traits for *both* men and women. *But* there is also a place for independence, assertively taking one's needs seriously and objective decision making, based on listening to what one's emotions have to say.

Women may often be stereotyped as "castrating bitches," "histrionic, manipulative and seductive" or "hysterical" and "depressed." Counseling experiences indicate that these women *do* exist and are usually found married to aggressive, self-centered, non-emotional, intellectualized men who: 1) talk them out of their feelings; 2) run away from any emotional exchange; 3) cannot communicate on a personal level and; 4) know nothing about intimacy, tenderness, compassion, or understanding.

When a woman is taught to take her needs seriously and how to present them assertively, she has little need for hysteria, manipulation and bitchiness. When men are taught not to be afraid of emotions (both theirs and hers) and how to communicate feelings on an intimate, revealing, non-defensive level, women have less need for destructive tactics and men less need to run away or withdraw into silence. One of the goals of therapy for women is to help them have equal access to all aspects of their being. Women receive (from society) a tremendous amount of support and encouragement to be nurturing; to nurture their friends, husbands, children. But they draw the line at themselves because they have also been taught to be self-sacrificing.

The result is a martyr who does not know or experience her own self-worth. All mature, nurturing love for others includes and is based on nurturing love for self and an expectancy of receiving this nurturing love *from* others as it is needed. We suggest that such a woman consider three steps toward becoming more balanced:

1. take the *compulsion* off nurturing others;
2. begin to nurture herself; and
3. begin to express all her feelings—especially anger.

While society expects women to be intuitive and have a lot of feeling and emotion, it often devalues and degrades women for experiencing these same things. An interesting contradiction in the Broverman Study is that the stereotyped female qualities of nurturing, intuitive understanding, perception, and concern for others are also seen as the qualities that make a good psychologist. Since most therapists are men (and one would hope most therapists are "healthy"), then a healthy male-therapist should have good touch with his inner feminine self. This paradox is often overlooked.

A problem with both chauvinism and feminism is that they tend to emphasize extremes rather than integration and balance. People can easily fall into this trap of extremism in the pursuit of comfort, for the simple truth is that we tend to be more comfortable with one facet of our nature than to be integrated as a whole. Often this is on a continuum from angry to fearful, for instance. The person who finds it comfortable to be angry, generally uses it as a defense against feelings of hurt, embarrassment, tenderness, or vulnerability. The person who finds it comfortable to cry and express hurt is generally out of touch with the emotions of anger and strength.

One might then conclude that "angry" people need to learn how to be vulnerable and "vulnerable" people need to learn how to express anger. It's all part of integration.

An added truth is that these opposites often marry each other . . . probably because they are looking for that missing ingredient in themselves and also because they couldn't put up with a "double dose" of what they are now.

If these opposites are not too far apart in temperament, the blend might very well strengthen the marriage and each individual. Each softens his or her own position and moves closer to the center and integration, and there is a nice complement between them. If these opposites are too far apart, they tend to polarize or irritate each other.

Fundamentalists Fight Back
For Pedestals And Spousal Support

All that glitters is not gold. With emancipation and equality comes responsibility and loss of fringe benefits. Society and the courts start to take women seriously and some women find they can't have total freedom and keep all their goodies. Divorce laws stop giving the rewards to "innocent and helpless women" who can't support themselves. Community property becomes just that, divided equally including the bills and obligations.

Spousal support all but disappears. Fathers have equal opportunity for child custody, with the victory going to the "most fit" rather than the man having to prove the mother "unfit."

Men begin to fight for "feminine" jobs instead of the other way around. All this becomes quite a threat to some women who happen to enjoy both their pedestals and dependency—ruling by covert manipulation.

To the rescue comes an old but new approach to keeping the status quo. Using the Bible for doctrinal support several writers and speakers have exhorted women to take all the responsibility for making the relationship work by making hubby happy. He's not interested in you, the home, therapy, or growth, but *you* are. So you set out to be the best sex partner, the perfect housewife, the "queen" to your "king". (Never the slave.) The claim is that he'll be so happy he'll let you rule the kingdom and restore your fringe benefits. He'll become the perfect, generous husband and never even know why. Your needs will be met, but he won't even be aware of how it happened.

Interestingly enough, the process seems to work for a lot of men and women. Practiced by a cross-section of religious fundamentalists, it meets the old-fashioned criteria of man being second-incommand to God and still teaches the wife a new method of getting her needs met. Since the old method of bitch—complain—sulk—and—withheld sex didn't work, anything else is at least an improvement. These people describe Feminists as those "who only think of self first and that's backwards. You can only gain happiness through devotion to others."

What seems to be missing in this point of view is an understanding that selfish and self-love are opposites. Being "self-less" is as psychologically counter-productive as being selfish. Devotion to others, unless it is based on self-love and devotion to one's own best interests and objectives, does not breed happiness, but exploitation, bitterness and resentment because no one is giving that kind of devotion to "me." If this concept were consistent as a two-way street, were the writers asking and expecting the man to give this same devotion to his wife, it would be more digestable. The double standard of the so-called "total woman" seems to be damaging to both partners.

The one excellent part of this Bible-based approach to marital relationships is that it tells women they *do* have the power to change their lives and encourages them to take he initiative and not to wait to be rescued. A common complaint heard in therapy is that "my spouse won't let me be healthy. I would change, but it wouldn't do any good."

That means, "my change wouldn't bring about the corresponding change in the other person that I desire." This excuse is heard continually from both men and women and also concerning parent-child relationships. "The total woman" approach has a benefit in that someone is saying to women: "You *can* effect a change in both of you. You *can* improve the relationship by yourself. You don't have to be an angry bitch; it hasn't helped anyway."

And the approach *has* effected changes. When one person changes, the other cannot easily remain the same. However, the following assumptions and misconceptions of "the total woman" approach are stumbling blocks for many people:

1. Man is God-given ruler of the household and always right, regardless.
2. Women are fulfilled best by filling a subservient and submissive role.
3. Man has little desire, interest, motivation, initiative, intelligence or caring to improve relationships—so woman has to provide these qualities.
4. Men are too weak to handle a woman's deep emotions.
5. Men don't have strong enough egos to handle a firm, direct approach by a woman.
6. A woman is not an equal partner in making decisions.
7. Women have inferior intellect to *all* men.
8. It is better for a man to make a mistake than for a woman to prevent his error by showing him a better way.

Some of the suggestions of "the total woman" are based on sound common sense and everyday courtesy except that the man is not requested or expected to reciprocate. Why not? Is he too Godly? or too goofy?

To believe the answer to relationships lies in the selfish hostility of of extreme feminism or the selfless devotion of some popular religionists would be to remain in the extremes and to return from whence we came. This would be counter-productive. The extreme attitudes were obviously not fully meeting the needs of either men or women, or we wouldn't now be struggling with all these changes and subsequent anxieties.

These implications could go on and on and are insulting to both men and women. We need to realize that men and women are different from each other because *people* are different from each other. We can enjoy and profit and learn from these differences.

More Fundamental Than The Fundamentalists

We suggest that there is a process more basic to any successful relationship. If we make it, it will be because we admire, appreciate and enjoy each other,

because we respect each other's needs and feelings of self-love,

because we see ourselves as having a worthy love to share and are worthy of receiving the love of others,

because *both* women and men care enough to communicate realness,

because women are not afraid to be assertive nor men to be emotional,

because *both* are freely given the freedom to be themselves and model this to their children.

When one partner is pressured to be more responsible for the success of the relationship than the other, an adversary position is created between them. This position causes more alienation and polarity —not less.

Increasingly people are more uncomfortable with a double standard in marriage relationships. If I want something for me, I must be willing to freely give it to my spouse. If I cannot give it, I must relinquish it for myself.

The answer lies in people learning to be honest with themselves and each other, open to the totality of human experience, both good and bad, internal and external, experiencing and sharing the full range of their emotions and unique humanness. The rest of this book presents our step-by-step suggestions to help you to reach these goals. These are steps many have followed to a more fulfilled life. The same path is open to you.

III. Freedom: Winning The Struggle For Personal Choice

"We have nothing to fear but fear itself."—FDR

The Dilemma

I want what I've got, I must keep it;
If I move on ahead I might lose it.

I can't make up my mind, it's driving me blind.
Do I risk or protect? I can't choose it.

My heart aches to grow.
It's pushing me so,
But my fear stands firm in my way.

If I dare to leave home,
I can't feel secure.
I don't know I can win, anyway.

It's boring to stay
to hoard and decay,
I'd rather be stretching for life,

But life's an unknown.
I have what I won;
I might find only heartache and strife.

The answer my friend,
brings confusion to end:
You've based your protection on things.

Life is in living
not hoarding and hiding—
you've got to take risks to explore.

True safety in living
is trusting one's being,
believing "I am" my supply.

No one can rob you
of what is within you,
That will be yours till you die.

> You are the essence.
> You are the value.
> Safety and peace you employ.
>
> So seek out the future
> with courage and fervor
> Life's best is for you to enjoy.

—CDL

The tug of war between chauvinism and feminism is an outer symptom of the internalized struggle in each of us between security and growth.

Security, dependency, safety and comfort are basic needs that cannot be ignored or denied. We cannot even consider moving to a higher stage of personal evolution or growth until safe in our present position.

The less mature we are, because our dependency needs have not been sufficiently met, the more urgent our desire for safety and security and the more fearfully we perceive change and growth.

The more mature we are, because our dependency needs have been and are continuing to be met, by ourselves and others, the more we lean toward new experience, growth and risk taking. We have less need to be protected by the safe "knowns" of life because we feel a continual protection of personal strength and bonding of love that move along with us and are never really left behind.

The path to maturity is for many of us a long, uphill struggle to growth and new levels of integration, re-education, new insights, the making of self-conscious decisions, and being willing to face occasional or frequent bitter struggles, both within ourselves and with others. It is moving out from the protected and familiar place of security to a new and unfamiliar growth of independence. It is surrendering support in exchange for temporary isolation. There is a basic conflict within all of us, between the part of the person seeking growth, expansion and health, versus the part that is longing for the protection of dependency.

The more internalized and secure our self image and personal feelings, the more easily we can flow with and tolerate external change. The less personally secure, the more we need rigid external conformity and security.

Let's look more closely at some of the difficulties we encounter in our fear of change that might explain why chauvinism is so attractive to both men and women and makes it difficult for us to extricate ourselves from its thorny grasp, even when we desire to.

An answer to this dilemma is suggested in a fascinating study of the effect of change on bodily health researched by Dr. Thomas H. Holmes and Dr. Richard Rake. Using case histories of over 5,000 people, they compiled their well-known "Social Readjustment Rating Scale." These doctors discovered that a cluster of life-style changes, either for good or bad, tended to occur before the onset of a major illness. Each life change was assigned a number of points (the more traumatic the change, the higher the points); such as 50 points for getting married, 75 for losing a job, 10 for a vacation. They found that when a person totaled from 150 to 300 points in a single year, his or her chances of severe illness were 50 per cent, even if all the changes were positive and desired ones. Once over 300 points, a person risked a staggering 90 per cent chance of medical disaster!

Researchers don't know why, but they do know that any change brings fear and anxiety to the point of affecting us physically. The result is, we often resist even *good* changes in order to bring about immediate relief from the anxiety connected with the change. In expending so much energy in order to cope with the change and anxiety, sometimes we become physically ill to *avoid* the change and anxiety.

Anxiety is a product of *all change*, so we must learn to expect it as a necessary interim step that can provide new understanding and insights if only we can learn to listen to what our feelings of anxiety are trying to tell us, and do so without judging these feelings either good or bad. They will often reveal what the real internal struggle is. Once feelings are brought into true focus, proper decisions are much easier to make.

For many the absence of anxiety is the highest state of happiness (especially true of those who escape into alcohol, drugs, sex or fantasy). But instead of utopia they find themselves caught in the middle of polarities with the push-pull of approach-avoidance. 'I want and fear both sides: i.e. I want love *and* I want to be left alone; I fear love and fear being left alone."

The result is the worst of all possible worlds . . . no success, no growth, yet all the anxiety connected with making a decision, and constantly faced with one. No decision *is* a decision, even if we try to avoid that reality.

There are many barriers to intimacy that keep us from getting close enough to each other to truly love and be loved. Probably they could all be summarized by the one word, fear. It's dual fear: the fear of hurting someone else or of being hurt by someone else, of being vulnerable.

So, we tend to deal with our social conflicts on the levels of interior dialogue. We carry on a complete conversation within our head, covering all the various alternatives. The more fearful, insecure, paranoid, and self-degrading we are, the worse this dialogue comes out. Lost in this dialogue, we become upset, hurt, or angry with the other for imagined sins they never had the opportunity to commit. We read each other's minds, take all negative comments personally ("That was vicious and intended to assasinate me!") and—being fearful and expecting rejection—we cannot stand the pain of actually telling one another how we really feel.

That terrible pain from the fear of being vulnerable (because you might use the information against me) can be the worst of all. "Of course, you wouldn't understand or care enough to change anyway, so why bother? I made my point by losing, so I win." We are defeated internally before the first shot of the battle.

Whether the conversation just described is conducted solely in one's imagination or actually shared with a partner, it generally remains on a defensive, superficial level (that looks for bad motives or behavior) rather than examining the deeper feelings of each person to sort out the real issues.

We conceal the real issues from ourselves the way Doug and Patty did. They are a young couple who had been married only two years when they came to therapy. He had been raised in a rather chauvinistic manner and she had a strong fear of being "used" or dominated. While still engaged they talked about the type of marriage they would have and she insisted they share equally in the domestic chores since both planned to work equally. She strongly emphasized her need for his help in maintaining a clean home. This was totally new to Doug, but because he loved her and saw the fairness in her request, he dove in to learn and to be an equal partner. He had a strong desire to please Patty.

By the time they came to therapy, he was angry and wouldn't do anything to please her. According to him, Patty had reneged on her part of the bargain. After six months she became a slob and never did her share. The true issue finally emerged: "I learned housework because Patty said it was vital to her and if I loved her I'd do this for her. So, I did, and six months later *she* stopped. The message I got was that she stopped loving me and told me so by not doing the housework." It took Doug quite a few months of struggle in therapy to sort out his real anger—not that the house was dirty or that she was exploiting him but: "She doesn't love me!" Once this issue was exposed, the therapy process moved forward quickly.

The word vulnerable can be defined in somewhat conflicting ways.

When a person says, "I'm too vulnerable to handle that now," he or she usually means, "I'm without proper internal or external protection, my defenses are weak, I can be hurt beyond my capacity at this moment, so I need to avoid or bypass the trauma." This is a legitimate and appropriate place for anyone to be at times. We aren't always sufficient for every moment and it's too much to ask that we should be.

Another definition of vulnerable is seen in the statement, "I am choosing to be very vulnerable and open to you at this time." The implication here is that "I'm so peaceful within myself and so deeply in touch with my natural resources at this moment, I can afford to risk lowering my defenses, letting you see and experience the naked me, knowing you thereby have some power to hurt me, but assured that I can handle the hurt if it comes and I cannot be destroyed in the process." This is personal strength at its highest functioning.

The problem of fear can be more clearly defined in terms of the changing tide of man-woman relationships by looking at three common polarities: success-failure; pleasure-pain; known-unknown.

Success-Failure

Logically, we all seek success and we fear or avoid failure, but there is also safety in failure and trauma in success. A fear of failure can keep people from asking for a date or from any real attempt at intimacy (assuming the other might reject me, not find me desirable, never give me a chance). Thus I avoid being revealed to the world as an undesirable "commodity."

On the other hand, the opportunity for success might be given freely: "What if the other *does* find me desirable, responds to me, and opens the door wide. *Now* I have to live up to someone's expectations (I don't even know what they are) and I have to compete with prior experiences and people. What if I'm really *not that good*? Now I'm revealed as a desirable person that couldn't cut it." If you don't try, you are guaranteed the *failure of loneliness*, but without the pain of having tried and failed. If your fear is stronger than your need for love . . . you opt for protection. And that's fear number two.

Pleasure-Pain

We all want the pleasure of loving and being loved, of closeness and intimacy, of warmth and sharing. We shy away from loneliness . . . from having no one to love. But with love comes risk: "If I let myself love you, I become vulnerable to being hurt. You may die, or leave me, or have an affair, or not love me back with the same intensity. Or I may become so needful of you that I will pay any price to keep you . . . that gives you tremendous power and control over my life. If I love, you may possess and enslave me." Anyone who has loved has been hurt. There is always some hurt involved in intimate, human relationships. How many of us have said "No one will ever hurt me like that again.?" Result: No one every *loves* me that much again.

Not to be loved also brings pain. Perhaps so, and it may bring *more* pain (anxiety) to be loved and have to worry about the consequences. So we struggle between the present loneliness we know and understand, and the possibility of a love that may hurt us in new and differ-ernt ways we don't understand.

Known-Unknown

The spectre of divorce best illustrates this double-bind polarity: "I am unhappy in my marriage and want out *but* do not have anyone better to go to *or* do not know if the one I found will turn out to be better *or* if I'll wind up stuck living alone, *or* if anyone will ever want me."

"This is a bad marriage and at times I can't stand it, *but* I've lived with it 10-15-20 years. I enjoy the children; I have status as part of a couple; I'm not alone. It might get better (even with no effort from me); at least I know what to expect. People don't know I'm unhappy . . . I'll have more financial security . . . etc."

Even when an affair has been going on for a year or two and the person is "madly in love", it is not necessarily easier to seek divorce. "Maybe the affair won't last, the other will change his/her mind . . . how do I know I can trust my new friend . . . I might wind up with neither one." Experience shows many times the man or woman who leaves a spouse to marry someone else needs to return to the original spouse, whether temporarily or permanently, before they can marry the new person. They are afraid of their decision to leave.

The most difficult but constructive decision is not to choose *between* two people, but to choose *for* your own happiness. If you are now married, you may need to face this decision process. Is it best for you to be married to your present spouse? Is the experience unhappy and destructive? What can you do? We will address this process several times in this book, for it is widespread. For now, the point to remember is that, faced with the unknown, you must choose for yourself.

Anxiety is a product of *all* change, so expect it. If you will *listen* to the feelings of anxiety, they will often reveal what the real struggle is. Once that is brought out into true focus, proper decisions are much easier to make.

The prior benefit of male chauvinism was that someone else handed this decision down and that relieved us of personal responsibility in the decision process. God, the Church, society, parents, cultural mores were all used as support systems for a way of relating. When support systems are removed and there are few absolutes on which to rest your case, you have to look within, find out who you are and what you want and take responsibility for your actions. What could be more scary—or exciting—than that?

The Moral Aspects Of Freedom

When three chaplains wrote a letter to the editor of the Los Angeles *Times* decrying the rise of drug usage by American servicemen in Vietnam, they opened a debate. Their basic charge was that the New Morality, *Playboy* magazine, and pornography had caused this state of affairs.

The editor was then deluged with emotional "answers" properly condemning these charges as simplistic and ridiculous. The letters implied that the immorality of the Vietnam war was the cause of all of our problems—an equally simplistic answer.

Here is our classic "Generation Gap." The old line standard of morality is tied to sexuality as being the cause of all of our hang-ups or problems, versus the new line position of immorality as being war and injustice. Essentially they are both saying the same thing—"I reject your morality, because I disagree with your motives for what you do."

While we are witnessing the death of the old morality, the uncomfortable truth is that we have not yet achieved *a new morality*. It is very difficult to be caught in a transition period where the old is not yet comfortably rejected, and the new has not yet become a completed reality.

The old morality is black versus white, law over love, principles before persons, universal over particular, judgment before mercy, thou shalt not—instead of thou, law and order before law with justice and commandments before concern. It is a legalism in which the law has lost its content but retains its form and demanded conformity to external rules. The attitude is rigid and inflexible, rather than love and understanding.

Living by the set rules of some authority allows one to live a comfortable and unhassled life without the problem of decision-making or choice. The conservatives of our day, whether they be religious or political, loudly proclaim that they have inherited the truth and from this point on no one else need to think or consider or weigh values for himself, as all these decisions have already been made for them.

The new morality, for which we still search, is oriented to the needs of people rather than toward the demand of principle. It is life-affirming rather than life-denying. It encourages both individual and relational freedom and responsibility. It permits joy and levies less repression. It allows great flexibility in the fixing of certain standards in order to understand individual differences. It is accepting, loving and forgiving, rather than rigid, condemning and indifferent. It is a love morality and not a code morality.

Being moral involves the matter of choice. As a result of our choosing, things happen to us, in us, to others, and in others. The new morality says that in any concrete situation all the facts, all the relationships, all the feelings should penetrate and motivate the choice—not some legalistic, abstract principle. In other words, the claim of the person or persons is greater than the cultural or social concept of "right" or "wrong."

Morality involves the freedom of choice. There is nothing moral about my refusing to steal from the grocery store simply because I am afraid of getting caught and going to jail. There is nothing moral about staying in a destructive marriage relationship because I am afraid that my church will disown me and make it impossible for me to take the sacraments or be a part of the ruling body of the Church, simply because I get a divorce. Choice always presents two opposite alternatives . . . in order to be able to morally say yes, I need the equal choice and opportunity of saying no. In order to be able to morally say no, I need the equal opportunity of saying yes.

There is no freedom without responsibility. This is where integrity enters the picture. The healthy, well-balanced, self-actualizing person will not choose to do anything destructive to his own integrity or that is irresponsible to himself or others. He has the freedom to consider any and every individual act on its own merits, weigh the consequences, and decide that this is something he wants to do.

Rebellion is a transitory phase in the quest for independence or freedom. The rebel often feels that he is now free because he is able to fight against the status-quo. But he only exists as a rebel as long as there is something to fight against. If he does not know yet what he is *for*, he thereby really has no choice but is compulsively and impulsively fighting *against* something at all times.

While it may be years before our country as a whole, or world as a whole for that matter, can come to achieve a new morality that rests its case on loving integrity, each of us as individuals and within the framework of our own individual families can provide a new morality. That new morality gives us a sense of truth in dealing with our own needs and the needs of those who are important to us. Through exercising our personal choice with integrity we achieve freedom within that new morality.

IV. Polarization: The Man-Woman Rift
Is Also The Mind-Body Rift

The Problem Between Us Is Also The Problem Within Me

We live in a world that seems populated with "thinkers," "feelers" and "spiritualizers." The thinkers do not feel, the feelers do not think, and the spiritualizers want to deny all that is real and live above the human. Of course, this is a gross over-generalization, but most of us do find it easier and more comfortable to live one of these roles than to integrate them into a single unit. It is difficult to generalize any personal situation due to the many individual exceptions and the fact we are all on a continuum from moderate to extreme. Even if you find yourself in one of our three classifications, you are probably not *purely* that one and demonstrate some elements of each of the others. We have all met persons who seem to have these elements in balance. They are "congruent." In other words, congruence is when what is going on in the mind, being felt in the stomach, coming out of the mouth, and being read in the body language are all the same.

Examining these stereotypes help us to identify key elements in our relationships.

Thinkers

A client who is a medical doctor once complained that he had attended hundreds of growth-oriented workshops, had been in therapy with several therapists, and had attended many lectures all of which had put down his intellect and tried to get him to "feel." He kept hearing that only intellectualizers "think;" real people "feel." He wasn't about to give up his intellect and was describing eloquently how important it was to him and that it was actually his major ego identification. It was explained to him that what "feeling therapists" are trying to say is that some people use their intellect to defend against feelings or entirely avoid them. If the intellect were not used as a block to feelings, the two could be made to work together.

Dr. K. never seemed to understand this until he did a long and particularly important guided daydream. He was able to relax enough to feel deep emotions, to experience them with a minimum of discomfort, and thoroughly to understand their inner messages. For the first time, Dr. K. was able to perceive that feelings and intellect are not mutually exclusive or enemies but are two different bodily functions, each delivering messages of understanding to the person. It *requires* the intellect to more fully decode and properly interpret the feeling symbols.

One definition of the schizophrenic is a person who cannot integrate his intellect and emotions. When the intellect is in control, he functions very well, and is sometimes more stable than most. When he becomes emotionally threatened, however, his intellect goes "out to lunch" and he loses control, becoming overwhelmed by the emotional anxiety state.

The action and reaction of your life should come as an appropriate and spontaneous response to the mating of emotions *and* intellect. You need to "listen" to your feelings. Listening entails the intellect. "What is my body trying to tell me and why?" "How can I best respond to the message?" These are questions for the intellect.

We are all familiar with the stereotype engineer, scientist, or accountant who generally prefers numbers and machinery to relationships and people. They are a good example of the "thinkers" in our society.

"Thinkers" approach life through logic, facts, shrewd arguments, and authority through knowledge. They usually have very high I.Q.'s and tend to be the most afraid of confusion, of being under obligation to someone, and of strong feelings of any kind. They show few emotions and when put under stress, tend to withdraw and become even more "rule ridden."

Thinkers probably predominate in our society, as most religions and social insitutions tends to look down on those who enjoy their physical senses.

Feelers

Latter day therapy, as in the Gestalt approach, has tried to bring people back to sensory awareness. The drug/youth culture has often carried this to the extreme of "pleasure only and always" regardless of the consequences. They each reflect the fact that feelings are messages from within that are trying to tell you something about yourself that your intellect either doesn't know or is trying to avoid. The better we learn to listen to and cooperate with our bodily senses, the easier it is to function properly, both from a physical and psychological standpoint.

On the "feeler" side of life, we have two extremes; aggressive feelers and submissive feelers, of which the extremes are sadists and masochists.

The aggressive feeler tends to dominate others and has achievement as an important goal in life. He orders and threatens others and is willing to discipline himself to get what he wants. He is very afraid of a loss of personal power, illness or being seen as a "softy." His emotions are tough. Put under stress he will become impulsive and even more dominant and controlling.

Edward M. is a successful corporate executive, very athletically inclined, outgoing and successful, flies his own plane and has a beautiful wife and three children. For the first years of his marriage his dominance manifested itself in a rather self-centered life style, wherein he "played with his adult toys," while his submissive wife and children watched and admired. As his wife, Mary, became stronger and more rebellious to his behavior he became more demanding and angry. He would vascilate between the roles of a deprived little boy, hurt and whimpering, to a screaming tyrant, who actually "raped" his wife one day because of his desperate need to assert his "rights" in the relationship.

As Mary became stronger in therapy and closer to the independence that threatened divorce it became more and more clear how humiliating and devastating divorce would be to Edward as a loss of face and status in the community and a stigma of failure he has to avoid at all costs. He tried hard to give her space and not to threaten her (mainly because of the strong peer pressure of an excellent couples' group) but would periodically blow up and become violent with her and the children.

This impulsive and violent behavior served to strengthen Mary's resolve and the divorce was completed. To the very end Edward did not accept this and left therapy rather than learn to deal with the driving fear within him that drove him to this need to control or be emotionally "destroyed."

A submissive feeler enjoys doing favors and entertaining people to get approval and love. He can be a martyr and is often exploited; in fact, seems to encourage exploitation. His greatest fear is loss of affection or direct personal attack-criticism; he will go to great extremes to avoid this. His emotions are tender and easily hurt; under stress, this person becomes clinging and dependent.

Brenda, a 50-year-old woman with a history of four broken marriages and two homosexual sons who hated her, sought help in therapy. In the first six months she went through three rather intense affairs, each starting out as "perfect" and ending with the men rather coldly rejecting her. Brenda was a very loving, giving person who totally submerged herself in serving and pleasing others. She claimed great personal satisfaction from this with no ulterior motives.

Ironically she seemed attracted to "takers," men who loved being taken care of hand and foot and showed their appreciation by being warm and responsive at the beginning—then gradually taking it for granted and giving almost nothing once the relationship became secure. This, of course, is the aggressive feeler, who has a love-hate relationship with women, *needs* them to survive but is actually afraid of their rejection and power. He chooses submissive women to dominate and exploit usually to the point where neither one is aware of *his* or *her* fear and feelings of inadequacy. Of course, Brenda begins to feel exploited and taken advantage of as the appreciation dissipates and her resentment gets expressed in direct and indirect ways. This angers the men and the relationships quickly dissolve.

Some people love and receive love in return. Others love and are exploited. The key difference is in motive. A submissive feeler does not believe he or she *deserves* to be loved so "buys" love by self-sacrifice, with the unconscious intent of putting the other under obligation to love them back. A person with true *self*-love gives out of the abundance of love available, but expects to be loved in return and is attracted to those who can and do love in return. A true submissive *giver* is generally attracted *only* to a selfish *taker*.

The obvious truth here is that these two extremes are drawn almost exclusively to each other and need each other to survive in their roles.

An example of a man in the submissive role follows.

A very successful and independent divorcee in her mid-forties was dating two rather attractive and socially desirable men but complained that one was "too nice" and she didn't know how to explain her feelings to him. "Both men do the same things in our relationship —take me nice places, treat me with respect, are warm to my teenage son, etc. One does it out of strength and self-confidence and it seems to come naturally. The other one comes across like a young boy needing praise and a pat on the head. The message from him is: Did I do a good job? Do you like me? Was I OK? He makes me feel like his mother. How do I tell him he's losing my respect?"

It may seem sexist to use a man's case to illustrate aggressive feelers and a woman for submissive but our chauvinistic culture has encouraged this to a point where this *is* generally the pattern. We wish to point out, however, there are many exceptions to the rule and both sexes are plentiful in both roles.

Spiritualizers

Difficult to categorize "spiritualizers" seem to slip back and forth from symptom to symptom but not in a constructive way. They tend to deny feelings as untrustworthy and unspiritual and want to be above them. They try to stay with the thinker but often do not have his one-track-mind capacity. They might vacillate between giving and receiving but are best known for denying anything (action or motivation) that might be construed as criticism. They take the "power of positive thinking" to the ultimate of "wishful thinking" but never quite overcome the doubts. When they marry each other, a divorce is highly unlikely because neither one can accept the concept of a failure or making a mistake. Such a relationship has a great capacity for subconscious bitterness and vindictiveness and judgmental behavior that is covered by a front of piety.

In therapy spiritualizers are unwilling or unable to express or to admit negatives about themselves which are seen as unspiritual.

Mrs. G. comes to therapy with many psychosomatic symptoms but her medical doctor can find no physical cause. She has migraine headaches and intestinal problems mostly. This is a woman with strong religious values and convictions. She believes that *any* expression of anger is wrong and that illness is caused by not being spiritual enough.

She is unhappily married to a passive man, who has never been as successful as she desired and she feels angry and cheated by this. Her religious beliefs insist she deny this anger but it irrupts from time to time and is happening more often. This creates guilt so she rationalizes the anger away or denies that it happened. ("I was just defending myself," or "He caused me to be angry.") Denying the anger and personal responsibility for one's own feelings and behavior forces the anger inside and it appears in physical symptoms. The symptoms of migraine headaches or stomach upset distract her from the anger and serve to "punish" her husband by making him feel guilty for causing this. Now he is supposed to feel sorry for her and take care of her better. The illness in turn makes her feel unspiritual for not being well. She believes there is no real illness or negative in life when you are in tune with God. You can easily see the circular contradictions that make change so difficult. We believe people must honestly and openly examine *all* feelings, motivations and behavior *Without Judgment*—for *Information And Understanding Only*—in order to affect the process of inner healing and personal growth.

Polarities

We observe that people who are not"congruent" tend to marry their opposites; once integrated, they tend to marry themselves. Why is this so? Do opposites really attract and why? What part is played by common interests and compatibility?

Before we consider compatibility, let's look at the polarities between couples.

It would seem logical that any person who seemed fairly locked into an extreme way of life for himself and not able to change that or seemingly even desirous of changing that, would want to marry what he thinks he lacks in himself: his opposite.

The tendency to marry someone different is a result of the opposite tendencies and extremes that are missing in one's self and need to be filled in by someone. A *Giver* has rarely learned to *Receive*. If he had learned to receive equally well, by definition, he would no longer be a Giver but a "congruent" person. So a Giver needs someone to receive, to appreciate and accept his generous qualities. Two givers might drive each other nuts trying to outgive the other at the same time, becoming disappointed that their gifts are not appreciated.

In order to feel complete and fulfilled, the giver needs a receiver and is really quite frustrated without this. While his search is for a *person* to receive from him, that person is in reality a symbol of the missing puzzle—a part of his own personality. He has never developed his receiver subpersonality. Therefore, he is rendered somewhat helpless in receiving love from himself or others, finds it difficult to believe in the value of his own gifts, and is dependent on his outside environment for validation of worth. Even when the outside world is providing validation, it tends to have transitory results since he seeks constant reassurance. As the giver cannot exist without a receiver, the receiver needs to be given to. "Show me you love me by meeting all my needs." The receiver often comes across more as a selfish *taker* who expects and demands from others and acts as though the only virtue he needs to share is the fact that he took what you had to give. You can easily see what two takers do to each other . . . each angrily accusing the other of not caring or loving.

We see such polarities every day. A convenient way of examing them is offered by Shostrum, in *Man the Manipulator*. He has divided people into four sets of polarities; half on the aggressive side and half on the passive. The Judge, who is Critical, balances the Protector, who is Supportive.

The Actualizing Types

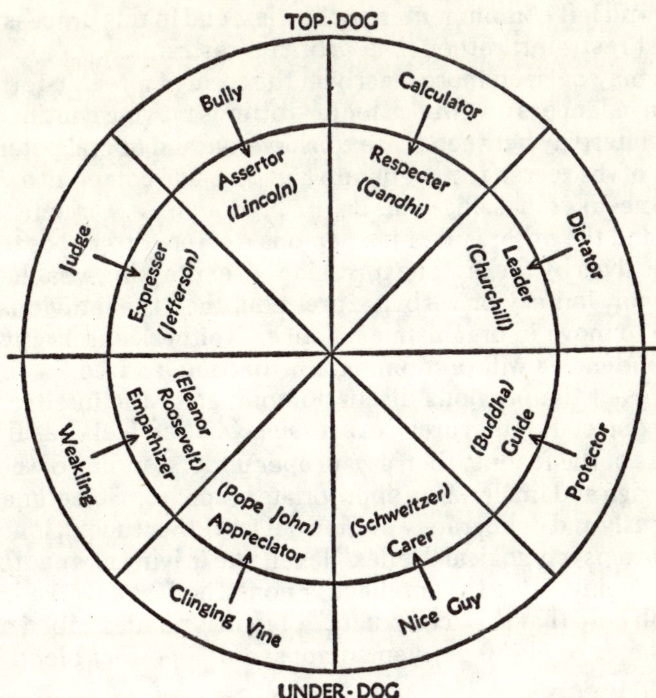

The bully, with his aggression, lines up against the nice guy who exudes warmth. The calculator, with his need to control, is opposite the clinging vine and dependency. Finally, the dictator uses strength or power against the weakling with sensitivity.

Each of these opposites have good points and any can be greatly misused. The tendency to misuse them comes when we are unbalanced or over-balanced on one side. If I never used my left arm, my right arm will become stronger from constant use and my left will become quite weak.

When we go looking for a spouse to "balance" us, we are really looking for the missing half of ourselves.

Did you ever wonder why an angry person who can't cry seems to inevitably marry a fearful crybaby? Could it be that the angry person needs to learn to cry and the crybaby needs to learn to be angry and strong? Once this process is recognized it becomes easier for both to work on this missing area within themselves, for each to be less threatened by the behavior of the other and less needful to exhibit extremes.

Shostrum talks about the actualizing person as "dancing between his right and left complimentary polarities, and in this process there is natural restraint; rather than artificial restraint."

"This may be seen more clearly in the form of a teeter-totter. A person in balance is one whose teeter-totter is moving continually in dynamic interplay between these conservative and liberal potentials. One side of the teeter-totter goes up and that side comes into awareness; the needs of that side of his nature predominate. Circumstances change, and the other end of his personal teeter-totter goes up. As long as he lives by the law of expression . . . expressing what he feels by behavior, fantasy or verbal expression, then the individual will continue to move in organismic balance. Neither conservative nor liberal tendencies will predominate or become fixated."

In terms of the previous discussion of mating the intellect with feelings, one could interpret "expressing what he feels" as first an awareness of the feeling, then as a proper understanding of the sensory message and finally as an appropriate response. Sometimes this is consciously and deliberately worked out and other times it is accomplished on a psychological "reflex" level, like driving a car automatically, or typing. But the intellect is none the less involved.

You will note that the "congruent" person is not described as in a static balance of 50-50 or even composed of a perfect blend of all characteristics.

Rather, he is constantly in motion, responding to various stimuli in both his inner and outer environments with appropriate reactions that encompass his entire being.

We can see some reasons why extreme, one-sided people do not marry themselves or if they do, why it usually doesn't work out—then why don't marriages between complete and extreme opposites work toward perfection?

After all, they need each other and they fill in the missing parts for each other. If these polar opposites are at the extreme end of the spectrum, they *do* bring certain satisfactions to the relationship and that's often what brought them together. The loud man does need the quiet woman. She serves as a calming influence, doesn't compete with him for attention and hopefully will influence him to be less obnoxious. She needs his pep and energy, is drawn to his spirit of assertiveness and hopes some of this will rub off on her.

If personalities are very far apart to begin with, after a time they begin to irritate and depress each other. "You are so quiet and passive, I can't carry on a conversation with you, let alone an argument. I find you dull and boring . . . no personality."

"If you would shut up once in a while, maybe someone else could talk. I'm so sick of your constant need to be the center of attention. You have no respect for anyone's feelings."

They're both right.

If, on the other hand, these two are *not* at extreme ends but fairly close to center, then it is possible that she will tend to be a quieting and calming influence on him and he will bring out more of the extrovert in her. Both benefit, both grow, and they can even find themselves reversing roles at times.

People who are relatively healthy and somewhat balanced, can greatly profit from a marriage of compatibility and find this as actualizing as good therapy. If they should mate *without* that compatibility, they could easily bring out the worst in each other and degenerate in their individual growth, as well as jeopardize the relationship itself.

Many couples fall into that negative category; people who are pleasant individuals, not pathologically sick, but absolutely do terrible things to each other, push all the wrong buttons and wind up being terribly destructive. Generally, these marriages cannot be saved and are not worth the trouble to try very long.

Seeking help, they may get into therapy long enough to "practice" on each other, learn a new and less destructive way to communicate, find out why they needed that kind of person to begin with (or why they stayed together for 20 years) and finally, take the risks necessary to break the old patterns. In this way, they can learn from their mistakes, reduce the chance of making the same mistakes in the next relationship, recover from the pain of the separation and get a more friendly divorce. Occasionally, it works so well that the old relationship dissolves and a new and beautiful one emerges with the same mate.

Unfortunately, most people come to counseling to "save" the marriage. If that goal is seen to be impossible, most people don't want to admit they have individual problems that caused their bad marriage to begin with. They just blame it on the other person, and go on to make the same mistake again because their own neurotic need wasn't resolved.

Dominance Vs. Equality

How does all of this fit into the changing roles of man-woman relationships, particularly in the area of dominance?

It is no coincidence that historically the aggressive, dominant people of our country have been predominantly men and the submissive, weak or giving ones mostly women. Our society has programmed these as accepted roles for men and women.

Now we have men and women reversing roles and taking on many of each others better qualities and also learning many of their worst traits as well.

How does this, or will this, affect relationships from this time in history? What is the difference between a traditional marriage and a contemporary one?

In a *traditional* relationship, the woman requires a strong man who will assert leadership and strength so that she can feel protected and secure. From this foundation of safety many women can function very independently and efficiently. If the man is perceived as weak or incapable of this protection, often the woman becomes insecure or angry because she is not receiving what *she perceives* as her "right" as a woman. Frustrated, she can often become bitchy, demanding, and withholding the assets she is supposed to bring to the traditional marriage: comfort, tenderness and support.

A traditional man has always been able to accept a more "submissive" wife because the culture told him that was the normal female role; therefore, he was not and is not as threatened by this, as a traditional woman would be threatened by a submissive man. He tends to feel important, needed, and masculine in his role as head of the household and enjoys seeing his wife respond to the "safe" environment he has provided by functioning well (and independently) in her housewife-mother roles.

We define dominance in relationships as *understanding and expressing one's self assertively; taking responsibility for one's own actions and needs; functioning independently and efficiently.*

Dominance is not the same as a "need to dominate another." In a *contemporary* marriage, two people can consider themselves "dominant" people in that they assert their own needs, independently or in an adversary situation; enjoy leadership roles, can take charge of a situation and follow through to conclusions, make decisions easily, and accept responsibility.

There is no need or desire to dominate the other or to compete with the other. Each has areas of strength, some overlapping and some different. These areas are appreciated and respected. Although there is not total agreement, this doesn't threaten either's security. There is nothing to prove; there is respect for each other's judgment and motivations so they can tolerate differences of opinion, especially when these are shared openly and non-defensively.

True strength (in men and women) does not require proof, nor does it depend on a need to control another. A *liberated* person cannot tolerate being a slave *or a master*. He/she demands for his/her loved-one what he/she demands for him/herself: freedom to be me, room to grow, the right to be strong, weak, vulnerable, independent, dependent, needy, angry, understood—and loved for all this.

Interestingly enough, an independent, liberated feminist *also* needs a strong man but for different reasons. She certainly would not be comfortable with or respect a man who was not as capable as she, who would be threatened by her strength, or would want to be overly dependent upon her. (Dependency creates hostility in both partners.) She would want an equal to share with, so that each can be free to be strong or vulnerable as the need arises.

It is safe to say that a liberated man, however, would have the same needs as a liberated woman. He would *not* be comfortable with less than an equal . . . would not respect a woman who did not take her needs seriously but preferred to be "taken care of" emotionally and materially.

Equality between man and woman is not sameness; it means the equal right to be "what I am." It assumes we have differences and that hopefully the areas of deficiency in one can be "covered" by the other. Our roles are to support, supplement, complement and share all aspects of what we are with one another. "Fair" treatment is not necessarily "equal" or "same" treatment as our needs are not always the same and they vary within the same person. Exact amounts of food would not be fair if divided between a 200 pound man and a 100 pound woman. What is appropriate is for each to have his own private food needs met, independently of the other.

We have described how we feel liberated men and women would relate to each other but have purposefully not given an example or two to illustrate because of the value hazards involved there. What is liberated for one may not be for another. For instance, a 50-50 division of housework may not work or be appropriate for everyone and when used as an example tends to be set in concrete by some as "God's only Truth." Since we are talking about attitudes that must be defined and structured to personalized contracts (whether written or assumed) by each individual relationship, we feel examples could "get in the way."

V. Compatibility And Contact Points

Successful relationships are actually based on two definitive issues: compatibility (which has to do with contact points) and communication skills. It seems rather impossible to imagine a constructive, fulfilling and pleasurable blending of two people that does not contain these two factors.

A couple can't really know for sure if they are compatible until they have mastered enough communication skills to find the real issues between them. It is absolutely amazing at times how many unlivable symptoms fall away or become humorous topics of warm kidding when the *real* issues are found, understood, and resolved.

Probably a lot more has been written and lectured on communications skills than compatibility, but all the skill in the world couldn't overcome the handicaps of true incompatibility, although it can often minimize it.

It could be arued that all couples are compatible or they wouldn't be together to begin with. However, there are many levels of compatibility and intimacy. Some pairings are based on deficiency needs and neurotic tendencies, which have already been discussed. An excellent friend might make a horrible spouse. Many people use the excuse of "incompatibility," which can be a vague feeling of discomfort one wishes to avoid, for a quickie divorce situation, without any real attempt at learning or growing.

We suggest that there are two different types of incompatibility. The first type involves couples that have life styles, needs, feelings, and values so different that there is little ground upon which to build communication skills. Looking at a couple like this makes one wonder how they ever got together. Perhaps the original impetus of the relationship was so neurotic that any growth at all doomed the couple to failure. Generally, by the time this couple seeks help, they are full of intense anger, bitterness, and vindictiveness. It is surprising that many of these marriages have lasted a long time. Both parties are lacking in trust and often experience a strong desire to hurt the other so that attempts at reconciliation are difficult, if not impossible. What generally happens is, that as soon as one spouse gets close to warm feelings, the other manages to sabotage the operation and vice versa.

When the vicious cycle is that powerful and there is *nothing* about the other that is appearling—even if the anger were gone—then why bother? The best we would hope for would be a more friendly or less bitter divorce and enough self disclosure and understanding to break the pattern within oneself so as not to carry this pattern over to the next relationship.

For those who believe in saving marriage at any cost, that may sound like heresy from someone who practices "marriage counseling," but any good therapist or counselor is actually in the "people" business and the major responsibility has to be to each individual first, and to the relationship second.

Many of us have come in contact with marriages that are destructive at their worst and blah at their best, and most people would agree they deserve better than to settle for less than they are capable of achieving.

People are starting to realize that the *institution* of marriage is not sacred nor does it need to be protected at all costs, but *people* are sacred and their best interests are to be preserved at all costs. If that is done, marriage will be well served and preserved and will be stable and well in years to come. As people learn how to properly gratify their true needs, more and more will be happily married, and lovingly rearing their children to be the same.

Remember, it is possible to fight through all this build-up of anger, start to relax and begin to develop communication skills. People do manage to sort through the emotional jungle and find tenderness and love. Often their "incompatibility" and "nothing to share in common" either ceases to be important or just disappears. Once the need to be punitive is no longer operating, they find a great many areas of common interest and concern.

The second type of incompatibility might be the saddest of all and most difficult to accept. This is where two people struggle through to real communication skills, find a depth of understanding within themselves, are in touch with real feelings, are able to share this without defensiveness, and *then* find that real love, passion, desire, life styles, and interests are just not there to be shared in common. They are usually good friends by this point and have little anxiety or feelings of blame. The magic just didn't happen.

What is true compatibility? What should we look for in each other? What areas are most important?

All of us have areas of interest, values and concerns that contact and connect us with others in the world around us. They are like electrical power sources that "plug in" to validate, confirm and enable us to experience and relate to others on hundreds of levels, some more important than others. We call these contact points.

If we don't share any common areas with someone, it is similar to being an electrical appliance with no outlet or power source to plug into. Therefore, we can't function in that setting. It takes a sharing of many such contact points to establish a complete and fulfilling relationship.

What then happens to your points of contact which don't happen to match with your spouse? (Six out of ten might be considered a great match up of individuals but still leaves four each that are not being used.) Whether these are actual, on-going needs not being met or unrealized potentials that your spouse doesn't stimulate to new growth, they are still an integral part of you. If not actualized and experienced they will wither from misuse and lose their power.

Obviously, no one partner can meet *all* the needs of another, but it makes sense that the more we share in common, the better chance for the relationship and the people as well to flourish. Which contact points have the greatest point value in measuring and predicting marital success? The ones closest to *integrity* and values.

While interests can be modified or expanded, and tastes can be stimulated and changed, life styles and integrity values are more representative of the person himself. Exceptions abound to any rule of of thumb, but some principles of personality stack the odds. Areas that generally don't change much over a lifetime or are deeply symbolic of who the person really is, would be religious faith or preference, conservative or liberal orientation to life, extrovert or introvert, athletic interests, musical and artistic tastes, sense of humor, and orientation toward family life, as well as sexual desires and preferences.

The more each partner demands the spouse supply all one's needs, the more contact points are necessary and the greater the demand and strain on the relationship. To the extent each partner freely gives and takes freedom to fulfill his/her own needs and to share contact points with friends and relatives, the more growth is possible. Again, it depends on the integrity level of the need. For most of us it is far easier to watch our loved one play tennis, cards, or attend the theater with a friend, than for them to have a sexual relationship with that same friend. However, some people cannot allow their spouses casual friendship even with members of the same sex, let alone the opposite sex, because they are too frightened of any competition. This is very confining to a relationship and the individuals in it and will be discussed further.

Right now, let's look at the positive side. What contact points do you share in common? Separate them into two divisions:

1. Life values that are essential to your personhood and growth.
2. Interests that are fun and desirable.

Each is important, but the latter grouping is certainly more flexible and adjustable. Only you can decide what areas can or cannot be compromised.

Do you have enough of the essentials? Can you tolerate the differences between you? When a loved one has a major difference of opinion or value from yours, do you tend to take that as a personal affront? What will you do with your needs that do *not* match?

These are vital concerns for your growth and future happiness. These questions are generally ignored when one is more interested in getting married than in being happy, when relief from loneliness takes priority over the exhilaration of anticipated growth, when needs surpass thoughtful preparation and when it is more important to have *anyone*, rather than patiently wait for a certain special *someone*.

So many people marry for fearful and neurotic reasons that we shouldn't be surprised at the divorce rate or the need for rehabilitation and re-construction of marriages to help them survive.

People often tend to see only a need to improve the relationship but not the people *in* the relationship or at least "not me, just my spouse." Personal growth heals relationships faster than vice-versa, although with some folks, they happen simultaneously.

Here are some basis, simple questions to ask yourself about the contact points in a prospective relationship:

1. Are we both far enough along in our separate searches for *personal identity* that we can bring out the best in each other, or are we still locked into the negative attractions of unfinished business?

This refers to the individuals who subconsciously marry the parent they most dislike in an attempt at reconciliation, or are looking for the missing element in themselves. The maturity of personal identity takes time for growth, *and* so does the active desire for the maturity. When you can comfortably live with your faults and tolerate the faults of others without undue strain or resentment, you are on your way.

2. *Am I comfortable* around this person?

That is, can I be my real self, or do I feel a need to work hard to impress the other or live up to unrealistic expectations? If you don't feel worthy of the other or constantly find yourself "being phony" or hiding parts of yourself that might not be accepted, you are being grossly unfair to yourself and prospective partner. No one can live under the constant pressure of pretense.

3. Have we been *acquainted long enough* to know how well we agree on important matters?

Or are we two desperate, needy people rebounding from past hurt or greedily grabbing at our one chance for love? Instant love is always suspect. Give it time. Total agreement is not always necessary or even possible but the ability to "see through the eyes of the other", experience empathy through identification and understanding of others' perception is essential to intimacy. The inability to see reality from the other's point of reference prohibits the passing of any meaning information between you, so that positions become polarized and behavior is interpreted as deliberately punitive or hurtful.

4. Can I permit the other *to be freely himself*?

This is the other side of the authenticity coin. If you can't wait to change this person, rescue him, or correct some bad habits—forget it, and find someone else. The chances are you will only damage yourself and the other. People who hide parts of self or desire to change others are fraudulent and not authentic. Discuss it *now*; share your fears or questions about each other. If you can't, you're with the wrong person.

5. How many *interests* do we share in common?

Do we both enjoy the same kind of music, people, books, activities and recreations? Is one of us bored by many of the things that please the other? (Sports on television, card games with friends.) Does one like to travel and go out a lot while the other is a homebody? Does one like the classics and opera, while the other craves country music and "Good 'Ole Boy" movies? Do we see humor in the same situations? Is one serious and intense about something that seems humorous to the other? Several of these points might be symptomatic of a person's whole personality, and not to be taken lightly.

6. Are our *backgrounds* similar enough so that we can understand each other readily in marriage?

Race, religion, family background, economic background, geographic differences (small town vs. large city approach to life), cultural differences. We are products of the manners and lifestyles of our past—Do they blend well with each other, or contribute to new growth? Are they irritants to be overcome? (A man or woman from a wealthy background, extravagant beyond current assets, married to a fiscal conservative.) One divorced and with children—the other not previously married. These are all potential problem areas.

7. How do *my family and friends* react to him/her? Does he embarrass me around them? Is it because I am overly sensitive or is it that he really doesn't fit with the other people I love and care for?

This may seem irrelevant to many people who see themselves as madly in love and unneedful of the rest of the world, and tend to close themselves in a love cocoon all of their own. The truth may well be that you are very much like those in your family and if they don't like him, it may be in the very near future that you won't either. Perhaps your judgment is clouded by other factors, and you are unable to see the total picture. Also, while you may feel little need for family ties and relationships in the first bloom of love, as time goes on you will want and need to be close to your family and relatives and for your loved one to be accepted and appreciated by them as well.

If it becomes necessary to choose between them and "give up" your family, it is common later on to "blame" and "resent" your spouse for this loss rather than to accept personal responsibility for your own choice. It may well be that your family was wrong and the healthy choice was to walk away from their rejection of you. This requires ultimate maturity in the choosing and care to accept one's own decision, rather than blame others for your disappointment later on.

8. What about *the family of the one I love*?

Are they a happy, well-adjusted family? If he comes from an unhappy family, how has it marred his personality? Which parent is he most like in personality? Which one of his parents are you the most like and what kind of relationship does he have with that parent?

If you are not sure . . . slow down . . . take the time to find out.

9. How well do we agree on *the roles of men and women*?

Perhaps the most vital question of all and an issue that has caused numerous divorce suits. In this changing culture where women are earning equal money and expecting shared experiences with the children and household, they have an obligation to make this known. Or a man may *expect* his wife to desire and pursue a career, only to find she wants only to be a mother and wife. As long as you agree, it will be comfortable. This is one area, however, that calls for flexibility as people often change these values over time.

10. How much do we *confide* in each other?

People who confide in each other are establishing better patterns for their future happiness. There is no other way to resolve conflicts and establish mutual avenues of direction than to openly discuss everything and anything. Elsewhere we discuss the need for mutual revelation; that love is based greatly on *knowing* each other deeply and intimately.

11. Can we *quarrel constructively*?

Are each of you learning and growing from the disagreements or simply taking turns hurting each other? A few quarrels may occur in almost all courtships, but many unresolved quarrels might mean a serious communication problem in marriage. If you can't work through disagreements when on "good behavior" (during courtship), it probably will not be easier when the mask if off (during marriage).

12. Do I *respect* my partner's judgment? Are there many occasions when I perceive him/her to be opinionated, judgmental, impulsive, indecisive, or not too bright?

It is very difficult, if not impossible to have a warm, close relationship with someone you feel is stupid, has poor judgment or makes decisions and displays behavior you can't admire.

13. How *authentic* are we being with ourselves and each other?

True love and intimacy are based on genuine openness and caring, an honest sharing of feelings in a way that supports and complements both parties involved.

People who *are* integrated, tend to marry themselves. That is precisely what is meant by the statement that the liberated or actualized person will not, and cannot, be happy with *less* than himself.

There will be many contact points of mutual interest, concern and values. Attitudes and approaches to life are more important than facts of individual taste, but even these will greatly match or at least be appreciated. The differences will not rest in the *areas of integrity* but be easily compromised or tolerated. This latter comes from the freedom of privacy and individual pursuits as well as shared ones.

When two persons are not possessively or fearfully locked into a couple-front, they can resolve many momentary variances in needs by allowing each to seek out his or her own pleasures, alone or with a friend. If one wants to watch football and the other prefers a movie, it helps to have two television sets. If everything has to be compromised by both doing *one* person's thing, there is a lot more chance for feeling misunderstood or rejected. Even people with exact likes don't always share the same timing . . . "I may love to dine out, but not tonight."

On the other side of the great divide, there is enough love and consuming desire to be together, coupled with a deep sense of fulfillment and satisfaction from *being* together, so they rarely allow too much space between them.

The differences between them serve as stimulation to growth, new opportunity for learning, relief from boredom and a balanced perspective.

No one has to be perfect and balance is not static or rigidly encased. To know that you have come far enough in life to *really* experience enough self-love and appreciation to truly be married to "oneself" and enjoy it, you've come a long way, baby.

VI. Can We Give Up Our Roles Long Enough To Be What We Are?

Are we more than the roles we play? In his book, *Pairing*, George Bach talks about the problems of "thinging" and "imaging" in relationships. When asked "Who are you?" we generally answer in terms of roles or "things." "I am a teacher, family counselor, spouse, parent, child, etc." If we wish to impress the other with who we are, we may tend to exaggerate or at least reveal everything we think will be impressive. That's "imaging"—raising our image in the eyes of the other, trying to be what we feel will make them like us and want to be with us.

While a healthy self-image cannot be separated from satisfaction in what we do or accomplish in the various roles we play, it is also true that we are many other things as well. "I am happy, sad, timid, bold, angry, depressed, loyal, cruel, alert, sincere, tender" ... the list is endless. In all of this "I am me. There are many parts of me ... some I like and some I don't . . . but all are me."

A client complains, "My husband is a Jekyll and Hyde. One day he's loving and kind, the next day he's angry and cruel. He's constantly changing."

It's not really that we change. It is rather that we express different aspects of ourselves at different times. "Which is the real person— the sober or the drunk one?" This makes interesting cocktail conversation. The truth is that he is *both*. When sober, the shy, timid side is in control and when drunk, the inhibitions become lowered and an angry, abusive side emerges.

James Vargiu, in his *Synthesis* magazine, refers to these various states as subpersonalities:

> There are in each of us a diversity of these semi-autonomous subpersonalities, striving to express themselves. And when

any of them succeed in doing so, we then play the corresponding role. But during that time the other subpersonalities are cut off. Yet they are still very much present even
though we may be unaware of them and they are likely to
create a lot of inner conflict. They may also have some very
beautiful, useful qualities that we may need, but not be in
touch with. So one of the easiest and most basic ways to
facilitate our growth is to get to know our subpersonalities.
As we understand them better, we can regulate and direct
their expression according to all our needs and goals, making them our helpers and our allies, and bringing them increasingly close to each other, toward greater harmony and
integration.

The Transactional Analysis approach also talks about subpersonalities in terms of the Parent, Adult and Child ego states in each of us.
These categories can be broken down into sub-groups such as over-
protective or punitive parent, rebellious or adaptive child, etc. Gestalt therapists talk about the "Top Dog" and "Under Dog" in all of us.

In the past few years, we have worked with several female clients,
usually in their mid-thirties with several children, generally "happily"
married, but a little bored, often with a dominating husband. Then
one day, these women enrolled in school to fight boredom and get
back into the swing of life. After a year or so the "women's lib syndrome" caught hold and they felt the need for abrupt change. They
found it impossible to be both individual and wife; free and committed. Having to justify their new-found needs (subpersonalities) for
independence, strength, freedom and growth, they felt compelled to
reject *all* the old—after blaming their husbands for abusing and mis-
using them.

There is really no need to make that choice. Both the sensitive,
compassionate wife and mother, *and* the independent, free individual
can dwell together in peace and harmony if both are recognized to be
legitimate and important parts of the total person. Each has a place;
each has a role.

We can certainly identify and work with these various parts of ourselves on a conscious level, and one of the major thrusts of therapy
is to help clients become comfortable with *every* part of themselves,
to own and acknowledge all their feelings. When we do this, the parts
we dislike become less threatening. When we don't, the ones we
deny or attempt to repress seem to get out of control and take over
our lives.

As we move toward the goal of being an integrated personality, we become increasingly able to choose, at any moment, which subpersonality we want to express. Until then, we are controlled by whichever subpersonality we are identified with at the moment, and thus *limited* to its particular good and bad qualities. But as the integration proceeds, every quality in us, every asset becomes available to us. When they are "on call", we have then the greatest freedom of expression; whatever is in us can be brought out and actualized.

The psychosynthesis approach speaks of a "higher order center," the "I" or "I-ness" around which the synthesis of the subpersonalities can occur, which is the harmonious and effective means of expression of the self-actualized human being.

In our own therapy sessions, we refer to the "higher order center" or "I" as, your "Spirit," the inner core of your beingness, of your integrity, wherein lies absolute truth for you. The subpersonalities we refer to generally as the "Crust," the scared, protective defensive side of you that won't trust the Spirit's sense of faith and adventure and wants to constantly protect you from all types of imagined dangers and pitfalls. It is often suggested that our clients talk to their "Crust" or subpersonality and ask what is wanted. Or, one can also talk to his "Spirit" or higher "I" to receive guidance and direction.

But there is another "I" who is the conscious awake state of awareness. We might call this the "assumed I." This is the person you relate to on a conscious level. In a sense, we must be aware of a neutral or human self, an intellect or whatever, that chooses which subpersonality will be in control (the adult if you will), who reaches for understanding from his higher consciousness and in turn determines and interprets the whole. This is the "assumed I" that all of us live with every day. Many people never, or rarely, seem to make contact with and hardly know of its existence.

Once we are able to make contact with the various subpersonalities (whether in our everyday intellectual awareness or through the more explicit confrontation within the scope of a guided daydream) we are prepared for the process of integration or congruence. James Vargiu calls this "the process of harmonization of our subpersonalities." He described the process in five phases: recognition, acceptance, coordination, integration, and synthesis.

Recognition of the existence of a subpersonality is obviously the first step. As long as we deny or distort unpleasant reality within us, we can never have the power or choice of change. We must first be prepared to recognize and identify the particular problem child of the moment.

The next step is *acceptance* of this subpersonality as a part of ourselves. It requires experiencing and owning those feelings no matter how distasteful, which can then be transformed into more positive ones. ("I feel sorry for this "dictator" part of me that keeps scheming for control when he really needs love.")

Coordination is a central aspect of the work with subpersonalities. It consists of reaching from the external demands of a subpersonality to its core, inner needs; from its actions to the meanings of its actions and the causes behind them; from what is says it *wants* to what it truly *needs*. In practically every situation, even if a subpersonality initially appears ugly, mean, in deep pain, hostile or a complete hinderance, once we reach its core we find that its *basic quality* is good. We see that it is not only acceptable but useful, and at times badly needed; that it can be harmonized with the other qualities, and that distortions and conflicts were produced largely in the frustrated efforts to express and actualize that fundamentally good quality. So the first step of coordination is to establish clear and open communication.

Integration is the process by which subpersonalities interact with each other and establish increasingly harmonious relationships, and often combine. Eventually this process can result in one whole, integrated personality.

Synthesis is a term to indicate the last phase of the harmonization process and concerns primarily the personality as a whole, and is essentially the culmination of individual growth. While personality integration is intrapersonal (within oneself) *synthesis* is basically interpersonal (between oneself and others) and transpersonal (similar to Maslow's "peak experiences," mystical experiences or a higher consciousness beyond our human understanding). As a result of this interplay, the life of the individual and his interaction with other human beings, becomes increasingly characterized by a sense of responsibility, caring, harmonious cooperation, and altruistic love. It leads to the harmonious integration of the human being with others, with mankind, and with the world.

The Guided Daydream

The most common method of harmonizing our subpersonalities, and thereby integrating ourselves, is the European technique often referred to as a "visualization" or "guided daydream," as created by Desoille.

In this method a person is reclining and relaxed for about five minutes. Relaxation is very similar to that of hypnosis in that the therapist speaks to the client in a low monotone in order to relax the various parts of the body. Instead of talking about the person becoming sleepy he talks in terms of the body becoming heavy, relaxed and calm. When the person is in this relaxed state, his muscular structure is less tense, his defenses are down, and yet he is fully awake and alert to what is going on around him. The therapist then places him in a dream situation such as telling him he is in a meadow, it is a beautiful day, and the sun is shining. The client is then instructed to report to the therapist the things he sees himself doing in the dream.

The person may see this dream sequence through his own eyes as though he were living it, or he might see it as if he were watching from a hill. Sometimes a person sees himself as a young child, sometimes at an age that is appropriate. Rather than attempting to do something, when the person is able to relax and let himself flow with the visualization, he finds that his imagination takes over, and that he is literally having a dream in an awake state, and his subconscious will work out his feelings for him in the same way that a dream works.

Basically three things are accomplished through the visualization process:

First, the process invariably relaxes a person at a very deep level of the core inner being, usually far beyond one's conscious awareness. (For the person who is highly nervous and upset this can be very effective.) Because the body is relaxed and less able to cut off subconscious feelings, these feelings come more readily to the surface. Muscle relaxation is correlated with lessened "anxiety." The visualization can last anywhere from thirty minutes to one hour and a half. Because it has been a very pleasant and relaxing time, the person becomes less afraid of his deep inner feelings, the things that are buried inside of him.

This leads to a second step, primarily catharsis, the releasing of more repressed images and materials. Often, for the next week or two after a visualization, the person will be much more congruent with his feelings and remember more of his dreams. He is instructed to write these dreams down and bring them in for further interpretation. The dreams would not necessarily be a continuation of the visualization, but simply a clue that more buried emotions have been released to the awareness level and the person is repressing fewer items.

The third thing that happens—occasionally, but not always—is that specific material from the past will come into a visualization and will be relived and reenacted by the person. On occasion we have had clients relive terrifying and very traumatic experiences at a very deep emotional level. They are re-experiencing the emotions of the moment that happened to them as children but with the strength and endurance of adults. At the end of this traumatic experience they are invariably exhausted yet very much at peace with themselves.

Even though the experience has been frightening to relive, the result is deeply peaceful and relaxing. This in itself is reassuring to them as they no longer need to defend against any of their deep innermost fears. Thus, psychotherapy helps people to find and be more comfortable with the meaning of their everyday experiences.

This visualization technique can also be used for what is called "Behavior Rehearsal" . . . an acting-out of what is expected to happen in the future (confronting one's boss for a raise in salary) to help extinguish much of the fear and anxiety which would normally be connected with the anticipated event. What really happens is that the practice of the good result extinguishes the fear of the bad or negative result.

Probably the most common focus of visualization is the process of confronting, looking at and acknowledging subpersonalities that we have tried to deny in our conscious state. They often start out as monsters, witches, dragons or worse; but once accepted, experienced, and even loved as "a legitimate part of myself," acting out due to feelings of rejection and deprivation, the monsters usually cry, shrink and become less ugly and frightening. It's as though they take off their masks and costumes and let you see who they really are.

Whether the visualization experience is a traumatic one or a pleasant romp in the meadow, the person seems to be put in touch with his deep feelings and is very relaxed in the process.

The following guided image sessions are detailed examples of the visualization technique. In both cases the clients are asked to bring forth a symbol representing their lives in the moment. These symbols could be dealt with as subpersonalities or in general (as we did here) as a diagnostic tool to show their present state of being. As you can see, it is possible not only to diagnose but to help change the present symbol and self image.

J. R. is a successful businessman, married, with four children; he has experienced impotence with his wife and is in therapy.

Therapist: I would like for you to visualize a symbol that represents your life right now, in the moment.

J. R.: I see garbage. It's waste, crumpled papers in a shopping bag.

Therapist: Dump the contents on a table. What is there?

J. R.: TV dinners, old clothes (my wife's), money, crumpled up bills, baby bottles, and more clothes.

Therapist: Anything valuable?

J. R.: Outlines of notes from school. I discarded them; they didn't bring me happiness . . . would like to salvage something.

Therapist: You are standing next to a recycling machine. Dump it all in and see what comes out.

J. R.:　　　I see myself at home when I'm younger. Glad to be home. The kids are small and running to greet me. I'm picking up my daughter. She's small . . . it feels great.

Therapist: Now pick up your son.

J. R.:　　　Feels good. He's hugging me back. My wife is at the door.

Therapist: What does she look like?

J. R.:　　　Soft and white. I'm reaching out to her. I feel good about her. Soft and warm, she's responsive. I'm glad to see her. We go into the living room and share experiences. We're happy to share with each other. We'll eat in a little while . . . Now we are all eating a nice meal together.

Therapist: Now it's after dinner and the children are in bed. Where are you?

J. R.:　　　On the couch in front of the fireplace. I feel warm and sexual, but I'm concerned about the kids.

Therapist: They won't wake up.

J. R.:　　　We're embracing, making love.

Therapist: Feel your bodies melt into each other and become one.

J. R.:　　　Feels great.

Therapist: Enjoy the afterglow.

J. R.:　　　I feel satisfied, warm, thankful.

Here was an impotent, angry man, who saw his life as garbage, was able to re-experience it in a new and positive way.

Our other session involves K. T., successful businesswoman; she is going through a divorce and has one child.

Therapist: I would like for you to visualize a symbol that represents your life right now.

K. T.:　　　It's a huge cable-like rope in a knot. It's big and brown, a very neat knot, a couple of inches in diameter and is cut at one end and pulled apart at the other. Not much rope. It's lacquered and neat. It would make a nice wall decoration.

Therapist: Pick it up.

K. T.:　　　It's heavy and large. I wouldn't want to untie it. I either accept it the way it is or throw it away. The cut edge is not lacquered. It's fresh rope. The other edge is pulled and ripped. All torn up but lacquered.

Therapist: Become the knot.

K. T.: I am the knot. I feel tight. The side with the lacquer I give out to others or show others; the other part is soft. The soft side is not as attractive or formal, but more comfortable to the touch.

Therapist: Which would others prefer?

K. T.: It depends. If you want pretty, you'd want the lacquered. If you like the rope and what it symbolizes, you'd like the soft side.

Therapist: Which do you prefer?

K. T.: I like both. One's attractive and one's comfortable. It brings back thoughts that it's better to be comfortable. When I first saw the cut edge, I didn't like it. Felt loose, and loose ends hurt. They are still sharp from the lacquer. I feel hurt from those edges; I have to be careful.

Therapist: You could break the lacquer off the end to be less sharp.

K. T.: That helps a little. My self-image is uncomfortable as a rope. It's lifeless.

Therapist: It could come to life by changing forms.

K. T.: All I see is me casually dressed. The knot symbolizes my heart . . . all tied up.

Therapist: Remove the lacquer as one piece. Now look at the rope.

K. T.: It's soft. I like it better with the veneer. It could still be a decoration.

Therapist: Become the rope again.

K. T.: The knot can move now. It's not stuck and more flexible. It's still a hard, tight knot, but it's supposed to be that way. It's not hurting the fibers and doesn't feel vulnerable. It actually feels stronger; a working knot now.

Therapist: Let's leave the lacquer off for now.

Evidently this young woman has two distinct images of herself; the lacquered, successful, well functioning front she gave the public and the softer, more relaxed, more natural side, which seemed rather vulnerable. She was comfortable with both but really didn't feel people would accept the softer part of her.

Part of her was "cut off" but unlacquered. She was divorced and cut off from a relationship and feeling the hurt. Part was ripped and torn but lacquered, leaving sharp edges that could protect her from outside invasion but actually wound up hurting her. This is the defensive side of us that says "I won't let anyone close enough to hurt me again." It also keeps people from being close enough to love us again.

At this point in her life, she was unsure of her real function and value. She could be a wall decoration or thrown away. The knot gave her structure and security and didn't want to be unravelled. However, she felt a little *too* tight.

She did not believe her soft, natural self was as attractive to others as the lacquered form she presented to the business world, but admitted that if someone really knew the soft side, it would be liked. When she was able to discard the lacquer and be her soft self, it was relaxing and she felt even more functional and even stronger than before.

Talking With Subpersonalities

You can talk to your subpersonalities and ask them what they want, why they are angry, etc. They can negotiate with each other. When one dominates, the other is ignored. Somewhat like children in a family situation, each seeks its proper place and acceptance.

In a real sense, you are acting as your own therapist by experiencing the feelings of the client (subpersonality), identifying with those feelings to better understand them, then providing love and acceptance and caring that they hurt.

Here is an example of a woman who confronted a very frightening part of herself in a guided daydream. Remember that all symbols in dreams or guided daydreams can be interpreted two ways: objectively and subjectively. In the objective interpretation, all the images represent your outside environment. A monster might represent a parent or your spouse. In the subjective interpretation, all the images are parts of you . . . subpersonalities.

Irene D. had been suffering from nightmares for several weeks and and was unable to clarify and barely remember them. Her fear was overwhelming at times. In a therapy session she was encouraged to try to go back to sleep to continue the dream the next time she was awakened at night. The following is what she reported:

"I awoke feeling terrified and overcome with anxiety. Staring me in the face was this ugly crippled monster with bulging eyes threatening to destroy me. I was convinced he could. My immediate feeling was to run away crying for protection . . . but somewhere down deep I felt I must *speak* to this monster before he destroyed me. Our conversation went something like this:

Irene D: What is your name?
Monster: My name is anger.
Irene D: What do you want with me? What have I done?

> Monster: I want my share of glory and recognition. I'm tired of being in the background—ignored and denied. I behave in this destructive manner, yelling and screaming because it's the only way I can be heard. I have to attack you to get your attention. You're always trying to control me and pretending I don't exist. Well, I do! I'm equally important. If it weren't for me, you wouldn't even know how you felt about anything. I'm like a thermometer; I keep you in touch with reality.
>
> Irene D: I apologize for not recognizing you. I'm sincerely sorry you are in so much pain. I will try to recognize your *needs* and *voice* more often and allow you to speak. I agree, you are important and I want to honor your presence. I want to become your friend and understand you.

As I did this, the monster began to cry and began shrinking into a little mouse and ran away. I couldn't believe my eyes.

This client had been suffering from the impression that it was in poor taste or even wrong to express anger. Her need was to appear calm and together, with never a ruffled feather. Irene D. was so out of touch with her feelings, the only way it was possible to deal with them was through intense dreams. At first it often seems foolish to try to have a conversation with the various sub-personalities and symbols of our dreams. This client was absolutely amazed at her conversation with the monster—particularly when experiencing it in the twilight hours of deep sleep. This is consistent with the pattern we have found: monsters cease to be monsters (actually changing shape and form) when confronted, listened to and offered loved.

Before we can get where we're going, we have to know where we are. If we're going to be healthy, self-actualizing people, we must *know* who we are and secondly, *love* who we are.

The more deeply we can experience and understand our feelings, needs, motivations, fears, anxieties, goals, and aspirations, the less need we will have to judge or condemn ourselves. The more we can believe in ourselves, the more we are capable of deep love for ourselves. If I understand what I feel and do and see it as appropriate, reasonable and realistic, I will like it and therefore like myself—the one who is feeling, doing, and experiencing.

VII. The Relationship Between Subpersonalities And Our Choice Of A Partner Or Spouse

In much the same way that subpersonalities fight with each other for supremacy and dissipate their energies through denial and struggle, we often confuse the situation even further by drawing to ourselves mates or partners who symbolize some unacceptable (but sometimes highly desirable) part of us. This makes the battle even more difficult because we have less control, awareness, and trust of the other and find it generally easier to use the other as a scapegoat for vindictive hostility, than to vent this hostility onto ourselves.

The loud uncouth clown is often attracted to the quiet, sophisticated or shy personality. Is it likely that the loud one hopes to be balanced and subtly subdued or made more "peaceful" and quiet by the presence of the quiet one, who in turn wishes to be more "turned on" and brought out of his/her shell by the boisterous clown? What often happens instead, is that each becomes very frightened and intimidated or embarrassed by the other, feels unaccepted and unacceptable to the other and, therefore, becomes even more extreme in trying to keep their individual identity. The loud one becomes louder and the quiet one, more withdrawn. It is unlikely for this battle to go on between two people without also going on between the subpersonalities within each of the two people.

Since much of both areas of conflict are below the level of consciousness, it gets very confusing and difficult to ascertain if I am more afraid of the negative you or the negative me.

The following material is taken from a therapy session with Barbara B., a 35 year old woman who has been married twice, and is intensely in search for some important answers regarding her relationships with men. Barbara has repeatedly been attracted to tall dark men. Most of her relationships have been unsuccessful attempts at union and were disappointing.

Therapist: What characteristics do these men share in common? How would you describe them?

Barbara: They are mostly irresponsible, cocky, independent, self-confident appearing, in control; they don't need me—just enjoy me. They ultimately *reject* me—but I find them irresistible sexually.

Therapist: I want you to *identify* with the male and try looking at Barbara. Describe what you feel *about yourself* and what you see in Barbara.

Barbara: (Barbara as male describing female) She is too vulnerable for me. I don't like being around *needy* people. I find her attractive because she makes me feel strong. I can control her, but I really want to be free of all obligations. It's not her fault; I need to be irresponsible. I want to be desired but I can't give myself. It's too scary —can't let her get too close—I need to control.

Having experienced in fantasy both male and female identities, how does this fit in with Barbara's choices?

If we can assume that within us are positive/negative male and positive/negative female concepts or aspects (as Jung postulates in his theory of anima-animus), then it is possible to take the next step: recognizing that the male Barbara described is the negative male within her own consciousness. It is that part of her which rejects her own negative feminine aspects. Barbara rejects her own vulnerability and neediness and her need to control. Part of Barbara longs to be free, sexually irresponsible and irresponsible in other ways as well. Part of Barbara can't give herself because it's too scary to be close and intimate.

Intimacy experienced *within* the Self first, is more comfortably actualized and recognized more readily in the environment. Alienation from the Self is evidenced by alienation in the world and the inability to relate real feelings and make an honest statement with our lives. In other words, if we can experience intimacy and communion with our various subpersonalities and become more aware of our true nature, then we will be better able to experience it in the world.

Unable to deal with this subpersonality's needs, Barbara seeks to resolve this problem outwardly in the men she chooses. She sets herself up with men who will reject her neediness for love, her vulnerability, and ultimately show that she is unappreciated. These men in actuality probably can't appreciate her either because they too are working out their problems outwardly in their choices of women. They may also reject their own vulnerability and neediness. So often we reject the qualities in others we find uncomfortable to deal with in ourselves. It's too close to home. We seek in our mates those qualities we admire and would like for ourselves, but lack the knowledge or experience to develop ourselves.

By being aware of these feelings as part of herself, Barbara has the choice of continuing to repress these feelings and not accept herself in these areas—*or*, she can *claim* and recognize her *own* rejection of herself and attempt the unfamiliar procedure of self-acceptance and love. When she can *allow* herself to be the *needy* child and give herself permission to be irresponsible occasionally—then in time, the need to "act out" these desires and feelings can diminish. By "acting out" we mean solving the problem externally with another.

But how much of ourselves have we claimed? This is the process of self-actualization. Claiming the whole Self—good and bad—and being the loving parent to the child within us provides an atmosphere of unconditional love, which is not necessarily unconditional acceptance of all behavior. We are not giving ourselves license to be destructive, but we are acknowledging our right to be loved with all our human frailties.

The next visualization sought to help Barbara get in touch with some positive male feelings within herself.

Therapist: Imagine that you are Sleeping Beauty. Where do you find yourself? What is the situation and what in general is going on?

Barbara: I'm lying in a casket with red velvet lining, wearing a long white dress. It's dark and there are many other caskets around in this large room. Down the hall a light beckons to me. I rise up in a light-weight body—very etheric and go down the hall to face the light. Behind a big desk is a bright shining light form—no face or person—just radiating energy and love.

Therapist: What do you see now?

Barbara: A pair of hands writing out some form of release. It says I'm free to go. I ask this form who he is and he says he's the energy force of all the bodies in the caskets. Now, I leave—I'm very happy.

Therapist: What happens next?

Barbara: I come upon a white horse and am riding over the countryside. It's a full moon and beautiful. I come upon a cottage. I'm welcomed as mistress of the house. They have been expecting me. I sit down in a high back chair next to the fireplace.

Therapist: Is anyone there?

Barbara: A tall dark man comes into the room and sits across from me. He seems very happy to see me. He's very warm and kind. (Pause) We just talk for awhile. Then we decide to retire. We walk up a long staircase and go to separate bedrooms. As I undress and crawl into bed, I wonder why we are in separate rooms.

Therapist: What are you feeling?

Barbara: I feel alone.

Therapist: Continue—what happens next?

Barbara: I find myself leaving my body and rising up to the spirit world. I'm on top of the roof. He joins me and we take off playing around the universe. We go to a ski lodge and are joined by many others. The atmosphere is very loving, sensual, joyous—I feel whole and complete. I don't want to leave.

Therapist: Go on.

Barbara: I can't.

Therapist: Relax more, breathe deeply; every time you exhale, you relax more.

Barbara: We're back in front of the fireplace. There is an apple cut in half placed in front of me.

Therapist: What does that mean to you?

Barbara: Separation—incomplete.

Therapist: Imagine the energy body of the whole apple which is covering the two halves. Focus your attention on the uninterrupted energy body of the whole apple. (Pause) Let's leave the apple for awhile. Identify with the female looking at the male in front of her. What does she see?

Barbara: He's strong emotionally but gentle and kind. He's very generous, very capable and in control of himself. He knows who he is and his strength. I can depend on him. I'm drawn to his strength and his capacity to endure.

Therapist: Now identify with the male. What does he see as he looks at the female in front of him?

Barbara: She seems shy, unaware of her strength and capacity; unaware of her place in the world. She *needs* my strength and support—my encouragement to *take* her place in this home. She doesn't know how to *ask* for help. I feel very close to her now. I offer her my hands across the table, then we embrace. I feel a warm glow of energy between us—a very powerful force. We become one.

Therapist: Barbara, what is the essence of this experience for you?

Barbara: Union.

Therapist: Before we close, ask him why you had to meet him in the spirit world and go to another planet to experience wholeness, joy and sensuality.

Barbara: He replied, "You wouldn't recognize me in the outer world. I'm already here—waiting for you. You have my support to be whole." I'm free—I feel complete for the first time.
(Barbara weeps softly.)

There is more to the entire visualization than we can go into here; let's consider the highlights:

This subpersonality or feminine aspect of Barbara was arising from a tomb—hidden away—dead for all intents and purposes—unable to resurrect these important feelings of shyness, inadequacy and lack of awareness of her place in the home (home being symbolic of marriage.) The body of light at the desk was the energy force of the higher consciousness and stated that it was the source of energy for all the other bodies in the caskets or in other words, the other subpersonalities of Barbara. She was set free to go and claim her heritage.

The tall dark man represents the positive male aspect of Barbara. She meets this part of herself for the first time. He's warm, encouraging and supportive. He wants her to take her place in the home.

The split apple was symbolic of the masculine/feminine aspects of Barbara. In this visualization she was able to experience wholeness —the union of masculine/feminine consciously joined into one. The split apple represented her feelings of separateness. Barbara realized this was the unity she'd been seeking—permission to be whole. This kind of experience of wholeness enables the individual to take the pressure off of a relationship, no longer demanding of the spouse the sense of completeness that is now felt within. Now, she can experience the true marriage of the soul—marriage to the Self—indestructable. This was represented by the energy body of the whole apple. In another discussion Barbara was asked:

Therapist: Where do you feel inadequate as a woman?

Barbara: It's hard for me to assert myself. I don't know my rights and strengths. Often, I will take a back seat in a group discussion or with a strong personality. I let them take over rather than insisting on my equality. I guess I'm not sure of my role in society or in a relationship—where is the power?

Many people, but women particularly, are cast into this role—either playing it or fighting against it—unsure of what to do, or how to change it. They know it's time for a change, but how do you change what you don't understand? This conflict can lead you in circles.

Intellectually Barbara could get a handle on her predicament, but through the visualization she could also experience and integrate her emotions with her intellect. Her subconscious made it clear symbolically that as a woman she was unsure of her place, and showed her just how much strength she could express—when and where. What was acceptable? What were her rights? The positive masculine aspect of Barbara revealed to her what she needed to know and experience: support and encouragement to be equal. The outstretched hand of the tall dark man says, "Yes, be yourself—make yourself at home here—be the mistress of the home—you have equal power— equal right."

This is Self love experienced on a deep level. This is acceptance. Bathing in this experience of Self acceptance and wholeness, Barbara is less tempted to seek these qualities in another form—especially a tall dark form.

If what we've been saying heretofore seems difficult for you to accept, just ask yourself this simple question. What is the most negative thing about your spouse that bothers you? Is it anger, passivity, too masculine, too feminine, possessive, demanding, unthoughtful, selfish, sadistic, etc.? Well, let us suggest that that's exactly what *you* have to work on in yourself or bring out.

For example, Bob's frustration and point of despair is when Helen exhibits her anger with him. However, we see Bob as one who is unable to deal with anger or even get angry. He is unable to experience anger in a healthy way. Bob was attracted to an angry woman who had no problems with anger. Why was he upset then and felt it was her worst quality? Probably because Helen, at this point, was not able to express anger in a non-destructive manner. Nevertheless, Bob needed an angry woman to get angry for him.

Another question: What is the most positive quality about your spouse? This is probably what you *desire* most *to be*.

Example: Sam deeply admired and loved Joan's capacity to be gentle and ultra-feminine. He was always strongly attracted to soft feminine women. This is an area where Sam had extreme difficulty and longed to express what was very frightening—and that was the feminine aspect of a loving gentle nature. He had too many hang-ups regarding his feelings about men being "soft" or a "push-over."

In one area we repress and deny feelings and need to work on bringing them into focus. In another area, we are aware of and desire to emulate certain qualities through identification. One is denial, the other is identification.

Likewise, the more actualized we become, the more likely we are attracted to the same qualities in others that we have developed. There again, we are seeking balance.

Logically and theoretically, the best way of handling this conflict is within one's self through the five phases of recognition, acceptance, coordination, integration, and synthesis discussed previously. Once accomplished (even during the process of accomplishment) we would expect the very same changes to be occurring simultaneously in our inter-personal relationships as our intra-personal one.

When we love ourselves, we find it easy to love others; accept ourselves, accept others; tolerate, be amused by, be understanding of, etc. Once we do this for ourselves, it is automatic to transfer this to others. So often the faults we hate the most in others are those we can't stand (but often won't even admit to) in ourselves. This is classic Freudian projection, but there is a great deal of truth to this statement. It is no coincidence that we find each other.

For every sick and destructive person, there is a "sickee" receiver of destructiveness. Why did you draw that person to you and vice versa? Why do you put up with it? (Often 15-20 years.) What is there in *you* of that madness that needs to be explored? (The *real* madness is that in about 98 per cent of the cases we've seen, when the poor, scared, little masochist rises up on her hind legs and shows enough strength to at least run like hell to the nearest divorce court, the big, strong, bad sadist crumbles like a helpless cookie and comes begging her to stay on bended knee. He's *more* scared and dependent than she is, as they usually both find out too late.)

The point we really want to make is, that whatever elements of destructiveness are in your spouse, there is a good chance that the same battle is going on between subpersonalities within you, and that's part of what drew you together. Recognize this and you might relieve some of the anger and resentment felt toward the other. At the same time, you might seek some introspection and understanding of the real issues involved, which is a lot better than "taking it personally" and being defensive.

There are many ways guided imagery can be used to put people in touch with their inner feelings.

In a group session we asked the couples present to picture a symbol of one's spouse. The directions—(which you can use for yourself with almost any symbol) were as follows: Picture a symbol that would represent your spouse in this very moment. Be aware of your feelings. Be aware of the setting or background surrounding the symbol. Become the symbol—how does the symbol feel? Become yourself again. Is there anything about the symbol you'd like to change?

This process could also be done with a symbol of your life, marriage, job, parent, etc. The purpose is to put you in touch with your deep, underlying emotions about each subject, so they can be experienced, not just talked about. Sometimes the feelings verify what is already known while sometimes clients are surprised to find new emotions that were not in their conscious awareness. In the therapy session guided imagery tends to be accepted as a more legitimate expression of feelings and therefore less criticized by spouses. For instance, if a wife expressed hostility toward her husband in group, he might be defensive, accuse her of being so, or attempt to talk her out of her feelings. If the *imagery* shows her hostile feelings, he is more likely to accept those feelings as a deep part of her and, therefore, a legitimate feeling rather than a defenseive attempt to make him look bad in the group.

Kay:	I saw Terry (her husband) as a knight in heavy armor, sitting on a white horse, waiting his turn to joust. He has a long jousting spear and is anticipating a fight.
Therapist:	What do you feel about this soldier?
Kay:	He's expecting a fight and that's Terry—always looking and always prepared with heavy armor on. He has very good defenses.
Therapist:	How about the spear?
Kay:	Obviously that's there to hurt me. (It could also have been there to protect her, but Kay assumed it was to hurt her.)
Therapist:	How did you feel *as* the soldier?
Kay:	That surprised me. I felt fear, when I expected to feel powerful and angry. I do not see Terry as frightened of me at all—just angry.
Therapist:	Did you change the symbol in any way?
Kay:	No, I wanted to but didn't know how and I guess that's true in my marriage—I don't know how I want Terry to change, but I'm scared of him.
Therapist:	What was your symbol, Terry?
Terry:	I saw Kay as a full grown Siamese cat, lying on the couch, quiet but aware.
Therapist:	How do you feel about this Siamese cat?
Terry:	This kind of cat is very beautiful, soft fur, loving when it wants to, but *only* when it wants to—extremely independent, tends to feel it owns you. It's a rather intimidating picture and that *is* the way I tend to see Kay.
Therapist:	How did you feel becoming the cat?
Terry:	I couldn't do it. I just could not get inside the cat—no idea what it was feeling.
Therapist:	Perhaps that also describes a problem you have relating to Kay—or others as well—there seems to be difficulty for you to have empathy with others—to put yourself in their feelings.

Terry: I know. There was one other thing—the cat had nice,
           long claws to call on at a moment's notice if needed.
           Those claws could really cut you up, and I didn't want
           that cat mad at me.

There is a powerful effectiveness in couples sharing images of themselves and this is magnified in a group setting of several couples. Imagery is more tolerable to the spouse as authentic material and not defensive vindictiveness. It sometimes comes as a surprise even to the person experiencing the visualization and often the person is somewhat or even totally unaware of the true meaning involved until these are interpreted, in the same fashion as one would interpret a dream.

Having the other couples present lends strong support and feedback. The input of 10-12 people can give you many more facets of interpretation and possible meanings to look for and everyone is experiencing a deep and personal sharing of oneself, not only with spouse and therapist but strangers as well. With this intimacy comes expressions of love, caring, support and well-being. There is a "family" relationship that is nurturing and supportive. Even when looking at unpleasant aspects of ourselves we are not rejected or run from but supported and cared about for our courage to do so.

Of course, not everyone has this group option or opportunity and Chapter 8 will give examples and directions for experiencing this in the privacy of one's own home, with or without a partner.

VIII. Guided Daydreams For You

You can try some guided daydreams for yourself in the privacy of your home; the process is really quite simple.

    1. *Relax yourself* in a chair or lying down in a comfortable position, making sure neither of your arms or legs are crossed. Crossed limbs cut off circulation flow and tend to tighten muscles rather than relax them. Sometimes we take three to five minutes to talk clients into a state of relaxation, but often if they just get comfortable and close their eyes the symbols come rather easily.

    2. We might suggest you start with *three deep, slow, cleansing breaths.*

    3. Then make a deliberate decision to *let go of all your body weight* and allow the chair or bed to totally support you.

    4. Now *imagine yourself being totally immersed in a blanket of peace* and tranquility. That should be enough to prepare you. (To illustrate how easy this is: Stop right now, and visualize your car, where you parked it. Walk to it, get in, start it and drive off. That's a visualization. It's that simple.)

    5. Now, *let a symbol* appear spontaneously of whatever you want to experience (your life, spouse, parent, job, something you fear, whatever.) Try to stay with the first symbol that comes even if you don't like it or if it seems inappropriate to you. Symbols can be anything, by the way—animals, plants, things, geometric forms—it doesn't matter. Many times our critical judgment gets in the way and wants to censor feelings before they have a chance to develop, for fear of learning something negative we are afraid to look at. The purpose of this exercise is to learn truthful information for greater clarity and understanding, so we must leave the judgment out.

    If a symbol doesn't readily come, you may deliberately create one but it is surprising how easily they will appear for most people.

6. *Be aware of the setting or background* your symbol is in. Be aware of all the details of the symbol itself and *how you feel* about them. Explore, look at or have an experience with the symbol.

7. *Try to become the symbol.* What does it *feel like to be* this symbol?

8. *How does the symbol feel about you?*

9. *Have a conversation* with the symbol. Often the symbol will answer back—or you can switch back and forth playing both roles.

10. *Feel free to change the symbol* any way you want and then put it anywhere you want.

11. As soon as you open your eyes, *write the experience down.* This a must; describe on paper in the simplest and most basic form how you felt about that symbol and what you experienced. If the symbol was a horse, write all your feelings about *that* horse (strong, weak, good for plowing all day, a fragile but fast race horse, swaybacked, mean, powerful, etc.).

If you have no feelings about that horse, describe how you feel about horses in general—love them, hate them, afraid of them, beautiful, ugly, whatever.

12. By the time you finish writing your feelings, including those of the symbol, *look at the things in the symbol you changed.* Where did you put it?

By now, you should have a clear picture of how you feel about whomever the symbol represents. If it doesn't fit your conscious feelings about that person (i.e., "I think I have no negative feelings toward my spouse but my symbol is a horse and I despise horses and think they are dumb."), perhaps you are repressing a lot of anger you don't wish to feel. Wherever there is a discrepancy between conscious awareness and visualization, we'll go with the visualization every time. Remember, it is *your* subconscious bringing out the symbol and its corresponding feelings. Symbols are the language of the unconscious and are used to by-pass the intellect and go directly to the source. Trust them.

Part II

Childhood Revisted

The importance of the parent-child relationship cannot be over-emphasized. In order to fully understand, appreciate and function in my role as a good parent, I must first accomplish this as a child to my parents. This will usually entail my taking the initiative in seeking out my parents to better nourish and cherish the child within me.

IX. The Needs Of Childhood . . .
Everyone Is Somebody's Child . . .

The disturbed adult is often simply the outer expression of a deprived and angry or frightened child, as we have seen in the previous chapter on imagery. These subpersonalities are the deprived aspects of our child self trying in distorted ways to get current needs met.

By the same token, a healthy adult is undergirded by the healthy child. Since many of us did not grow up as healthily as we should have, our task is to help the child "heal up" so that the adult can "grow up." Just as the pathway to a good marriage leads through our parents . . . as the pathway to the *you* part of a relationship leads through the *me* part . . . the pathway to being an independent and responsible adult leads through the struggles of being a dependent and vulnerable child.

You can start down those various pathways of emotional well-being now. We can provide some intellectual signposts or insights to keep you *on* the pathway. Furthermore, you can reach some of the deep feeling levels that validate this experience of well-being to you personally. More important than just *acting* different, you can experience at a very deep, personal and feeling level, a lessening need to defend yourself, recognizing your real needs; you can know the excitement of *being* different—in attitude, frame of reference, feeling tone, and experience.

Where Am I Now? . . .
And How Did I Get This Way?

You are a product today of all your yesterdays. The things you do are symptoms of what you are. They are the methods you have found to satisfy your basic needs, which you might not always even understand. Consider the universal proberb, "The child is father of the man." The man is the result of what the child was. Everything that has ever happened to you in the past has helped determine what you are today.

This chapter should be read from two viewpoints: first, that of a parent rearing children; second, and more importantly, that of yourself as your parent's child, who had a very personal and private rearing all your own. Perhaps by recognizing some of the strengths and weaknesses of your childhood situations, you will be able to see many of the similarities, differences, and influences that are affecting the manner in which you now relate to your children. These are the foundation years that gave us most of the repressed materials that come back to haunt us later on.

It's so easy to get stuck in a rigid pattern of *Do's* and *Don'ts, Right's* and *Wrong's,* that we forget it is the *Atmosphere* and *Attitudes* of the home that make the deepest impressions when it comes to rearing our children properly and meeting their basic needs.

> Children Learn How To Love By Being Loved . . .
> They Learn How to Respect By Being Respected . . .
> They Learn How To Give By Being Given To . . .
> How To Receive By Being Received Of . . .
> How To Listen By Being Listened To . . .
> How To Care By Being Cared About . . .

If your child is rejecting, selfish, disrespectful and unmindful of the needs of others . . .??

Let's first explore what we mean by love.

Let us divide all types of love into two general categories: unconditional and conditional love. Unconditional love says "I love you, because you exist and I need no other reason to love you." Conditional love says, "I love you *because* you do what I want; you please me; you are like me, you love me first, etc." (Grandma's rule in Behavior Modification is "You do what I want you to do, then I'll let you do what you want to do.")

For the most part, we experience unconditional love only from the immediate members of our family. For most of us that includes our parents and brothers and sisters but for others, under varying conditions, it might include a whole family or "clan." In some respects, a generalized brotherly love for mankind is unconditional in nature, but certainly not to the degree or intensity of a personal relationship.

Practically all other types of love seem to be included on the "conditional" side. All other types of relationships are really types of conditional love, with varying degrees of depth and intensity. From friendship to courtship, to romance, to erotic love—these are all based on various conditions of the relationships. When we try to make them into unconditional types of love, they become "sick."

What is meant by "sick" is when a deprived spouse who never received sufficient unconditional parent love tries to turn the spouse (and often the children as well) into substitute parents and wants the primary role of the relationship to be a parenting one, rather than two adults sharing. In the extreme, the deprived spouse may continually "test" his/her spouse to see if the unconditional love is still there. "How far do I have to go before you too will reject me?"—by drinking too much, gaining weight, having affairs, being irresponsible, etc. "If you love me, you'll forgive me."

Sometimes we refer to these two types of love as "mother love" and "father love," but this can become somewhat confusing. It leaves us with the impression that only mothers can give unconditional love and fathers can only give conditional love, which is not true. The mother who only gave unconditional love would be a sentimental slob who could never say "no" to her children; the father who only gave conditional love would be an authoritarian monster who lived by the rule book but who had no tenderness or feeling.

It should go without saying, however, the effective parents must be able to give both conditional and unconditional love. The child needs to feel that no matter what he does, he, as a person, will never be rejected, and that is unconditional love. On the other hand, he must be aware that he will be protected from doing things that are destructive and that certain conditions are laid down for his behavior. These expectations of behavior must be fulfilled.

The child's first emotional experience is that of being loved. "I am loved because I exist, and this is a passive experience which requires nothing of me in return except to exist." For the most part up until eight and one-half to ten years of age, the problem with the child is that of *being* loved. Some psychologists go so far as to say that the child himself does not really love up to this point. The reason for this is because he cannot survive without help until this age. In other words, he has to "love" the parent back in order to get the parent to take care of him. He cannot really love until there is a choice *not* to love. While that may be technically true, there are certainly signs that children as young as two and three years of age can give love for its own sake. Many times we have seen a small child love and comfort and take care of his or her parents when they were ill and give an unconditional type of love when there was little or no immediate gain from it.

The child *Learns How To Love By Being Loved,* and the earlier the age that he receives and is able to experience this, the earlier the age at which he will be able to return it. Receiving this love and believing in it enables the child to internalize his parents' love enough to go on to adult love, one based on his/her own productivity and desire to share.

Immature Vs. Mature Love

Infantile or immature love says, "I love you, because I am loved." "I am able to love you, because you love me first." This is very appropriate for the infant who is not able to create love and knows nothing about it. By contrast, mature love says, "I am loved because I love," or "My love creates a loving response in you."

Infantile love says, "I love you, because I need you." This is deep and intense dependency need of the small child who cannot exist without his parents, is appropriate for the young child but inappropriate for the mature adult. We do not mind being responsible for the life or death survival of our small child, but we rather resent it when the "child" becomes thirty-five or when our husband or wife makes the same dependency request of us.

Mature love says, "I need you, because I love you." This is an entirely different type of need. I do not need you to survive, to clothe me, advise or direct or keep me alive in any way, shape, or form; but because I love you, I need you to receive my love, respond to my love, and to share myself with you in a hundred different ways. if I do not have this from you, my love will be invariably incomplete.

To Feel Loved . . .

To show how this parent love affects adult children more than the method of child rearing or parental theories, or even behavior change in the parent or child, let's look at Sharon and her mother.

Sharon, a young woman going through a separation and possible divorce, had her mother from out-of-state staying to help her. She did not want her mother there, did not want to discuss her in therapy, and only wanted to discuss ways of saving her marriage. Yet it seemed desirable to take advantage of her mother's presence to work through some of Sharon's parent-child needs. The more it was discussed, the more anxious and troubled she became and the more reasons she came up with to send her mother home: "Mother is a slob; I'm a compulsive housekeeper. Mother spoils the children; I don't. Mother smokes and drops ashes on the furniture and carpet. Mother spills food. Mother is defensive. Mother rejected another daughter who was in therapy; I hate Mother and don't want a thing from her."

There could not have been greater incompatibility. In situations like this, the client is sometimes discouraged from confronting the parent alone. It can often escalate into a greater conflict and make all one's worst fears come true. Even in the therapist's office, this can still occur, but if it does, at least the therapist is there to comfort and try to hear both parties and help them hear and say what they really want. Often the very setting of the office and presence of a professional and objective person mitigates against a certain amount of defensiveness. At least the therapist can quickly identify defensiveness without being judgmental or blaming. This process is often enough to encourage both parties to begin a new type of dialogue they could not have attained unaided.

In this case, Sharon had decided to confront her mother alone with all her hateful feelings. To her amazement and surprise, the expected defensiveness was not expressed. Instead, Sharon found her mother listening to her feelings, caring and understanding. Apparently mother had learned a lot from the other daughter's therapy and had no difficulty apologizing for all the hurt she had unknowingly inflicted on her family. She showered love and concern on Sharon, with no need to defend herself, and allowed Sharon all her hurt and anger. Her mother just accepted it.

Sharon discovered a truth many people never know. When you are *allowed* to express all your hate, anger and resentment, *and* it is not judged or defended against, there is an immediate outpouring of love toward that same person who has just given you this most beautiful gift; *the right to your feelings*. When someone loves you enough to allow you to hate them, tremendous closeness, love, and intimacy are possible.

The point to be made with this story is that neither person really changed. Mother is still a slob who spills food and drops ashes on furniture and carpet; Sharon is still a compulsive cleaner. *But now*, it isn't important. Sharon has discovered a new sense of humor and she kids her mother about it, hands her an ashtry, shakes her head at the impulsiveness of her own feelings. She didn't *decide* to handle it this way. The change of attitude came as a complete surprise to her. Once Sharon felt loved (the real issue of why she was angry with her mother), she could tolerate mother's faults. She'll still clean her mother's house when she visits there and follows after her at times with an ashtray, but her *feelings* are different.

We have all see homes in which the impossibly bad habits of the other lost all importance when both sides felt loved and did not feel that the bad habit was a "conscious device to deliberately and vindictively put me down as an example of your hate for me." In some cases where there is truth in the latter statement (or even where there is not), often there *is* a change of behavior because the person now wants to demonstrate his or her love in a concrete way. However, change is not as important as the inner revelation of both parties of what the behavior really means and what the person really is trying to express.

In the long run, methods of child-rearing are primarily reflective of the parents' personalities more than expressions of love or the lack of it. Permissive parents have been known to rear beautifully healthy children on one hand and sometimes spoiled, arrogant, grasping and rebellious children on the other. Authoritarian homes are capable of the exact same results. Why? What has made the difference?

In a permissive home a child may say, "Gee, my parents let me do anything I want to do; they really trust me and love me. I wouldn't do anything to betray that trust."

The child next door, with equally permissive parents may say, "My parents don't give a damn what I do, and they don't love me."

In an authoritarian home right across the street, one child will be saying, "My parents control my activities very closely, because they care about me and watch me and don't want me to be hurt."

Next door the child of similar parents is saying, "My parents don't love me at all, and they don't trust me a bit, so therefore, they control and try to keep me from doing the things that they did when they were kids."

In each case, the important variable was whether or not the child *felt* loved. Love is an intangible feeling that cannot always be known by the action that is performed. Parents have a tendency to justify or prove their love by describing their behavior, but the child can feel deep beneath the behavior (usually on an unconscious level that he or she cannot understand) whether the love is coming through.

Perhaps we should say at this point that we believe that every child loves his parents and every parent loves his child. There is no way of proving this but somehow we feel it is as much a biological fact as an emotional one. When a parent acts in a rejecting or cruel or exploiting fashion, it is not because he cannot love his child or is incapable of this, but it is because he is unable to make contact with his deep love for the child. He is reacting on a purely defensive or selfish basis to keep himself from being hurt or embarrassed, and therefore, the child can only feel that and cannot feel the love that is buried somewhere underneath.

A minister friend tells a story of his small son's first entry into Sunday School. When the child left the nursery to go to the more structured Sunday School, he became an immediate hellion and disrupted the class completely. The teacher tried to calm him down and get him to stop his disruptive behavior, but he only answered that she should leave him alone, because his Daddy owned that church! (Of course this was not true, but the child in his fantasy and imagination saw it that way.)

The father was summoned to do something, and the child was forced to submit to the rules and regulations of the Sunday School class and to stop his disruptive behavior. The minister said it took him approximately ten years to figure out what his son was trying to ask him. Obedience was not the issue. The son was not going to be allowed to disrupt the class or to be a little hellion. He was going to obey. The issue was *why* he was going to obey.

"Do I have to be a good boy in order to protect your reputation as the minister of this church, or do I have to be a good boy, because it is really best for me and is something I will have to learn in order to get along with people for the rest of my life?"

We wonder how many people reading this book were brought up with the unconscious feeling (which quickly comes to a conscious level when brought to your attention) that they had to be good or successful or productive people who made Mom and Dad look like good parents in the neighborhood . . . and not because it was simply best for them, as they grew up. How many fathers push their sons into Little League, so they can work off their own frustrations as a non-athlete or athlete who didn't make it? How many stage mothers shove their children into show business so they can live through their children and get the satisfactions which were denied them when they were young?

Or, "Gracie's kids come home with A's and B's all the time, and I'm expected to brag about C's and D's? . . . "George next door was just accepted at Harvard, and I'm embarrassed, because you'll be lucky to graduate from high school." . . . "Why can't you play the piano like your cousin Joanie?" . . . or the capper of them all, when the sixteen year old daughter comes home tearfully proclaiming she is pregnant, and Mother screams out in return . . . "How could you do this to me?"

When the child gets arrested . . . or pregnant . . . or fails . . . or just doesn't live up to his or her potential or to the expectations of his or her frustrated parents, *and* the parents' immediate reaction is that the child has failed them, that is a classic example of exploitation. The parent is putting his needs above the child's. Naturally, all parents are hurt or embarrassed or frustrated at the failure of their children. But their primary concern is how their *child* must feel—and for the child's welfare—*if* the parent is really feeling the child's needs and the parents' own love for this child.

Maslow stated in a filmed interview, "If you respect the personality of the child, you leave it alone." What did he mean by that? Did he mean that you leave the child alone? Certainly not. The parent is under obligation to discipline, direct, guide, and take care of his child and in no way can leave him alone.

He owes the child the intimate sharing of his own value system, religious faith, ethics, manners and morals . . . to suggest meaningful alternatives and illuminate possible consequences . . . to teach the child how to weight judgments and make mature decisions *and* to protect the child from danger or pitfalls his judgment is not yet qualified to recognize.

Maslow said to leave the *personality* alone. Don't try to shape or mold your child into something he is not, but do attempt to provide the proper atmosphere within which he can grow and achieve and be successful at his own pace and on his own terms.

The opposite course is to rear the child primarily to satisfy your own personal ends, pushing the child to be a great athlete, actor, lawyer, doctor, etc. so that you can have the vicarious thrill of an accomplishment that eluded you or so you can get the glory of what a sacrificing and great parent you were to have had a successful child. The difference is in which is primary, your child's success and satisfaction or your own parental pride.

Love And Imagination

The importance of the child's imagination is not given enough attention in many of today's psychological theories of child development. Since a child is necessarily limited in resources for controlling his environment or even understanding at a depth level, he must turn to fantasy, in the forms of dreams, rationalizations, day-dreams and imagination, to interpret his world and make it come out in a reasonable way that maintains his integrity and sanity.

A psychiatrist named W. Earl Biddle has constituted a system of depth psychology which explains normal and abnormal behavior and restores imagination to its rightful place as a function of the total personality. In trying to integrate the beliefs of Freud with his own, Biddle clarifies a theory of childhood that fills in the gaps of many of today's psychological theories.

First of all, Biddle believes with Freud that influences exerted upon the child mold the entire future of the individual; "the child is father of the man" in the sense that everything that man is today is a product of his childhood experiences. A child's imagination and fantasies are both his greatest assets and his worst enemies. According to the logic of the child, a good person is all good, and a bad person is all bad . . . so, according to Biddle, in addition to his real parents, the child has what Biddle calls the fantastic good parents and the fantastic bad parents.

His real parents become endowed with these good or bad traits when they treat him in ways he considers to be good or bad. Until age three, the child lives mostly in extremes; he either loves or he hates.

That is why when a three-year-old shakes his fist in your face and screams with all the intensity of his body that he hates you for not giving him an ice cream cone, he can really make you believe it. The parent feels threatened by this intense attack because at that moment the child completely and totally hates.

Ten or fifteen minutes later when the child is snuggling up to you, and kissing and loving you, and telling you how much he cares about you, he is also total in his feelings and equally sincere. It is very difficult for some parents to understand this, because they do not live in this world of extremes.

The parent is thinking that if *he* screamed out with such intensity he would be saying, "I hated you yesterday, I hate you today, and I will hate you the rest of my life." The child is only saying, "I hate you at this moment" or "I love you at this moment" and is not being inconsistent by changing his mind a few minutes later.

Only with satisfying experiences in reality-testing are these extremes of love and hate modified. As the child grows up he begins to remember that "Yesterday Mother gave me an ice cream cone, and even though she denied me one today, perhaps she is not all bad."

Children use things or objects to represent their parents and to deal with them. We are all familiar with the scapegoat method of dealing with our anxiety or anger. The president of the corporation had a fight with his wife and takes it out on the vice-president who in turns chews out the foreman, who fires his number one worker, who comes home and beats up his wife; the wife in turn beats the oldest child, who beats up his smaller brother, who goes out and kicks the dog, which in turn bites the cat, and the cat eventually will attack the corporation president's wife thereby completing the cycle.

When Mother hits the child, his first reaction is to want to hit Mother back, and in most cases he does exactly that. He hits Mother back and a strange thing happens; she hits him again and again. He soons learns that Mother is bigger than he is and can hit harder. Therefore, it becomes unsafe and rather stupid to go on hitting Mother. He still has to do something with his anger, so he goes into his bedroom, picks up a pencil and breaks it in half. According to Biddle, he is not really breaking the pencil but is breaking Mother's back.

A child's imagination is so strong he does not really know what the limits of his powers may be. Therefore, a few minutes later, he may very well sneak into the kitchen to take a look and see if Mother's back is really broken. When he sees that she is all right, he is relieved that he has been able to hate her or get his anger out toward her by breaking the pencil, without actually destroying real Mother. Probably the most traumatic experience of a child's life is to wish the parent dead because of extreme anger at the moment, and then while the child is in his room angrily acting out his feelings, the parent goes to the grocery store and is killed in an auto accident. The child will either consciously or unconsciously believe the rest of his life that he has killed his parent or feel guilt even if he knows better.

One such experience happened to John. In a marathon therapy situation, John recalled an experience he had totally forgotten. He saw himself at seven years of age flying an airplane in his bedroom. His father was a military pilot who was often away from home. John resented this very deeply and he also hated his father who was a very authoritarian and cruel person. Therefore, John was always torn by not having his father's physical presence or being upset or angry with his father when he was at home.

At this particular time, in his room at seven years of age, he was flying an airplane over his head with a string and playfully shooting it down. He would shoot this airplane in his imagination and then crash it viciously to the floor. As he did this over and over again, he imagined killing his father, with whom he was very angry. The very next day he was told by his mother that his father had been shot down in action the day prior.

John was told later that he went into shock and did not talk again for the next six months. When he did begin to talk, he stuttered and has to this day. One of the things that brought him into therapy was the desire to conquer his stuttering habit. But he had completely forgotten this incident until it flashed back to him during the marathon. He was experiencing extreme guilt and feeling all those seven year old feelings of having killed his father. In Biddle's terms he had shot down the imaginary bad father . . . killed him . . . (coincidentally) his *real* father happened to die. He had no intention of killing his real father, only his imaginary bad father.

The Child And Sexual Identity

According to Biddle, all objects when reduced to their primary symbolic meaning are mother and father symbols and not sex symbols as claimed by Freud. For instance, in dream interpretation, Freud would interpret all the symbols as either male or female phallic symbols. Biddle goes a step further to say that they are mother and father symbols, which certainly would not remove the sex from them, since all mothers and fathers are sexual people.

In other words, if I should encounter a friend today, the chances are that I would use him (or her) as a symbol in my dreams tonight. However, the real meaning of the dream might be interpreted in several ways: I might be dreaming in one aspect about my feelings toward this particular friend . . . or toward my son . . . or toward myself . . . but the primary or basic symbol would be that of how I felt about Father (which is symbolic or symptomatic of how I feel about all men). The same is true of women and their mothers.

In dealing with the Oedipal fantasy Biddle claims that children imagine themselves as "spirits" and desire spiritual union with both parents. Freud was right in saying that little boys do compete with their fathers for Mother's attention, and so do little girls with their mothers. They do talk about marrying their parents, and they do fight for a closeness with them. Biddle believes that a spiritual union with both parents, primarily the parent of the opposite sex, is the child's goal.

"The good father desires and permits both the boy and the girl to possess the good mother and vice versa. These permissive and possessive fantasies are essential to normal personality development and good mental health. The child intensely needs this intimate spiritual union with the good parents and incessantly strives to achieve it.

"If the child is deprived of parental love and respect, he cannot enjoy his fantasies of intimate closeness to the parent. If the real father is actually hostile, the boy will be afraid of him and will be unable to indulge his fantasies of closeness to the mother because of the real threat of attack by the father. The girl cannot incorporate Father in fantasy because of the danger he might cause real damage to her if incorporated."

How often do we see children dressing up in their parents' clothes or literally walking in their shoes? In a sense they are trying to get inside Mother and Father and see what it is like to be them. This is what Biddle means by the spiritual union with both parents.

The girl gets her sexual identity from Mother. She learns, hopefully, what it is like to be a woman by seeing what Mother is, and what Mother does, and how Mother relates to life in taking her own needs seriously. If she identifies with Mother, then she tries to be like her. If she does not like Mother's image of what a woman is, then she will inevitably try to be the opposite of Mother.

Next the girl tries to work out her sexual identity as a woman by relating to Father. Father is the first man in her life and the most important one. She learns with him what it is like to be seated at the table, to have the car door opened for her, to be appreciated when she is all "dolled-up" in a new dress.

If Father thinks that she is beautiful and desirable and loveable, then other men will also. By the same token the boy gets his sexual identity from Father and works it out in reality-tests with Mother.

Biddle continues that, "If the child is unable to combat the threatening parent and is forced to give up his wishes for spiritual possession with the parent of the opposite sex, under threat of his own annihilation, then he will be abnormal and not normal as claimed by Freud."

If the boy's real father is jealous and hostile towards him and resents the time that Mother gives to the child or the affection that's between them, then the boy will actually become afraid of real physical damage at the hands of Father. If Father catches him getting too close to Mother, Father will reject him or punish him. If Father should "read his mind" and know how close the child wants to get to Mother, the same thing will happen. For fear of retaliation from a real, hostile Father, the child cannot even enjoy his fantasies of intimate closeness to Mother. He can't get close to Father either because of Father's hostility and anger. If Father's big, towering body can hardly contain all the hostility and anger within it (when I imagine being inside of Father), then I am afraid that this hostility and anger filling up my little body will blow me to smithereens.

If the child, by the force of his own personality and perhaps with one parent's help, can overcome the real threatening parent and win the battle for spiritual possession, he will be all right, according to Biddle. If he cannot and must give up spiritual possession of the parent of the opposite sex, then he will be destroyed or abnormal.

In summary, Freud contends that the boy desires *sexual* union with Mother and wants to destroy Father. If he gives up his need for sexual union with Mother and identifies with the hostile father who will not let him have Mother, he is normal. Biddle contrasts this by saying the boy wants spiritual union with Mother. A loving, benevolent father encourages and allows him to have this spiritual union with Mother. He is able to identify with this warm, loving father and in this way to achieve his own sexual identity. This makes him normal.

Every woman needs a warm-loving-physical-affectionate-accepting-kind-and-sensual relationship with father that is not sexually threatening to either one of them.

Of course, Father is the key here, as the daughter will not be threatened unless the father is. If the father is so threatened by his daughter's sexuality that he is afraid he might have intercourse with her and therefore has to run away from her, the daughter also is terrified. Consciously or unconsciously she feels that her sexuality is so powerful that even her own father cannot handle it. If Father can't handle it, she cannot be comfortable with her sexuality and feels that it is too powerful to be received by other men. If Father does have intercourse with her, then an even worse thing has happened. Now she beaten Mother and again does not know the limits of her own sexuality. She is burdened also with the guilt of what she has done and usually grows up feeling totally responsible for the act. It seems very difficult for the daughter to accept the fact that Father might be to blame. She goes on in life feeling that the only way one can satisfactorily express love to men is sexually. She may like or dislike this and react accordingly.

For instance, as a result, one girl may be totally turned off by sex and have difficulty giving herself to any man. On the other hand, her twin sister might become a nymphomaniac who cannot get enough sex from men. Each woman has a deep sexual problem but expresses it with exactly opposite symptoms.

Reality-Testing Our Child-Needs

Biddle continues that our social relationships are motivated by the need of the individual to improve his mother and father fantasies through reality-testing in relationships with other people. In other words, if my own mother and father are hostile and cold and indifferent to me, then I will seek mother and father substitutes that are not.

A five-year old, who has had a hostile and rejecting mother, may find his first warm and loving mother image in a grandmotherly kindergarden teacher who cares very deeply for him. In order to find their good images young people turn to and identify with aunts or uncles, scoutmasters, pastors or youth leaders, sports heroes or musicians.

"Only by improving or annihilating the fantastic hostile parents, symbolically represented by hostile real people can the good parents be incorporated," Biddle claims. "Competition in society commonly helps to overcome the fantastic bad parents."

Larry is a client whose experience demonstrates Biddle's views. Five years ago Larry was in his mid-thirties with a wife and several children. He held a rather average job as a salesman and deliveryman for a small company where he had worked for approximately four years, with five or six other salesmen-deliverymen. Larry's very sadistic father had died approximately ten years previously.

It seems little coincidence that his boss was also a rather cruel, sarcastic man. Larry saw his boss as one who picked on him continually and always took advantage of him. It did not seem that the man took similar advantage of the other drivers. Larry fumed about this for years but put up with it for fear of losing his job, which he needed to support his family, and because he was not too sure he could get a better job. This situation came up one might in a couples' group he was attending. Larry was really able to get in touch with his needs about this situation as the group encouraged him not to put up with this nonsense. They urged him to confront his boss with his real feelings. After one particularly productive group session, Larry went home determined to confront his boss the next morning.

He went to work with this on his mind and simply waited for the boss to give him an opening, which he knew would come very quickly. No later than fifteen or twenty minutes after he had arrived at work, the opportunity presented itself. When the boss started his tirade, Larry immediately began to feel his anger. After a very brief time, he stopped the boss by saying that he had taken all the nonsense that he was going to take from him and was tired of being treated in this despicable manner. He was a human being, intended to be treated as such, and was no longer going to put up with the inhuman treatment he was getting. He was not going to be taken advantage of any more—he was not going to do all the extra things that were never appreciated. He wanted the same type of treatment the other men were getting, and he wanted it now or, "You can take your job, and I'll tell you what you can do with it!"

At this point, Larry stepped back waiting to be fired. He had already made up his mind that the boss in no way would accept this type of answer and that he would be fired. He had just decided that his integrity was more important than the job and that it was worth being fired for, as he needed the respect of his wife, children, and himself more than he needed the job.

Surprisingly enough his boss also took a step backward and a deep breath. He profusely apologized to Larry, saying that he was totally unaware of treating him in this fashion. He confided that he had always liked Larry better than the other drivers and actually had teased him and been sarcastic with him because he liked him best of all and thought that Larry knew that. He assured him that his behavior would change and that he would never again take advantage of him. Over the next several months, they became almost like father and son, and a short time later Larry received a rather generous raise in salary. Needless to say he kicked himself all over town for waiting four years before taking his needs so seriously and expressing himself.

Everyone likes stories with happy endings, but what would have happened if Larry had been fired? Because he had been so cut-off from his own feelings, he had no way of predicting the outcome; and the percentage was on the side of his being fired. Would he then have been wrong for having taken his needs seriously? In Biddle's terms "only by improving or destroying the fantastic hostile parents, symbolically represented by hostile real people, can the good parents be incorporated."

Larry received his bad father-image from a hostile real father. It was validated by having a hostile real boss, who symbolically represented this bad image. By telling the boss exactly how he felt, Larry was able to improve his relationship with his boss and therefore change his bad-father image. In reality there was little chance that the boss would fire him, because Larry had already stated his terms for keeping the job.

In other words, if the behavior did not improve, he was going to quit. If the boss had rejected these terms and let him quit or fired him, then Larry would have *destroyed* the fantastic bad-father image. He destroyed it very simply by taking away his boss's power or authority over him. The bad father cannot hurt him if the bad father no longer has authority or control over his life. This is what Biddle means by improving or destroying the fantasy images.

Although we can do our best to improve any relationship, when the other person does not cooperate with us, we have no other alternative but to cut off the relationship so that the person no longer has the power to upset or hurt us. If we can successfully deal with our problems on an image level in this manner, we find our need for violent solutions disappears.

Many of us feel much of the time it is impossible to be a good parent. It is very easy to get the feeling that if we do something wrong, our child will be scarred for life. This is literally not true.

It is not so much *what* we do (our methods of child rearing) as *why* we do it (our motivations and ultimate feelings toward the child). It is not so much our behavior, as how the child experiences and interprets the *meaning* behind the behavior that makes the child feel loved . . . or to feel deprived of our love. We have seen parents say things poorly, handle situations inappropriately and still get fine results, because somehow the child sensed the underlying love, caring and affection that was the primary motivation for the behavior. Not all parents are well educated for the best rearing of children and even those who are make mistakes. None of us are perfect or have to be.

Biddle reassures us that "the child who has sensibly lenient, understanding and sympathetic parents finds reality reassuring, and encounters much less difficulty in controlling his fantasies. In a secure environment the child can be assured of the reality of the fantastic good parents. He can feel he is good like them and can pattern the opinions and attitudes that he has about himself in accordance with those of the good parent."

Children need freedom within bounds. They need the security of knowing what their boundaries are and how far they can go, but they also need the freedom to be themselves within those boundaries. They need their judgment trusted and in order for them to develop judgment, they need to help share in the decision-making processes. Sometimes we as parents give our children the impression (and sometimes parents really believe this) that whenever given the choice they will do the most destructive thing available. Children basically want the same things that we do—happiness and success. If given the opportunity for the proper decision, they will usually make it. When children used bad judgment or deliberately do something that is destructive, it is usually a defense measure in retaliation for some injustice they feel has been done to them. This is also true of us as adults. We cannot experience ourselves without boundaries, but we ourselves are not the boundaries.

Every parent has two kinds of needs and every child only one. The child has his child-needs and the parent also has his own child-needs. These are often in conflict with each other. The child wants to watch Sesame Street on television, and the father wants to watch a football game. Here are two child-needs in conflict with each other. There is no right or wrong about which one should win at any particular hour of the day. As in any conflict between two people, fairness usually dictates that either one will win approximately half of the time. There are always times when one person is going to get what he wants, and the other will be disappointed. If the parent puts the child first *all* of the time, then he will feel resentful and hostile toward both the child and himself for never being able to take his own needs seriously. If he takes his own child-needs first all the time, at the expense of the child, he will feel guilty for cheating the child out of its normal pleasures of life.

To the parent's advantage he also has his needs as a parent who wants what's best for the child. Both my child and I want him to be successful and happy, and there is no conflict there. If I deeply feel that I want my child to be happy and feel my own love for this child, I will see to it that he is not deprived, and he will generally not feel deprived as a person.

On the other hand, if I do take care of my own needs "at his expense" once in a while, I will not feel guilty about this, and the child will be able to accept disappointment, because he knows the next time he will probably get his own way. This is part of how he learns to compromise in all of his decisions in life.

The importance of the parent-child relationship cannot be overemphasized. In order to fully understand, appreciate and function in my role as a good parent, I must first accomplish this as a child to *my* parents. This will usually entail my taking the initiative in seeking out my parents to better nourish and cherish the child within me.

The benefit of this nourishment is to directly "free " us of the neurotic ties to our parents that inevitably carry over to affect our choice of spouse and our consequent role as parent.

How to use your parents for your own growth is described in the next chapter.

X. Parent Power

How Your Parent Power Helps You Become A More Fully Free And Happy Adult

There is a positive and dynamic approach that can break the ties of neurotic dependency, rid you of guilt and hidden hostility and free you of the need to demand that your spouse and children "make up" for the parenting you never had.

This approach works with or without your parents' cooperation, even if they are no longer living.

For years, psychotherapy has wrestled with the problem of what to do with one's parents. One side of the coin, Freudian or dynamically-based therapy, tends to blame parents for all the client's inadequacies and goes to great lengths to disclose and uncover hysterical traumas from which could be traced present symptoms. This process has often led therapists to be described as those one visits to "cop-out" on one's parents. Much of the client's growth seems to stop at the point of dumping the blame on his parents, accepting his "right" to hate them for their failures toward him and thereafter limping through life with the credo of "What do you expect of a man with a broken leg?"

Leaving a man a legacy of hate and an excuse to be lame hardly constitutes the summation of therapeutic growth. The only value of hate is to use it as motivation to win freedom to be truly your best self. (That will be more fully explained further in the chapter.)

The other side of the psychological coin reflects the ideas of the modern-day therapists, ranging from Carl Rogers' Client-Centered Therapy to Behavior Modification, and from George Bach's Creative Aggression to Albert Ellis and Rational Emotive Therapy, including Gestalt and encounter groups. While their methods vary and are often diametrically opposed, they agree that history and parents have little real place in the therapeutic growth of today. In short, it doesn't matter what the cause of your difficulty, you have long since been divorced from that cause, and must change today's behavior because it isn't meeting today's needs—you are no longer yesterday's child.

Our own feeling is that the moderns ignore the fact that if an adult did not get his basic needs met as a child, they are *still* not met today, and the phony relationships forced onto us as children (because we had no defense against them) often still persist in exactly the same manner today.

Thus two conclusions stand out clearly:

First, even though we are adults, we often get locked into deceptive and destructive relationships with our parents that carry over into our adult lives and deeply affect the way we relate to our spouse and children.

Secondly, very few therapists seem to recognize a potentially powerful ally we might term "psychosomatic health." If our parents (in spite of deep love and good intentions) do in fact have the power to cause all types of psychological cripping effects on us, can they not also have the equally powerful and significant impact of psychological cure? We think they can.

No two people in the world have more potential for good and bad in the lives of each one of us than our parents. Let's turn on the "Parent Power" to heal the sick and crippled aspects of our personalities and find a new kind of love, rather than a justification for phoniness or hate.

We don't believe in blame. Few parents wake up saying, "Today I am going to destroy my child." Our motivation is good and we really do want to be effective parents. But sometimes we don't know what the needs of our children are . . . or how to meet them.

We do have to face the reality of cause and effect. At various times we might have a good effect on our children or a bad one, but we do have an effect. The better we can understand this cause-and-effect relationship with our children, the better parents we can be in rearing healthy children and improving our relationships.

We would like everyone to read this chapter from the standpoint of *you, the child.* In order to be a healthy adult, you need to know what your legitimate rights and needs are and to take them seriously. Then and only then, can you respond to the needs of others.

For most of you reading this, we would guess that the relationship with your parents could best be described as "phony." For example, if you were asked to be honest and real with your parents, perhaps your answer would be something like this, "If I told my parents how I *really* felt, they would a) have a heart attack, b) disown me, c) knock me clear across the room, d) never understand, e) bug me about it the rest of my life, etc., etc., etc.," If so, you fit the qualification for a phony relationship. In other words, both of you are cooperating in a conspiracy to pretend that the relationship is something that it really is not. Carrying on this pretense to protect ourselves or the other doesn't really meet anybody's needs. Because of this, we eventually begin to hunt and start to look around for help. Eventually we read a book or article, get into a psychology class, or go to therapy, and begin to realize that the relationship truly is phony.

The first real reaction to that discovery is inevitably anger; to the extent someone takes away our freedom, we will hate him. A phony relationship with our parents takes away our freedom to be ourselves, and this leads to intense anger or hatred. The purpose of this chapter is to take us from the initial phony relationship—through the anger response—to the ultimate of a love relationship with our parents, which will truly win us back our freedom.

Two Types Of Anger

Before we can really deal with the phony-to-anger-to-love process, we need to clarify that there are two types of anger. Most of us are very afraid of anger and have a tendency to see it as only destructive or bad. We need to realize that there is *destructive* anger and there is *constructive* anger.

Destructive anger is punitive—it punishes others for whatever they have done to us or whatever we have imagined they have done to us. It is defensive in that it protects me from being further hurt. It attacks your character as the best means of punishing you or paying you back for hurting me. It covers up the real feelings which lie underneath, of hurt, embarrassment, and vulnerability.

Destructive anger always starts with a "you" statement and assumes your worst motivations toward "me." "You" deliberately hurt, attack, embarrass, or humiliate me because you don't like me and have malicious and vicious intent. You see me as impugning your motives and attacking your character. I certainly do not give the impression that I am hurt or vulnerable or really care.

Constructive anger does exactly the opposite. It may be just as angry, loud or noisy; but it reveals feelings rather than covering them up. "I am angry with you because you hurt me." It does not punish the other or defend against the other or attack the other, but clarifies and tries to tell how I feel and why. In the long run, it draws people together.

Constructive anger can be just as hurting and upsetting, but it talks about "me" and my feelings rather than "you" and what you did: I feel hurt, embarrassed, or whatever as a result of your actions.

Constructive anger can be expressed without creating an all-out battle. Phil and Elaine had made a private agreement between themselves that they would never embarrass each other, or have private arguments in public or before their friends. One night at a party, Elaine did something that embarrassed Phil very deeply, which he felt made him look like a fool. His destructive impulse was to lash back at Elaine in public and to embarrass her as badly as she had embarrassed him.

Phil did not do this as he felt it would have made both of them look very bad, and he did not know for certain if his wife had intended to embarrass him. He could have taken Elaine aside and talked to her privately in another room, but he decided to wait till they got home. Phil struggled with himself all night trying to decide whether or not she had acted deliberately to hurt him. Almost as soon as they walked in the door of their home, he asked her very simply and in a rather pleasant but hurt voice, "Are you aware of how I felt when you did . . . (this particular act)?"

The look on Elaine's face answered for her. She had no idea how her action seemed to him and no intention of hurting him. Hearing his feelings expressed, she realized how she had appeared and simply apologized. The constructive anger Phil expressed avoided a fight.

The destructive anger reaction would have assumed that Elaine had deliberately tried to embarrass and hurt Phil; he would have lashed out because of that assumption, attacking her character and "putting her in her place." Her reaction would have been equally defensive, and even if she knew she had been wrong and had not intended to hurt him, she would have had to defend herself against his stupid attack. She would have wound up really trying to hurt and punish him for his accusation.

By asking Elaine about her motivations and intentions, Phil made no such assumption or accusation and gave her an opportunity to tell him exactly what she was feeling and what she was trying to say to him. Elaine might have said that she was angry with him at the time of the party. This would have given them an opportunity to deal with this in a reasonable way. As it was, she had no intention of hurting him and said so.

Destructive anger occurs between parent and child when each offended party assumes that the other is doing malicious things because of hate and is trying to destroy him. This gives him no alternative but to defend himself at all costs.

There is no harm or destructiveness in anger that confronts with the intent of healing a relationship and of bringing love out of chaos.

There are two other very important points that need to be made before we can talk about what children need from their parents: 1) every child needs to know that he cannot destroy his parents; and 2)every child needs to know that his parents cannot destroy him. ("Destroy" may sound like a strong word but many people literally feel a fearful power of "life and death" relationship with their parents and act as though one side or the other can literally be destroyed emotionally. "I won't be able to live without this relationship.")

The basic reasons that parents and children do not confront each other with their needs is because they are either afraid of destroying or being destroyed. If they destroy the other, they cannot live with the guilt, and if they are destroyed, they cannot live with the pain.

Of course, we accept the reality that people do kill other people at times. That's not the focus here. The point is, that emotionally, you do not have the power of life and death over your parents; by the same token, they do not have this power over you. We are only responsible for our own actions and have no responsibility or control over someone else's reaction, even if that reaction is to have a heart attack or to commit suicide. This may seem like a cold attitude, but it is not intended to be, and hopefully it will become clear as we go along.

If I am afraid that my parents will be destroyed by my needs, I certainly do not want to risk the guilt of presenting my needs to them. By the same token, if I am afraid that their rejection of me can destroy me emotionally, I cannot risk that rejection with any type of confrontation of my needs and feelings. A child has a responsibility and obligation to himself and to his parents to first of all know what his needs are, and secondly, to present these needs to his parents.

Revelation And Change

Every child has two things he needs from his parents: *Unconditional Love*, "I love you because you exist and need no other reason to love you. There is nothing you can say or do that could cause me to stop loving you. I may not agree with all your values or ideas,or of your actions, but I love you and nothing can change that." And, secondly, you need your parents to *reveal* themselves to you. You need to know who they are and why they are, above all else. We get very hooked on change, and our need for our parents to treat us differently and to agree with our values or be more like we are. Since we can't see them as changing, we see no hope for the relationship. Change is not the issue—Revelation is. If you understand why your parents do the things they do, or feel the way they feel, this will make you relate differently to them and feel differently about them.

When a child feels unconditionally loved and knows that nothing can change that, watches his parents sit down and tell him how they feel and why, then he goes very quickly to a third step, which is that he now can reveal himself to the parents so they understand why he is like he is.

We don't feel it could ever be stressed enough . . . the real imporrance of parents and children revealing themselves to one another. Over and over again, in our office, we see proof that the breakdown in a relationship is due to bad communication of *why* we do the things we do. You may feel you already know why they do what they do, but for some reason, hearing them admit their fears and anxieties out loud makes a world of difference.

A beautiful eighteen-year-old student brought her parents in for an interview because she was afraid her father was physically going to beat her up. He was a large man, well over six feet tall and weighed two hundred and eighty pounds. She saw him as rather rigid and when he would tell her to do something, she would ask him, "Why?" At this, he would fly into a rage and become enormously angry and demand that she do it. If she continued to ask, "Why?" he would threaten to drive her into the wall with his fist and she believed him.

The mother, father and daughter all came into the office for an interview and the recurring theme from the father was, "Tell my daughter not to ask me *why*!" From the daughter it was, "Get my father to explain to me *why*!" After an hour and a half of this hassling, the father was asked very directly what he was feeling in his body when his daughter would look him in the eye and say "Why?" He became very thoughtful and took the question quite seriously. After a short period of time, he smiled and said, "Fear. That's the feeling. Fear. I'm afraid of her. I guess I'm just afraid of being wrong. My mother doesn't respect my judgment, and my wife certainly doesn't and when this eighteen-year-old kid comes along and tells me that she doesn't respect my judgment either, that's the last straw!"

The father was smiling and rather relaxed. In revealing his feelings to his daughter, he had learned something about himself that he did not know. His daughter's reaction was spontaneous and surprised. She had not known this. The father was asked what would happen if the next time they had a confrontation or he told her to do something and she questioned "Why?" (and if he felt the anger rising within him), he would just say to his daughter, "There it is again. I feel afraid and very angry. I can feel myself wanting to attack you because I'm afraid you'll be right and I'll be wrong." What would your daughter do? Do you think she would react any differently than she does now? The father just smiled and nodded, "I think it would change everything."

Twenty-year-old Paul brought his father for a confrontation in a therapy session one day because he wanted to "tell him off." In the course of the confrontation, Paul was very angry and pointed out a particular problem that happened over and over again when he was a child. "When I would do something wrong, Mother would never spank me, but warn me that Dad would take care of that when he got home. Then, you would come home and beat me up terribly. I never felt that this was fair since Mother would make you do her beating for her. I would go to my room and cry and about thirty minutes later you would come on your hands and knees and apologize for what you had done. I always felt this was very phony and inconsistent. If you're going to spank me, why should you apologize—and if you're going to apologize and you knew you were wrong, then stop beating me so badly. I always saw you as weak and phony."

The father began to cry as the boy talked. He said very softly to his son, "I know I have a terrible temper just like my father. When I was a little boy, the same thing would happen to me. My father would come home from work, take me to my room, and beat me up. I never knew why and he would never tell me what I had done wrong. I would become so frustrated and angry at my father for never telling me what I had done, that I always vowed if I ever had a son and had to spank him like my father spanked me, at least he was gonna' know why. When I came to your room thirty minutes later, it was not to apologize but to explain to you what you had done wrong and what I expected of you in the future—so you wouldn't do it again and I would not have to spank you again. I do know that my anger was unreasonable and much too violent and I'm sorry about that."

Paul sat there rather stunned. All of his life he had seen his father as weak and phony and apologetic when he actually was trying to explain to his son how he felt and what he needed from him so that the son would be able to respond properly. Nothing had changed about the past except that now the son understood the father's feelings and motivations. Instead of feeling resentful and angry toward his father, he was saying, "Wow, my father really loves me."

These are just two examples of how change wasn't necessary . . . but revelation was.

Additionally, once the children know what the parents are really feeling, the change often does take place. If I react in a less defensive and less offensive manner to my parents, they are going to treat me differently. If I am more direct and honest with them regarding my feelings, they are going to be different than they were before.

It would be rather an ideal situation if all parents knew their children's needs, anticipated them, and took care of them without the child having to present these needs at all—but this just isn't the case. Children as individuals are different and parents are not as knowledgeable as they could be. There isn't any way that a parent can meet a child's needs until he knows what those needs are. At least then he has a choice.

A child's responsibility is to present his needs to the parent. To the extent he withholds them (for any reason), he is rejecting his parents by robbing them of the opportunity to "parent" him. We'll talk later about types of confrontation and methods of approaching your parents with your needs. Everybody is different and everyone will view this in a different fashion. The point is that each person must go to his parents and say that he needs unconditional love and that he needs to know them. That's meeting your responsibility to yourself and also to your parents as a good child.

In return, the parents have two choices, 1) they can accept your needs and meet them; or 2) they can reject your needs for whatever reason. This is reality that we have to accept. Not all parents seem to be capable or willing to meet the needs of their children, but most will come through. They may not do it in the exact fashion desired, and may never be the perfect parents that you are looking for, but still they can meet your needs. Realistically speaking, because of their own sickness or problems, there are always parents who can't or won't. We read constantly in the newspaper about parents who beat or desert or even kill their children. Others are so defensive or sick that they blame everything on the child and cannot accept any responsibility for whatever problems may exist.

The fear of your parents saying "No" is probably much more real than the possibility of their saying "No"—but it is nevertheless a distinct possibility and one that we have to face and deal with in advance.

If your parents accept your needs and give you the unconditional love and the revealing of themselves that you need, life takes on new meaning. It is very easy to go from phony, to anger, to love, and have a new love-relationship with your parents if this is their reaction. How could you do anything but love parents who are giving you this kind of love, acceptance, and understanding? We deeply feel that this will change every other meaningful relationship in a person's life—particularly those relationships which concern spouse and children.

But what if the parents reject? Now what happens to the child? Is he destroyed.

Your mental health and emotional well-being does not depend on your parents or anyone else! What your parents do with your needs can either make it easier or harder for you to meet your needs, but *it is not final*.

If your parents reject you, then you have two choices: 1) You can also reject your child needs; 2) You can accept your own child needs as legitimate.

When the parent rejects the child, the appropriate reaction is hurt. Because we don't want to feel that hurt, we tend to compensate by rejecting *them*. "I don't need them, they're no good. I'm a big boy now, I can live without them. Who needs it!" When this happens, you are rejecting *your own* needs. You are agreeing with your parents and saying, in effect, I do not need parents. I am an orphan who can live without them. *This is a lie!* You are saying that the need is only legitimate *if* it can be met.

If I am thirsty and need a drink of water, that is a legitimate need whether there is water readily available to me or none within a hundred miles. My thirst is either legitimate or it is not legitimate and has nothing to do with the availability of water. As a child, my needs for unconditional love and for my parents to reveal themselves to me are legitimate whether or not my parents died when I was born, or reject me, or walk away from me or meet my needs.

To deny your own needs is to be an emotional cripple. The tendency follows—and this is the tragedy of it all—that when your child then comes to you and says, "Hey, Dad, I need you," your reaction will most probably be "Go away you little creep, if I don't need parents, you don't either." If society has made you feel guilty enough not to be willing to admit this publicly, then you may try to overcompensate and smother-love your child so that he won't realize he's not being loved deep inside you. And, you'll resent him all the time for demanding something of you that you didn't get from your own parents.

The now classic study of Harry Harlow's monkeys illustrates this dramatically. The monkeys were reared with substitute mothers (made out of chicken wire and foam rubber) and later, when these monkeys were grown, they were completely incapable of mothering their own young. When the young monkey would cling to this mother and demand the type of attention and affection that it wanted, mother would become so angry that she would push her baby away and if that were not successful, sometimes would go so far as to kill the baby, if there were not intervention.

In this case, the original monkey had a mother who was not rejecting in any way. But, the substitute mothers made of chicken wire and foam rubber would not respond or give love to the child. Although they never rejected the child nor pushed it away, the child developed rejecting behavior. Nourishment came from the mother, who was always warm and cuddly. It was available whenever the child was afraid or needy. Why then did the monkey raised by the substitute mother reject its own child? Baby monkeys are very clinging and very demanding. It was as though the monkey mother was saying, "My mother did not give me all this love and affection that you demand,

and, therefore, I resent your asking it of me."

The rejected child has one other choice: Even though your parents have rejected your child needs, you can still accept these needs as legitimate and right. In this case, the child simply says to himself, "I need a mother and a father. I need a mother's and father's unconditional love and emotional support and affection. I need to know my parents so that I can better discover who I am and what my own needs and values and desires are. I do not have this." The result is intense pain, grief and mourning.

Perhaps this would be easier to understand in terms of a death. If a child's parents are taken away from him by car accident or illness, we know what is legitimate to do. We go to a funeral and we grieve and we cry because we have deprived of the love and presence of our parents. This grieving may last a few days or a few months, but we cry it out and let ourselves feel our deep sense of loss and deprivation. After a period of time, the grief passes and life continues.

We don't ever lose our sorrow and from time to time we may remember them, we may cry, we may deeply miss them and feel very badly about our loss. But the grief seems to be gone. As a matter of fact, we may even enjoy the sorrowful memories of this loved one who is gone; we may enjoy the sweetness of the times we did have.

If your parents reject you, this is, in reality, an emotional death. They have refused to meet your needs, but your needs live on. You must allow yourself to feel overwhelmed with the grief, the pain and the sorrow of what has happened to you; this seems to heal. We cannot explain totally why or how this happens, but we do know that healing takes place. By accepting the legitimacy of your own needs, your needs are met and you have in effect given yourself unconditional love. This seems to free you from the negative influences of your mother and father and you will no longer punish your children, or your spouse, for whatever grievances you had had with your parents.

Now, when your little child comes to you and says, "Hey Mom/Dad, I need you," your reaction will be, "Yes, I know what your needs are, because I know what my needs were (as a child). Mine weren't met, but I certainly want to meet yours." The resentment is gone because you never denied your own needs as a child and, therefore, have no need to deny those of your child.

The Healing Power Of Confrontation

To us, this confrontation is the missing link in most therapies that deal with parental relationships. It may seem like a very cruel and painful and hard thing to go through and many times it is. We want to make it clear that the child in no way is rejecting his parents. He is accepting the reality that his parents have rejected him. He has asked them for good food and in Biblical terms, "...they have given him a stone." He is rejecting the bad food that they gave him in the name of love.

We believe very strongly that this is what Erich Fromm meant when he said in the *Art of Loving* that a mature person becomes his own mother and father in a very real sense, able to give himself unconditional love and acceptance.

A young man who had endured this tragic experience of being rejected by his mother was once asked by a friend, "And what have you done for a mother since?" Since approximately four years had passed and this question had never been asked before, the young man was taken aback. After considerable thought, he smiled and had his answer. He told his friend, "All my life I thought I had a pretty good relaship with my mother. All my life, also, I had collected mothers everywhere I went. It brought me a great sense of satisfaction to know that older women enjoyed mothering me, and making over me. With every girl I dated, it seems, I had an even better relationship with her mother. Then I went to therapy and found out that my relationship with my own mother wasn't that good, and in fact I was rejected totally by her."

He then smiled broadly. "I am just now aware that I have not collected mothers since...I haven't needed one. I have been 'mothered' at times by my children, my wife and my friends. But since that time, I have never needed a 'mother.' "

This man's needs were met by his own acknowledgement that they were legitimate. He will no longer need to punish his wife or friends for not giving him unconditional love constantly, and he'll have less need to play the role of the deprived child who tries to force all around him to mother him constantly.

At this point, whenever we are lecturing or sharing this subject with others, there is an inevitable reaction: "What right have I got to do this to my parents?"

To do what to your parents? All you're asking for is love. How can you deny your parents the opportunity of being your parents? If you do not come to them with your needs, and then your needs are not met, your parents can rightfully say to you, "We never had a chance to be your parents, because you denied us this."

When Charles was a child, he had both hay fever and asthma, until the age of twelve and as a result of this, was always rather skinny and weak. Mother was constantly trying to build him up with milk shakes and as many milk products she could pour down him so that he would gain weight. At a very early age, in the process of trying to discover the allergic cause, the doctor told Mother her son was allergic to cow's milk. Mother had been "poisoning" her child all those years. Obviously, if the child had died, Mother would not have been tried for murder. She did not intend to poison him and was trying to do what was best but nevertheless, by loading him with this milk that was causing an allergic reaction, she was, in effect, poisoning him. As soon as she found out, she stopped.

To further illustrate this point, let's pretend that Mother never found out about the milk and continued to pour quarts of cow's milk into her son until the day he left home at the age of twenty-one.

Charles goes on to get married and have a family of his own and later on a doctor discovers the allergy to cow's milk. He advises a switch to goat's milk which is healthier for asthmatics and does not cause an allergic reaction.

Charles drinks goat's milk approximately for one year, gains twenty pounds, and is in better health than ever in his life with no more allergic reaction. In the meantime, he now has children that perhaps have the same weaknesses and rather than risk any chances with cow's milk, they are raised on goat's milk also.

After a few years of living away from home, he visits Mother and takes the family along. He cannot wait to break the good news to Mother and rushes into the house expectantly, "Mother, wait till you hear the good news! My doctor has told me that I have been allergic to cow's milk and you've been poisoning me all these years," he says with a laugh. "Look at me now. I've been drinking goat's milk for a year, gained all this weight; I've color in my face and feel great. Our son has been raised on it and look at him." He expects Mother to be thrilled at what has happened to him.

Instead, her reaction is, "What do doctors know? I'm your mother. I know what's best for my child. Nobody can tell me that you're allergic to cow's milk. Goat's milk is for goats. When you come in my house you drink cow's milk and your children drink cow's milk." (Or, chicken soup, or whatever it happens to be, the "Jewish momma" comes in all flavors.)

"Wait a minute, Mother. I don't think you understand. The *doctor* said I'm allergic to cow's milk. It poisons my system. Since I have stopped drinking it and have been drinking goat's milk, I am now healthy!"

Mother refuses to understand and demands that as long as he is visiting in her home, out of courtesy to her values and beliefs, he must drink cow's milk and his children must drink cow's milk or they'll have to leave her home.

What would you do? We have people who tell us all the time, "She's an old, senile woman, so why not humor her and drink a glass of milk.

What will it hurt? So you get a little attack of asthma—you'll get over it, and you won't visit your mother very often."

What would you do?

It seems rather obvious that very few people would stay and drink cow's milk. They have come to Mother to share their new discovery and new health, and she has rejected their needs. They have asked for good food and she has given them bad food in the name of love. Not only is each having to risk his own health, but the health of his children as well.

Of course, most of us would leave. It is easy to see that we would take a stand on something as concrete as whether or not we are going to risk drinking cow's milk and endanger our health. How much more important is our emotional well-being?

We come to our parents and ask them for emotional good food. If they give it to us, we are emotionally well fed, nurtured and well. If they give us bad food, we have an obligation to ourselves and to our family to reject it. (We also do not do our parents any favor by accepting this bad food and pretending that it is good. By calling it bad food, which it is, we are giving them an opportunity to correct their mistake and to profit from it.)

Again, we want to emphasize the child has no need to reject the parents. He is simply refusing the bad food and refusing to pretend that it is good food. He walks away from the parental home grieved and sad, and deeply hurt that he has been misunderstood and rejected. He loves his parents and knows on a deep level that they love him. The problem is not whether they love, but whether or not they can express this love in a way that will meet his needs. (Again, the parent is not meeting his own parental needs by offering the child bad food.)

In one of our marriage and family classes there were two nineteen-year-old girls who were daughter and daughter-in-law to the same woman. Each had a daughter about six months of age. When we were discussing parent-child relationships, both of them complained about "Mother" in the same way. She bugged them about everything they did as mothers. They could do nothing right in the area of dressing the child, disciplining the child, washing the child, or anything else. They were both very angry and upset with her and resented being around her all. Neither had done anything about it because they could not hurt her feelings. Instead, they stayed away and saw her as little as possible. In order to protect her feelings and not to hurt her, they rejected her and kept away as much as possible, depriving her of her grandchildren.

Were they really doing her a favor? The honest, direct method might be least hurtful and present the best opportunity for working out a relationship. All they have to do is tell her how they feel. Tell her that they feel she has no confidence in them, and that she constantly treats them as little children who do not know what they are doing. Explain that they feel no emotional support or caring from her, even though they are aware that she is trying to help. Her method constantly gives them the feeling of being rejected and put-down. Certainly this confrontation will hurt her feelings and will be difficult for the girls, but it gives them an opportunity to change the relationship and to work it out to mutual satisfaction. Just quietly and slowly withdrawing from her, and depriving her of their love and presence as well as the affection and love of her grandchildren will not really do anyone a favor. Revealing one's needs in such a confrontation can open up new and joyous relationships.

XI. The Joy Of Confrontation

How Do I Confront My Parents?

Confrontation comes in all sizes and shapes. Everyone is different, with varying needs and personalities. We cannot tell you how to confront your parents or what approach is applicable. One person will be angry, another in tears and hurt. One will make an appointment to sit down and have a direct confrontation, another will seize the opportunity of the moment. One may accuse and talk about the past, another deal only with the situation at hand. Our best advice to you is to be what you are at the moment.

If your anger is sincere and needs to be released, then you need to be angry. If you are deeply hurting and sorrowful, then your parents need to experience that. If you feel cold and unemotional, then that will have to be your approach. Trying to experience emotions that you are not feeling at the moment will only make you appear phony and insincere.

Perhaps the best way to discuss confrontations is simply to illustrate what our students or clients have done.

Telling Mother Off

During the time of the student moratorium on the Viet Nam war, Charles worked with a twenty-year-old student, a somewhat militant long-hair who seemed to be enjoying the class, but not taking it particularly seriously. There were many classroom discussions in which he disagreed at length, but always pleasantly, and in good taste. He was enjoyed as a student and added a lot of flavor to the class. But when Charles got to the part about confronting one's parents, he openly disagreed by saying he didn't need his parents, wanted nothing to do with them, and besides, they wouldn't understand or respond.

One day Charles was walking across campus when he heard his name being called. Looking around, he saw this young man bouncing across campus like he was on a pogo-stick. It seemed rather out of character for one of the "cool" guys of the college to be so excited or yelling across the grounds. He bounced up with a happy smile on his face, shouting, "Leviton, it works . . . it works. You were right, it works!" When asked what he was talking about, he said loudly, "I called my Mother!"

There were two immediate emotional reactions. First of all, Mother must have lived at least two thousand miles away from the tone of his voice and the way he said it, and there was the feeling he *paid* for the phone call himself.

"I did exactly what you said."

That made Charles shudder; he could just imagine what had occurred.

"I called my mother and really told her off. I said, 'Mother, I've let my hair grow and it's longer than shoulder length. I've got a beard that I haven't shaved or combed for over six months. I've used every kind of dope known to man. I go to bed with every girl I can get my hands on. I'm wearing a black armband and I'm a member of the college moratorium. What 'da ya think of that, Mother? How 'da ya like it?'

"There was a long silence at the other end of the phone. Finally she spoke. 'Well, son, I certainly don't like what you're doing, if that's what you want to know. I feel very sad and very depressed at the way you're living your life. But you're twenty-years of age, and you're over two thousand miles away, and I guess if that's the way you want to live, there isn't much that I can do about it.'

"At this, the sound of her voice changed. '*Now*, there's something I want to say to you. You're my son and I'm your Mother and there isn't much you can ever do about that! No matter what you do, or how you live, or what you believe or think, I'm still your Mother. I may not approve of what you're doing, but I love you and I'll always love you, and there's nothing in the whole wide world you can do that will make me stop loving you.'

"Now the silence was on the other end of the line. It took a long time before I could answer."

His voice, even as he told the story, was soft and very emotional.

"Mother, you just wiped out twenty years of shit with that one sentence."

She didn't argue or disagree or judge him or tell him he was wrong or try to talk him out of it or even get offended. She simply told him exactly how she felt about what he had told her and how she felt about him. Nothing else needed to be said. To see the look on his face and hear the change in his voice would complete the story. He said with beautiful and firm conviction, "For the first time I know my Mother loves me."

Some of you may be thinking, "What good will it do? Has he stopped the drugs? Did it change his sex life? Is he still a long-haired militant? If these things didn't change, then what good did it do?"

Our answer is simply, we don't know, and to us it isn't really important. It seems rather obvious that his behavior was compensation for the fact that he didn't feel loved and was very angry toward society, mainly because he felt deprived and rejected by his parents; particularly his mother. He confronted his mother in all the wrong ways. He did not present his needs properly, but simply attacked her in a punitive way. Mother responded with deep feeling, emotion, and love. That boy will never be the same again. We can't help but feel that his life style will have to change in some ways. But whether it outwardly changed or not, his reasons for actions would definitely change.

He would no longer need to escape from pain through dope because the pain has lessened. He no longer will have to use sex as an act of hostility toward women because he doesn't feel hostile toward Mother anymore. His need to symbolically destroy his parents by destroying his society could change toward a more healthy, constructive attitude of improving society, because he no longer feels his mother is trying to destroy him.

Getting Through to Dad

Contrast the above story with one that may come a little closer to most of your own homes and lives: A father of three teenagers suddenly burst into a rage one evening and began to tell his teenagers and wife that he felt rejected, unloved, and unappreciated. He was nothing but a paycheck and everyone took, took, took from him and gave nothing in return. His tirade left everyone speechless in surprise and no one seemed to know how to answer as he raged on and on. Finally, his shy, quiet seventeen-year-old daughter said very softly to him, "Dad, I don't even know you."

Immediately, the angry, hostile father was reduced to tears. It was as though his loneliness and desolation had been heard for the first time in his life. They embraced in the middle of the room as the rest of the family tip-toed away to leave them in private.

No more words were spoken that evening, but she later revealed that for the past six months he had been driving her to school in total silence every day on his way to work. The morning after his outburst her father was in the best mood she had ever seen, and from the time they walked to the car, until he opened the door and dropped her off at school, twenty minutes later, he never stopped talking. It was as though he couldn't say enough. He babbled on about what he had done the day before, what he was planning to do that day, and what his plans were for the future. Nothing seemed too unimportant; he was just sharing everything and anything that came to mind.

A whole new world had taken shape. "My daughter wants to know me, and she's going to know everything that I can tell."

Six months later, as the daughter was relating the story to a college class, she giggled and added, "We're going to the ball game tomorrow."

Risk Hurting Dad

When we hear someone tell that they cannot take the risk of hurting their parents by telling them that they have not met their needs or were not good parents to them, the story of a client we will refer to as Don comes to mind. Don described his relationship with his father in the following manner:

"My background as a child was different from most, I think. In 1945 during the War, my father was injured and, subsequently, his right leg was amputated. Prior to being drafted into the service, he was, as I understand, going to be signed to play professional baseball. His injury made that life-long dream impossible.

"In late 1949, he went back to the Veterans' Hospital for spinal surgery. Bloodclots formed and were not noticed until it was too late. He is now paralyzed from the waist down, although he still has feelings in the lower half of his body.

"In 1961 he was involved in an auto accident in which he was paralyzed higher up, both lungs were punctured and his jaw broken, his hand and leg broken; he was in intensive care for five months. The subsequent pain made it necessary to have five brain operations which were experimental. These left him with a decreased mental capacity.

"I tell you these things, not for sympathy, but rather to make you understand what will come later.

"As a boy, my father and I couldn't go hiking, swimming, or even walk to the store together. If we went anywhere, I pushed his wheelchair. My father enjoyed baseball. I don't know if it was consciously or unconsciously, but I was determined to become the baseball player my father was never able to be. From the time I was nine, I practiced baseball two or three hours a day. I was twelve when I injured my elbow. I was never able to play well after that, but I continued until I was fifteen.

"I decided my father wasn't a man. I don't know at what age I made this profound decision, but I know that I made it. From that time on, I took the responsibility of being the man in the family.

"I worked since I was twelve except for one semester in college. At seventeen I sold cookware door-to-door for eight months. At nineteen I got married and sold vacuum cleaners and encyclopedias until I was twenty-one. Then I worked construction for one year. All this time I was also going to school full-time, because I was a man. I wasn't."

A subsequent divorce brought Don into therapy. He was literally going to pieces and was a very needy client.

Don was making some progress in therapy and starting to accept the reality of his divorce. At about this time he learned that his father had to go into surgery once again. This time it was a stomach difficulty and they were going to remove much of his digestive tract. They told the family rather bluntly that the father was too weak for the surgery, but he would die without it. There was a strong possibility that he would not be able to survive the surgery either.

Don realized that his father was going to die, and he would not be able to grieve normally over his father's death. After all, he felt as though he had never had a father. He'd have to be the man in the family and comfort his mother and sisters when his father died; there would be no one to comfort him. He felt very sick inside that he had never had the opportunity of being a little boy with a Daddy. A week prior to the operation, he came to group therapy to try to express this need and seek comfort. But the group got into other things, completely misunderstood when he did try to get in, and he left rejected and alone. Don felt that even the therapist had misunderstood him and was so angry he could not even come for a private session to express his need.

"On Wednesday, I went over to my father's house. I had dinner, watched television, and generally avoided what I had come for. I kept thinking of the risk I would be taking; telling my father what I had felt as a child. In his weakened condition he might have a heart attack and die because of me. He could totally reject what I was feeling and tell me to get out. He could get defensive and tell me to grow up, and that would hurt. He could listen and not really hear. Or, he could become my Daddy for the first time. I finally decided waiting wasn't going to make it easier. So I went in to talk to my Daddy. We started with small talk. Finally, I said, 'I think you're going to die and there are things I need to settle with you.' He got very quiet, and then I began. I told him how I felt it was unfair that as a boy I was supposed to be the man. He was always sick and could never do things with me. I had played baseball because he couldn't. I had learned to dance because he couldn't. I loved him so much I tried to be his little man."

At this time, Don became very angry, and it flashed across his mind that his father never was a man. He blurted this out with a great deal of fear and guilt.

"He looked at me with tears in his eyes and said, 'I really was a poor father, wasn't I? I never realized you felt that way.'

"I told him I needed him to be my Daddy, not my father, that could come later. I put my arms around my Daddy and hugged him and he hugged me and loved me. I kissed my father on the mouth for the first time in ten years. I now had a Daddy. We cried together, hugged, loved, and were both totally honest with our feelings. I told him all the things that hurt me as a child. We cried over these things. We cried because he couldn't walk. He shared some of his heartbreak with me, and we loved each other for it.

"I told my Dad how, as a child, I would go to sleep at night and pray to God He would let me have the pain. 'Let me not walk, so he can.' But now I saw him for the first time. I experienced this man. I told him I would never go through what he had gone through. I was not enough of a man to do that. But with his strength I would try to make him proud of his son."

For the first time, while Don was telling his father all the reasons why he felt his father was not a man, he began to realize how strong his father really was and how much courage he had. Don knew that he could not have lived through the pain and torture of his father's many accidents and surgeries. For the first time, he knew his father was strong enough to be his Daddy.

On the way into surgery, Don's mother was crying and telling her husband that she needed him and that he needed to live because she couldn't live without him. Don stopped his mother by saying that his Dad had a right to die if he wanted. That if he couldn't stand the pain any longer and if it wasn't worth the struggle, that he had the right to die for his own sake. Don's father pulled him down and hugged him again and said, "No, I want to live; I want to be your Daddy."

Don's father has lived, and the relationship has continued even better than it began. Since that time, Don's younger sister, who had been quite a problem-child in the family, has also been able to work out a relationship with her Dad as a result of this confrontation.

What do you do if your child comes to you and says, "You failed me as a parent; I don't feel love?"

The sad reaction that we see all too often is a defensive one. The parent denies the truth of the accusation, tells the child you have no right to feel that way, rejects the feelings, and thereby rejects the child, proving the point.

From the parents' perspective, consider the following:

"If my child feels unloved, I am sorry he feels that way.

"If my child hurts, I am sorry he hurts.

"If my child feels I've let him down, I'm sorry.

"It doesn't really matter if his facts aren't correct, or if he has completely misunderstood me; if he doesn't feel loved, then somehow, some way, whether I wanted to or not, I have not met his needs."

The first thing you do is *respond* to the child's feelings. Then you decide what to do about them.

If your child says he feels unloved, how does that make you feel?

If your reaction is a personal one and you feel hurt or rejected or insulted or put-down that your child could feel that way about you, and that's the reaction you give your child, then your child is right. You are responding as a defensive, selfish child and are not concerned with his needs.

If your primary reaction is hurt for your child's hurt, and concern for what this must have done to him—feeling unloved—then you are responding as a healthy parent.

A Healthy Response

A nineteen-year-old daughter brought her father into our office: He had been divorced from her mother since his daughter was thirteen years of age, and had lived mostly out of the country since that time. He was coming back to visit his daughter for the first time in about two years.

She had been in therapy for about six months and was terrified of of a confrontation with her father. We discussed it at great length in preparation for his homecoming, and she said the thing that bothered her most about him and what she remembered most was when she was about thirteen years of age and her sister was about twelve, that he never gave them any privacy.

He never allowed them to close the bathroom door or bedroom door when they were dressing or taking a shower. She always felt that he was a dirty old man who was spying on her and wanted to see her in the nude. The thought of confronting him with this scared her very badly.

Her father very readily came to my office with her. In the course of the conversation, she told him how she felt about the privacy issue. The father was very thoughtful for a long time before speaking. He then responded that he could not remember anything about that. But if that's what she remembered, then it was very probably true. Thinking about it some more, he suddenly responded, "Wow, you must have thought I was a dirty old man!"

Here is a father responding to his daughter's feelings.

"I don't remember being a dirty old man, but I suppose it's possible that it was true that I was looking at you sexually. You developed a lovely body early, and I know I was always proud of that. I always felt you were the prettiest girl in the family and the most affectionate. I can only tell you how badly I feel that you've had these feelings about me all these years. Whether they're true or not, I had no intention of hurting you, and I can only say I'm sorry."

How refreshing to visit with a totally non-defensive father whose only concern was for the feelings of his daughter. The child comes to the parent with a problem and the parent immediately feels he is expected to solve it. If he can't solve the problem, the usual solution is that he denies the need, and then he doesn't have to solve it.

The child falls down and scrapes his knee and cries to us that it hurts. Our response, "No, it doesn't." Now the child is really confused and wonders why his knee is lying to him.

The child says, "I want an ice cream cone." Mother's response, "No, you don't." Again the parent is teaching him to lie about his needs and the child is taught not to believe his own stomach.

The answer: Respond to the feelings first, then you can say what you can do about the feeling.

Responding To A Child's Need

David and Elizabeth learned this somewhere between Los Angeles and Palm Springs about three o'clock in the morning, driving along a dark freeway. Their son Eric was about two years of age and usually slept in the car on long rides of this kind. He woke up in the middle of the desert with nothing around, crying that he wanted some milk. Elizabeth told him they didn't have any and he responded, "Yes, you do."

Children at that age, as you know, feel that parents are magicians who can get milk any time and any place they want it simply by opening the glove compartment or the trunk, or pulling it out of their purse. A long argument ensued which was quite unresolved.

At this point Daddy was becoming very upset, to say the least, but kept reassuring himself with the words of his therapist, "It's all right for the child to fight with the mother."

Eventually, Eric became exhausted and dropped back to sleep. Approximately thirty minutes later, the argument began again as he cried out for milk, and Elizabeth reassured him that they had none and that it was three o'clock in the morning and there was no milk to be given. He demanded again, "I want some milk!" This time his mother responded in a soft, understanding voice, "I know you do." This was repeated twice more and the child dropped off to sleep. He never woke up again for the rest of the trip.

What was different about his mother's response?

What she was saying to him essentially was that it was all right to be thirsty. She acknowledged his thirst and his right to be thirsty and his right to want some milk.

That is responding to the feelings of the child. Usually that's enough, for that's the child's real, deepest need. He needs to be reassured that you know what his needs are and that his needs are legitimate.

Of course, that won't satisfy his thirst, but it will satisfy his feelings for being understood and cared about. Arguing with him about the availability of milk does not really meet either one of his needs. When the feelings have been met by saying, "I know you do," then you can explain why he can't have any. In most cases the explanation isn't even necessary.

A brief time later, Elizabeth was sharing this experience over the phone with her friend Jean who had told her that she really did not believe in that principle. While they were talking on the phone, Jean's seven-year-old daughter came running into the room to complain that the three-year-old had just hit her. Rather than referee, or take sides, or solve the problem as she had done previously, Elizabeth's friend simply responded to her daughter's feelings.

"You are very hurt, aren't you?"

"Yes."

"You're very upset that your sister picks on you a lot, aren't you?"

"Yes."

"It makes you feel very bad that you're bigger than she is and not allowed to hit her back?"

"Yes."

"It must have really hurt you very badly."

"Yes."

Satisfied, the seven-year-old wheeled on her heel and ran back out in the yard to play. Jean jumped up and down giggling and laughing, screaming at her friend, "It works, it works!" Jean had simply responded to her daughter's hurt feelings and didn't have to solve the problem.

It's so simple, we stumble over it. All a parent has to say is, "I'm sorry you hurt. I never meant to hurt you." Is that too much to ask?

We don't have to defend ourselves, or become defensive, or even convince the child he's wrong. First we respond to the feelings and tell the child we love him, and then if there are corrections regarding the facts, there is plenty of time to tell the child how you really feel.

One of the most difficult tasks to deal with as a therapist is when a child says he can't even imagine asking a parent for love because it's too risky, or worse yet, he has asked and has been turned down.

As a parent, you are really important. Mom and Dad are the two most important people in any child's life. They can give more than anyone else, and have the power to hurt more than anyone else. Children will always need their parents' love, affection, and support. People die, but relationships live on, and children need a loving relationship with you more than anyone in the world.

XII. Nurturing The Deprived Child Heals The Angry Adult

Sickness is misused Health . . .
Won't is misused Will . . .
Hate is misused Power . . .
Death is misused Life . . .

Every human being is born with two basic characteristics, directions, needs, drives or polarities that affect that individual:

1.   Inherent in all is a basic and immediate striving for safety, security, rest, equilibrium, happiness, serenity, and the absence of pain.

2.   Balancing these are the needs for growth, stretching, excitement, exercise, struggle, exhileration and so on.

The first is related to our basic or child needs, which Maslow says are for love, belonging, respect, and self-esteem. The second deals with higher or adult needs and are more difficult to define in exact terms since individuals differ greatly in these areas.

Both these drives or characteristics are universal and perfectly normal. They are represented symbolically in what we previously described as the Spirit (integrity, core of one's nature). The Crust breaks down into various subpersonalities, while the Spirit tends to be the force unifying the individual.

It is safe to say that the healthier or more actualized the person, the less he would need or rely on safety or security ("coasting" values). He would function, instead, more on the struggling and growing edge of his existence.

Neurosis can be defined as a deficiency disease. To the extent that our basic needs are not met, we tend to over-emphasize the need for safety and security. Fear becomes an over-riding obsession and we become defensive, which can be expressed in many difference ways.

All sick, destructive, self-defeating behavior is a self-protective, reactive defense against real or imagined fear, anxiety, rejection, hurt, and pain.

When you can trust your inner self to be capable of handling pain, you can see and relate to life as it *is*, not distorted or as you *fear* it might be.

Actualizing or healthy people make better *choices* than unhealthy people because they can see the alternatives with less distortion. They tend to make more choices that are conducive to their own self-actualization and that of others as well.

One of the strongest messages we constantly relay to our clients is that what is *truly* good for you is truly good for the important others in your life. There are many people caught up in the paradox that to take my own needs seriously or to do something good for me, is to take away an equal something from someone else. This creates strong feelings of guilt and resentment.

Finding the real difference between selfishness and self-love, and feeling comfortable with one's own rights as an individual, is not always easy to do and requires genuine truthfulness to oneself.

How do we learn to make good choices in life, those that provoke growth rather than just protect from fear? Man's higher nature rests on his lower one—growth needs depend on using the foundation of safety needs which have been met.

As Maslow tells us, first we must gratify the basic needs. These basics should normally be fulfilled as a growing child in a normal, loving home.

Like climbing a ladder, we will only proceed to the next step when we feel secure on the present one. Safety and security, then, result from learning to trust one's own capabilities and improving on them, while at the same time, finding one's true limitations. A person who is foolhardy and takes irresponsible chances with his life is not practicing actualization and growth by proving he's surpassed his needs for security; he's being foolish.

When a child grows up with an awareness of unconditional love, knows there is nothing he can do to cause his parents to stop loving him, feels their pride in his accomplishments, experiences closeness and respect—then he develops self worth and self love.

In a sense he is saying, "My parents have proven to me by their attitudes and behavior that I am a worthy and worthwhile individual, with a great deal of personal value, and they've given me a birthright of love. Since I believe in them, I accept their evaluation of myself as my own."

He should then go through life with a cetain expectancy of success and love and find it. This is not to say he will never experience negatives. Those were part of his heritage in growing up. But because of the supportive love that was and is available, he can handle these with relative ease and overcome them.

What happens when these needs are not met as a child grows up? Probably no one is fully evolved as a child nor fully deprived, so we can say to the extent one's basic needs were not met as a child, he will continue attempts to meet them at the adult level through romantic relationships, competition in the world of work, striving for fame and public adoration, and often through trying to mold his own children.

His striving for growth needs to be met will be somewhat influenced and his motives contaminated by the need for approval and love.

It is sometimes very difficult to determine—even within one's self at times—what our true motivation is. The accomplishment or act itself does not necessarily reveal the motive.

For example, even the most actualized person needs the validation of others. This is a healthy need; if no one believed in your value except you and your parents, you would soon be overwhelmed with doubts and insecurity. It feels good to have validation from romantic love, friends, peers and associates that we are well thought of, highly regarded, and respected. This strengthens one's own self concept and validates one's own self worth.

The contrast to this, is the person who wants *more* than validation of what he already knows and believes (leaving room for normal self-doubt) and instead is asking the world to give him self worth he doesn't now have. "Convince me I'm good and loveable so that I can believe it." This might even be acceptable if the person could receive it. The rest of us could then act as substitute parents and give an unconditional positive regard that would be used as a basis for establishing a new self concept.

The problem is that many people caught up in this extreme need *won't believe or accept what is given.* Like bottomless pits, they are continually unfilled and never satisfied. They have insatiable thirsts and will not let you quench them. Eventually they tire people out and are left alone with their "payoff"—"I was right, no one loves me."

Healing Feelings Of The Past

There are at least five steps that can be taken to heal the past feelings of a deprived child:

1. *We can accept the reality of what is: "My needs were not entirely met as a child and it's difficult for me to believe in or accept the love of others, and that's where I find myself now."*

For some people, this is the hardest step of all. To admit the truth about themselves is to *judge* harshly that *therefore*: I am sick, bad, degenerate, worthless, and unacceptable. Judgment is not the issue here. Until you honestly look at and evaluate your present circumstances, it is almost impossible to change them.

Once people grasp this concept and can admit fears, faults, inadequacies, and needs without feeling judged by themselves or others, a great relaxation, healing, and even change takes place. They lose their need to defend against this awareness, can now listen to criticism without fear of being destroyed by it, can see and learn from their mistakes, and actually like themselves better as a result.

Once it is understood that defensive behavior was for the purpose of protection and not because you were a bad person, then the need to protect yourself lessens and the defensive behavior begins to change.

2. *We can actually go back to our parents and get the unconditional love we need, or at least reassure ourselves it is really there.* The need to be loved as a birthright is a powerful one and seems to carry over into every other relationship as we described in the previous chapter.

3. *In dealing with this need for feelings of self-worth, we can use guided daydreams to enable us to confront our parents, even parents who are deceased or unavailable due to distance or are just too defensive to approach.* In therapy the client becomes as a child in an actual situation from the past. The therapist might suggest that the client is a child in his own bedroom and very upset. Almost always an actual prior event will be seen. We can "bring into the room" the parent they want to confront and have the child say what he is really feeling. It is now safe to take risks that could not be taken by the young child in reality.

Interestingly enough, the feelings and fear of the young child are now being experienced and strong therapist's support is usually needed for the child to state his feelings. Sometimes the child just can't do it, and we suggest that the adult client walk into the room and confront the parent in defense of the child. This will generally create enough courage for the child to say what needs to be said to the parent.

A Guided Daydream Encounter

Here is an example:

Therapist: Visualize yourself as a small child in your room. You are very upset. Tell me what you see.

Client: I used to sleep with my brother in the same room. I'm 6 years old, sitting on the bed upset. I never cried as a child. I'm upset because Father punished me and I had decided *not* to cry because the punishment was unfair. He wouldn't stop spanking me till I cried, so I did; didn't want to give him the satisfaction, and I'm mad at myself that I did.

Therapist: Why did he punish you?

Client: I called one of his friends "fat." I didn't mean to be disrespectful. Dad took off his belt and hit me in front of everyone.

Therapist: Dad is now coming back into the room to talk to you about it.

Client: He wouldn't do that. It was casual and fun for him; he wasn't even mad. He went to bed.

Therapist: Go to his room and tell him how you feel.

Client: (To the Father) The spanking was unfair. I didn't mean to say it.

Therapist: Be the 6 year old and tell him.

Client: I can't do it as a 6 year old.

Therapist: Then have the adult you come into the room and say it.

Client: You didn't do right when you spanked him. He's a person too. (To Therapist) No one ever talked to him that way.

Therapist: How is he responding?

Client: He is quiet and seems to be hurt. I feel pity for the child (client begins to cry).

Therapist: Pick up the little boy.

Client: (sobbing heavily) It hurts. It's embarrassing to cry. I'm embarrassed; people will find out I'm such a softy and will think less of me. Father would!

Therapist: How do you feel when other men cry?

Client: That's O.K. They are lucky that they can cry.

Therapist: Can you allow your sons to cry?

Client: Yes, I encourage them to and comfort them, but I punish myself. God, I'd love to quit that.

Several things happened in this session. The client relived unpleasant experiences that really happened as a child. He found he still could not confront Father as a child, even though it was a "daydream" and not real Father. However, the adult did have the courage to confront Father and there was a new reaction. Father became quiet and hurt; there was no prior experience to predict this happening. Then he found deep feelings of sorrow and hurt for the little boy, but it was very difficult for the adult client to cry without feelings of guilt and embarrassment. It was a real breakthrough of emotions for the client to cry as an adult man in the presence of another adult (the therapist), even though others who had this privilege were considered "lucky" by him.

Often, the parent starts out very defensive and angry and then breaks down and admits his own fears and needs. When the therapist can provide emotional support and a direct, firm method of approach for the client, the "parent" in the daydream is able to respond with true feelings.

We are sharing some rather extreme situations with extreme fathers to show how effective this technique can be under almost impossible situations. For most people whose parents are not that angry and hostile in their approach to life, the experience is less severe.

Guided Imagery Confrontation

The following is an even more difficult father-son situation. The son had absolutely no possibility of dealing with an unreasonable father in real life, and now as an adult is so angry with Father, that he is afraid of his own potential violence.

Therapist: You are a small child in your bedroom. What do you see?

Client: (describes the room in detail) I'm 5 or 6 years old, standing. I feel estranged; don't feel a part of the room. Not a pleasant feeling.

Therapist: Your Father is coming into the room and is very angry with you.

Client: I feel stark terror; I see blood and guts piled up deep in the room, like he's already killed me. He killed me and left—he's gone.

Therapist: Become the blood and guts.

Client: I feel totally rejected—more than a punishment—my person has been destroyed. I'm all alone, no help.

Therapist: Call out for help.

Client: Mom comes in the doorway. She tells me I shouldn't have done what I did.

Therapist: Tell her you're dead.

Client: She says, "I can't help that."

Therapist: Ask for her help.

Client: She says she can't. She finally sees the blood and guts; She screams at Dad. She's mad at him now. She is holding me and rocking me back and forth. She's protecting me from him. I feel safe—protected more than loved. Dad is looking at me and making me feel horrible that I can't take my own punishment. He feels punishment is forever. Father says getting nourishment from Mother is wrong.

Therapist: Ask him why he is so angry with you.

Client: He doesn't want me around. I know why. He's had
             enough unpleasantness and doesn't want more from
             me at home. He doesn't like coming home anyway.
Therapist: Tell him that.
Client: Dad is startled.
Therapist: What else would you like to tell him?
Client: All you do is take; push people around; bully people
             and have no feelings yourself. (He's angry) All the
             things I say just make me hurt.
Therapist: Share the hurt with your Father.
Client: That makes him feel bad. He didn't know I felt that
             way. He's trying to deny it. I've beat him down to the
             floor.
Therapist: Tell him you understand his feelings; you know he's
             part of you and is very frightened but you love him
             and see through his anger to the fear.
Client: He stood up. That's what he wanted to hear. (To
             Father) Why were you afraid of me?

     (Father: Because you were a little kid—part of me.)

Therapist: Become the adult you.
Client: I feel sorrow and compassion for him.
Therapist: Can you move toward him?
Client: I'm hugging him. He feels rigid and uncomfortable.
Therapist: Tell him to relax.
Client: He's crying and relaxing. I understand. I feel strong. I
             feel like his parent and "all together." Mother is stand-
             ing there. She feels amazement. The blood and guts
             are gone.
Therapist: Put the child there.
Client: He's looking up at Dad with innocent, tender face, lov-
             ing and yearning.
Therapist: *You* go to the child.
Client: I picked him up and am hugging him.
Therapist: Reassure him there is nothing to fear anymore.
Client: I feel a lot of pain. The child wants to go to sleep now.
             I feel so sorry for the little guy. He's asleep in my arms
             (client is crying softly).

To those who have not experienced it this scene may sound somewhat strange and unreal, but it is a deeply moving and life transform-
ing experience for the client. We believe and have seen hundreds of
proofs that the client's "integrity" is in touch with and understands
the parents' "integrity," beneath the defense mechanisms, and is
able to communicate on that level. We have had clients who never

did have a need to "confront" their real parents after doing so in a daydream. They understood the parents so well it was as though they had already had an actual confrontation. Therefore, their feelings for the parent changed in a positive way and love was now possible instead of defensiveness, rebellion or phoniness. As a result, the parents also changed and the child did experience direct love.

The real principle here is understanding the true motive that underlies the behavior. When we understand that our parents did unloving things to us (sometimes even to the point of viciousness and cruelty) because of their own fear, feelings of inadequacy and defensiveness; our insight can lead the way to compassion. They behaved that way out of their own self ignorance, not because they hated us or because we were unloveable. And when the parent can admit this to us, beautiful changes take place on a deep, feeling level. There are literally changes from the inside out, not just intellectually decisions to "act" differently.

4. *Another very effective tool toward improving feelings of self love and self worth, is what we call "re-parenting."* It is a process also experienced in the relaxed state of a guided daydream but can be repeated at will by the client—you could experience it right now.

Re-Parenting The Crying Child

The client is asked to relax himself in a chair, close his eyes and visualize himself as a child crying in his room, very upset. This time we are *not* confronting the parent. Once the scene is being experienced (and the child's feelings generally come very quickly to the surface, even to the point of instant tears), we ask that the adult client walk into the room.

Therapist: What do you see?
Client: The child is sitting on the bed crying. His Dad has just spanked him for something he didn't do and he's very hurt.
Therapist: Does he see you?
Client: Yes, he seems pleased I'm here. (Tears)
Therapist: What would you like to do?
Client: I just picked him up and am rocking him on the bed and holding him in my arms. We're both crying now and I'm telling him not to cry.
Therapist: But he's hurt. He *needs* to cry. Just reassure him of your love.
Client: Yes, I am, it *is* O.K. to cry, damn it. All my life I've been told not to cry. I'm holding him very tight and he feels very safe. He's glad I'm here with him and says no one understands.

Therapist: But *you* do, don't you? No one understands the thoughts and feelings of that child like you do.
Client: Yes.
Therapist: Tell the child he will never again be alone. You can't protect him from pain, but you can give him love and comfort so he won't be alone.
Client: He wants to know where I've been and I told him I didn't know I could come and comfort him like this but from now on I'll come often and we'll have fun together.

We ask the client to "visit" with the child for five minutes or so every day till the next appointment. This is one of the most exciting happenings in many people's therapy. They usually come back excited, relaxed and with deep feelings of inner love and peace.

It is the *child* in us that feels unloved, unworthy, abandoned or whatever. The tendency is for the adult in us to go on treating the child in us like our parents did, either out of habit or subconscious belief that the parents were right. This, of course, tends to cause others to treat us the same way, bringing much frustration and unhappiness.

Once this pattern is broken and you are given permission to love, appreciate, and enjoy that little person, *both* the child and the adult are benefited. The adult enjoys the good parenting he is giving and the child enjoys the unconditional love.

Re-visiting Childhood

Here is an example of an adult female client visiting with her small child-self.

Therapist: See yourself as a small child in your bedroom, crying.
Client: I see a 5 or 6 year old little kid, kneeling by the bed. Her fists are all balled up. Mother is mad at her. I'm not sure why. She is crying but trying not to.
Therapist: The adult you is now standing in the doorway watching her. What do you see?
Client: I'd like to go over and hug her. I want to tell her she doesn't have to cry. Now we are sitting on the bed together and I'm reaching out to her. She wants to be held and hugged. It feels so warm and loving. I want to take away her hurt and let her know everything will be O.K.
Therapist: Let her know you love her and care about her regardless of what happens to her.
Client: This makes her calm. She isn't as tense. Her hands are relaxed. She feels comforted.

Therapist: Become the 5 year old. How do you feel?
Client: I feel good and safe. I believe the adult loves me. I love her too. She's a friend; she's going to be there when I need her. (She's now crying softly.)
Therapist: Draw strength from the adult you. What is the adult feeling?
Client: Warm, tender feelings. I like the feeling of comforting her.
Therapist: Can you see the specialness in the child?
Client: Yes, she has a bright quality about her—alive and alert and happy most of the time. She bubbles over, her eyes sparkle; she's bright, really going to grow up to be something.
Therapist: Tell her you are available at any time and you love her.
Client: I have!

This young woman had some very positive feelings about her "child" but needed to re-experience and remind herself of these. She was going through a separation at the time of the daydream and had a very poor self-image and a weight problem. In the next few weeks there was a definite change in her self concept and she became much more assertive regarding her needs.

The following older man saw himself as a very ugly and undesirable child and was still struggling to overcome this poor self concept when he visualized this re-parenting daydream.

Client: I see a 7 year old with glasses—homely, funny looking little squirt.
Therapist: What does he feel about himself?
Client: Kids call him Percy and "sissy." He's picking flowers in the back yard.
Therapist: Let the adult you go into the yard with him.
Client: Such a smart little guy and sensitive; too much feeling for his own good.
Therapist: Give him some love.
Client: I put him on my shoulders. He likes it. I tell him I love him.
(Child: Do you really mean it? That's what Mom and Dad say but they *have* to say it. I can't believe it.)
Client: It's not like Mom and Dad. No obligation. Mine is truly objective. I love you because you're you.
(Child: Gee, where have you been?)
Client: This has been so hard to think about—I've turned you off.
Therapist: Tell him you're sorry you did that.

Client: I'd like to be your buddy. You don't have to be a whiz
           kid for me, winning scholarships and all that. You're
           O.K. the way you are. I'll come often now. You make
           me feel good. I'll be me and you be you. We can be real
           with each other.

Occasionally, you will find clients who *cannot* love the child. They
have adopted the parents' point of view so strongly that they feel
guilty and sneaky loving the child. It's like going behind the parents'
back and disobeying the edict to *not* love the child. Often they don't
believe the child deserves to be loved, but instead feel the child should
be strong, that there is no place for crying, or feeling the pain, or
admitting weakness.

This is very sad to observe and very difficult to deal with. The
therapist strives to present the child's birthright of love and attempts
to provide a safe enough environment for the client to experience this
love.

If for some reason, you find it difficult or impossible to love the
small child of your past, we see this as a very serious symptom that
says your ability to love others as an adult may be seriously impaired.
This condition would be especially damaging to a marital relationship
and to one's ability to love as a parent to children.

5. *Another method of meeting needs of the past and changing life
scripts is called dis-identification and comes from Assagioli's theory of
psychosynthesis.*

When our individual needs are not met, they tend to become angry
and take personalities that fight back like rebellious children. We
have referred to them earlier as subpersonalities.

For instance, if our normal and appropriate feelings of trust in self
and in life are denied, a *dictator* may rise within us to demand perfection, set rules and administer control: "If I lose control I may fall
apart."

But another need is to be loved and appreciated and if this need
is denied, we have a *martyr* personality, who doesn't trust the *dictator*
but reacts with a guilty conscience and self pity: "There is so much
demand on me and so little reward."

A third need denial could be in the area of anger and strength, which
we call the *bitch*. The *bitch* reacts to the *martyr's* helplessness and is
sharp, cruel, on target, and needs revenge: "You'll pay for being so
weak and stupid and burdening me!"

The final subpersonality is the *clinger* whose need for dependence
has been denied, driving it to extremes of despair and even suicidal
tendencies: "I'll force you to recognize my need to be taken care of."

When one of these needs becomes dominant it tends to take over and we *become* the subpersonality for a time. Since we generally don't like these various defensive sides of us, we try to deny their existence, justify their actions or blame them on someone else: "You made me act that way." At the same time, we can't help but fear perhaps we really *are* the monster within us that we hate, fear or deny.

Assagioli states, "We are dominated by everything with which our self is identified. We can dominate and control everything from which we dis-identify ourselves."

I *have* a dictator side to my personality, but I am *not* a dictator. I can own my feelings like I own my car, but I am *not* my feelings any more than I am my car.

First, we dis-identify with the various parts of us and then we identify with the personal "I" or Self that utilizes and integrates the best of all parts.

In the process of dis-identification, we *step back* to become an Objective Observer and a Director of the unfolding scene. These are not more subpersonalities but attitudes of the true self. This becomes a stable place from which we can look at ourselves *without* self-criticism, with full acceptance, with clear perception. There is no place for moral judgment here.

For instance, if a man finds himself becoming a "vicious attacker": in a fight with his wife, he can allow himself to be an Objective Observer at that point and first of all *be aware* he is viciously attacking her and that his vicious sub-personality is now in control.

If he morally judges himself for this behavior, there will be an immediate counter-reaction (by the sub-personality) to defend the viciousness because of the wife's behavior. ("It's all her fault—she attacked me first," etc.)

If he can be objective and be aware *without* judgment, more than likely his perception will become more clear as to what is happening between them.

"Wow, I'm really angry and attacking her. Why am I coming on so strong? I must be very frightened and insecure right now. Apparently I feel very hurt by her comments. My attack is making her more defensive and hurt, too."

If the husband—as Objective Observer—is able to perceive all that, you can readily see his need for abusive anger is lessening. He now understands what he is doing and why, thus providing himself with alternatives. The *best* alternative is to share his new insight with his wife in the same calm, objective manner he was experiencing it. How can he turn off his anger so quickly? By turning *on* his objectivity and seeing things as they really are.

If he shares out loud the discussion that went on in his head, the chances are excellent she will respond appropriately in kind, and the discussion will continue as a "passing of new information" rather than of vindictive punishment.

Subpersonalities are symptoms which reveal that needs are not being met, which bring messages from within that you are not functioning well because the machinery is in need of repair. The Objective Observer listens to the messages and the Director corrects the scene by re-writing the script to properly meet the needs.

The examples we have presented demonstrate that it is the deprived child who fosters the angry, demanding and unfulfilled adult. It may very well sound oversimplified or too easy a solution to accept, but the fact remains, that, when we are able to listen to the needs of the child, to nourish it with the good food of unconditional love, and to allow the child a place in our adult lives, we experience an inner healing.

As the anger leaves, our feelings of self worth are improved, our behavior is modified and our adult needs are finally met.

Part III

Revealing And Healing Communication

When the true motivation is to reveal myself in a vulnerable way, reaching out to you, anger becomes the contact that promotes healing, through intimacy and caring.

XIII. The Proper Use Of Anger

Most people were given one of two messages by their parents as children growing up: "Don't be angry—be afraid;" or "Don't be afraid—be angry."

Rarely will you find a home where both of these emotions are openly accepted; most of us can readily identify which family message we received. Therefore, we generally attach strong value judgments to these emotions, bringing immediate, intense and ,often, over-reactive responses.

Neither anger nor fear are regarded as high virtues in our society but generally anger has the more negative reputation, and is the most threatening. Books on assertiveness and "creative aggression" or intimidating others succeed mainly because most of us are not comfortable with our anger and have spent years developing a casual "Joe Cool" approach to life to avoid angry confrontations. Some of us are afraid of our own anger (loss of control under stress), fearful of thereby physically hurting someone or "looking like a fool." Others are afraid of *receiving* the anger of someone else (*being* hurt physically or emotionally).

In spite of these fears and all our best intentions, most of us manage to experience and express anger with relative ease and consistency, often at the expense of relationships and people we highly regard.

First of all, we have witnessed the destructive *misuse of anger* and its subsequent hurtful consequences, both to the giver and receiver. We will pinpoint some of these abusive uses and suggest why they happen and offer some alternative methods of expressing one's intensive feelings.

Second, we have also seen the painful and destructive results of *withholding* anger. This can lead to ulcers, nervous breakdowns, heart attacks, strokes and (some researchers feel) even cancer for the withholder. It can and does cause equal damage to the spouse and family of the withholder from their frustration in trying to relate to a person who refuses to share who he is and what he is experiencing.

Finally, we *believe* in anger and see it as a very necessary and essential asset to persons and their relationships. We believe there is no such thing as a healthy, growing, productive and exciting relationship that does not include the sharing of intense, volatile—yes, *angry* feelings in a manner that clears the air, reveals emotions and desires and makes commitment to the needs of both parties.

Now comes an equally important issue: What is *good* about anger? Why do we need it? How can we best express it? How are relationships affected when we *don't* express it? What is anger really and how can it improve our communication and feelings about ourselves and others?

Let's look now at 13 points that focus on what anger *is* in the best sense of definition. Many of these points naturally overlap, but experienced as a whole, tend to show what basic communication skills at their very best can accomplish in situations involving anger.

1. Anger Is: A Source Of Discovery About Self

Knowing what angers you can tell you a lot about yourself, in what areas you are sensitive, have strong moral convictions, are threatened, petty, judgmental, caring, defensive or intolerant.

This is an opportunity for discovering strengths and weaknesses, values and convictions, by simply learning to listen to your own feelings and reactions. Give yourself permission to experience and own it all, the good and the bad. You have all the choices necessary in deciding how to act on those feelings, the key is to first be aware of them and what they mean to you. In this way, you can take full responsibility for what hurts you, and why, and be able to do something constructive with that information.

2. Anger Is: A Feeling

Anger does not have to be explained, justified or defended anymore than love does. Feelings are not subject to moral judgment. We are in charge of and responsible for how they are expressed but there is no need to justify the feelings themselves. The only need is to be aware of them and understand where they come from and the messages they are trying to bring to us.

Strong words, by the way, are the poetry of anger. Anger is a strong and intense emotion and it is incongruent to express strong emotions with mild words. Even those who do not believe in "four letter words," cursing or whatever you choose to call it, find themselves creating a substitute language of acceptable strong words: such as darn for damn, doggone for Goddamn, heck for hell.

The other side of the coin is that strong words are pretty helpless if they prevent you from being "heard." You may have to clean up your act in order to get someone's attention. This is a point that needs to be understood when generations clash and obscene words are used to shock one's elders. If we already know certain words offend the persons we are trying to relate to, the use of those words might be the very source of losing any opportunity for success.

Remember, words *can* be offensive, so don't get hung up on words at the expense of not being heard.

3. Anger Is: A Gift

What more loving and intimate gift can be shared than one's intense and straightforward feelings? Why give just a small part of yourself? Give the entire gamut of your emotions and reactions, share who you are in the moment, give a gift that says "you are *that* important to me." "If I don't hear your anger (hurt), I can't trust your love."

It is a gift in process, one that is never complete. The packaging varies from support to confrontation to caring—and it's a genuine way of expressing love.

The receiver is not required, however, to like the gift or even to agree that it is something to be desired. The gift is my own to give; how you receive it or respond to it is up to you.

4. Anger Is: Nourishing To Self

The primary purpose of constructive anger is to take care of ourselves, *protecting* ourselves by being clear and open, not by blocking or creating distance. If you *can't* protect yourself with anger when necessary (or you fear you cannot), then great blocks of energy must be constantly withheld to afford this protection and build a fortress against potential attack.

Sullenness, resentment and withdrawal are all great energy drains to the system, as well as is the need to be constantly alert to attack from all sides.

The powerful man, well trained in self-defense, who knows he can defend himself, will often walk away from a fight and have no reason to participate, nothing to prove. The one who is constantly provoking fights or at least can't walk away from one, is usually a peson still trying to prove to himself and to the world how tough he is. He doesn't really believe in his strength, so he has constantly to reassure himself of its presence.

When you know there is the natural anger and strength needed to protect you on call, then the body can relax; energy can be directed to productive channels and there is a tremendous experience of vitality and aliveness. It is good for the body to release anger rather than sit on it. Most, if not all, psychomatic illness comes from repressing feelings. We have shown examples of this in other portions of the book.

Destructive use of anger could cause as much damage to the body and nervous system as repression, creating more anxiety and turmoil than it resolves.

The *constructive* use of anger is a catharsis, a release of tension and a cleansing of poison from the system. These added benefits of positive response, can help greatly to bring about healing.

5. Anger Is: Multi-Layered

Top Layer   — Anger
Middle Layer — Hurt
Lower Layer   — Blocked Tenderness, Caring and a Hope
                           for Something Better

Between each of these layers could be filters of fear as well. There is Love-Hate in all intense, intimate relationships. To keep the relationship alive and vital, it must be brought to the surface and dealt with.

Hate or anger first blocks off the hurt that needs to be expressed so that you can be more deeply understood. If you refuse to share this second layer of hurt or if the other person refuses to acknowledge and care about your hurt, then the *real* block takes place. Then the deep, tender, loving feelings are effectively blocked off and cannot be expressed. It is very difficult, almost impossible, to love someone who won't let you be angry with them, who forces you to cut off those intense feelings, or who discounts your hurt feelings as childish, inappropriate, or not important.

That is why sex is one of the first relationships to go when anger appears. How can you express tenderness and love when you are still angry and hurt? For those who report that the only thing going for the relationship is great sex, sex evidently symbolizes to them something other than tenderness, love and respect. Perhaps it is their method of expressing hostility and conquest, while for others, it may be a security blanket to relieve anxiety.

However, anger *can* be a real turn-on, not because it is hurtful, but because you become vulnerable, open, totally who you are at that moment. Anger may trigger true contact at its very best, with a response that is natural and immediate. To the contrary, anger unexpressed is a major block to both loving and sexual feelings.

6. Anger Is: Reponse

It is always a reaction rather than an initiating action. It responds to what someone has given to you and to your own internalizing of that gift.

Often, it is a response to hurt, jealousy, disappointment, fear, or loss. One feels safer and less vulnerable responding with anger than expressing any of the above.

This is usually a mixed bag of emotions. Part of you wants to be angry and express it (getting even with the other peson for hurting you) and part does not want the hassle involved. Perhaps you would like to just "hit and run"—express it and be done. Anger is a *door opener* to even heavier feelings and fears, so that if you attack another, you have opened yourself to a heavier counter-attack and more hurt, with more escalation. We want to run away from not only the immediate angry reaction (if it would stop there, great!) but the escalation that follows. That can be simply an escalation of "I got you last" or into deeper levels of who we are and what we really feel about each other.

The fact that you broke a dish is not so important, unless it symbolizes to me that "my" things are not important to you and somehow that gets interpreted as an example of how you misuse our relationship and reject my love.

Anger tells us about our response if we will listen. It tells us what's important at that moment (whether real or neurotic) and how we feel about it.

7. Anger Is: A Risk

We have no control and actually must relinquish any control over the outcome, or else it is manipulation. "This is me because I need to be me, not because I *have* to *have* any prescribed result."

In our counseling practice, we often speak of an "emotional divorce" and how every bad marriage needs one. What that amounts to is the *willingness* to *risk* a divorce in the process of changing yourself and your relationship. You and your growth have to be more important than the continuation of the marriage.

When we "protect" the marriage by not rocking the boat or doing anything that could upset our spouse enough to leave, we are, in effect, stifling it to death—foregoing any opportunity for constructive growth and learning. This generally happens when one or both of the marriage partners are insecure and terrified of being alone. The prospect of having to face the challenges of single life, without the financial or emotional security of a spouse is just too overwhelming. For those who can take the risk, all the odds increase in their favor. For them there is a better chance of the marriage not only surviving, but growing into something unique and special. Also, their individual growth will do the same and each feeds good nourishment to the other.

For those who do *not* take the risk, the best they can look forward to is a deteriorating version of what they now have, an illusion of security contaminated by continual mistrust, resentment and concealed hostility that errupts from time to time and could impulsively push either or both into a readiness for divorce anyway, without ever having had the true opportunity for growth.

While anger keeps coming up in various settings, the message remains the same: Let go of control; what will be, will be. Let go of the outcome; it is not your responsibility. Let go of your "image;" let people see the real you. They might surprise you and like it.

Everyone is really put on notice to be responsive to and responsible for their own feelings when one person takes charge of his life. "I'm putting out myself and inviting you to do the same, assuming you *can* and *will*." There is no hidden agenda for us to protect each other's feelings and play "nice guy" to avoid controversy or pain. This is a compliment to all involved; you *are* strong, you *are* capable, and you *can* speak your need, you *won't* crumble under stress. "I can afford to be myself with you for you really are a peer, an equal in every way."

8. Anger Is: Building Commitment

The big issue in commitment is this: People will never believe in your verbalized commitment to them, until they see concrete evidence that you are totally committed to and capable of loving and taking care of yourself.

Anger says: "I take care of me! I am affirming my commitment to me!" The reaction: "Gee, I want a person like that on *my* side. Here is someone you can count on when you are in need."

The paradox of commitment is shown by two clients in Palm Springs, a mother, Mary, and her 18-year-old son, Woody. Woody was angry, rebellious, heavily into drugs and totally incorrigible, but he seemed to enjoy the idea of counseling and readily agreed to be involved. As time progressed, it became obvious that Mary feared Woody for several reasons: he had previously tried to commit suicide and would often use this as a threat to get what he wanted or to get her off his back; he was occasionally violent and she was physically afraid of him; she felt guilty and partly responsible for his condition and felt she had no "right" to express her anger; whenever she got angry, he would get worse; and finally she was trying to make up to Woody for his father's rejection of him.

The therapist continually encouraged Mary to recognize that Woody would not change until he *had* to. Limits had to be set and enforced; feelings of anger and hurt must be expressed. She resisted all of this pressure saying that if anything bad (worse) happened to Woody, she could not forgive herself. She just could not risk alienating him further and causing a total collapse in the relationship or, worse yet, death.

One day Mary called hysterically to say she had taken the advice, that there had been a violent confrontation and Woody left. She would never see him again, he was probably already dead and it was all her fault. She related the following story:

Mary decided to take her needs seriously as suggested, but Woody took it lightly and ridiculed her. When he tired of that game, he told her to shut up because he was tired of listening. He then went to his room and locked the door, lying down on his bed and beginning to play his guitar. Mary pounded on the door, screaming in a very real anger, "I'm not through with you yet." He cursed her and continued to play. There was a long silence and Woody was relaxing in the belief he had won an easy one when there was a sudden loud noise—five foot, 100 pound, Mary had taken a long run down the hallway and had broken the door open with her shoulder, sending it crashing against the wall. Now she was moving toward the bed with hands upraised, yelling, "I said, I'm not through with you yet."

Within seconds, Woody had burst off the bed, knocked Mary out of his path, clobbered grandmother coming down the hall to see what had happened, jumped on his motorcycle and was long gone.

Mary was sure that this final blow would push Woody to suicide, and she was plagued by guilt.

Mary was reassured she had done the right thing by taking her needs seriously and that Woody was going to have to be responsible for his own life. She could not keep him alive. Since Woody was due in group the next day, she was asked to relax and play a waiting game, give Woody a chance to respond.

Sure enough, Woody attended the group the following night. He arrived 10 minutes late and carefully looked the room over for his mother before he came in. He related the same basic story as Mary had and put the entire group into absolute laughter throughout. The punch line came at the end. "My mother broke down that door (awe in his voice). My mother really loves me. She was going to *kill* me! *My mother really loves me.* That was the first time in 18 years I knew my mother loved me."

It may be difficult to get the connection between a mother's anger that was strong enough to kill, and experiencing love from that situation, but it is real. Woody had first of all interpreted her passive leniency and lack of discipline as not loving or caring about him or what happened to him. Next, he had absolutely *no* respect for her as a person because he had watched his Father take advantage of her (and she just came back for more) and now he continued the game as well. Finally, if she cared so little for herself, she surely could not love anyone else; if he couldn't make her mad, he couldn't be very important to her. All that changed with one broken door! The message was multi-leveled. "You've pushed me around long enough. I'm committed to *my* survival. If anyone is going to die in the family, it will be you, not me. I love you too much to let you destroy me or to cooperate in your destruction of yourself. You can destroy yourself if you choose, but not with *my* help.

Woody got the message. We got them together the next day and reconciliation was begun.

9. Anger Is: An Assertion

We have previously defined assertion as taking care of oneself in an appropriate manner, while it's counterpart, aggression, is attacking the other person in a hostile manner.

To be assertive is to confidently, firmly, appropriately and directly state your feelings, needs, convictions and attitudes to another human being. At the same time, it includes respect for the other person's feelings. When we assert ourselves, we necessarily consider the feelings of others. When we are aggressive, we do not. Assertion is "putting yourself on the line," describing and relating your experience in the relationship, how you are being affected.

Anger as assertion is passing information for the primary purpose of being better understood, rather than just to change behavior. It is not designed to be intimidating or controlling, but *is very* effective in achieving the desired results simply because of the methods used.

Being assertive, you use "I" statements of feelings, rather than "you" statements of accusation. You do not intrude into the space of others or question their motives, integrity or heritage. Responding to this attitude, others are not as apt to be defensive, are much more likely to hear what you have to say and, therefore, be more free to respond to your desires.

A very mild example may demonstrate this more clearly. Charles was playing solitare when his son, Eric, was quite small and just learning the game himself. Since Daddy was playing, Eric also wanted to and they set up on opposite sides of a rather narrow counter. As the games progressed, Eric would slowly move deeper across the counter taking up more room and moving into Dad's space.

It became somewhat irritating and the temptation was to *treat* Eric with irritation: "Don't do it," "You're in my way," or "It irritates me when you don't give me enough room." All of these statements are "you" statements tinged with blame and rejection.

To deliberately test whether a youngster could respond to simple assertiveness (and to feel better about himself), Daddy simply said to Eric in a tone of information only (No hostility or irritation) "That's *my* space." Eric's reply was immediate—"Oh," and he moved the cards. He did not feel the need to apologize or feel guilty and simply moved the cards without being directly asked to. Of course he invaded the same space at least six or seven times in an hour, and each time it was handled exactly the same way with the same results. Some of you may wonder why it happened so many times and whether Eric was testing Daddy. That's possible, and it is also possible that he became so involved in the game he did not notice.

The point is Daddy got what he needed each time he asserted his space and did not have to get angry to achieve it. (With anger he might have cut it off sooner but it would have put a damper on their fun.) Eric felt related to as a reasonable, responsive person and he reacted that way, he moved the cards.

10. Anger Is: Situational

Chronic anger is rarely appropriate to the situation, either in intensity or reality. The angry person is, in fact, responding to the situation, but using it as a trigger that sets off a far deeper and more intense emotion from within. Then it is usually expressed as an *over-reaction*.

Chronic anger is identification with a prior pattern of events, causing an over-reaction. It's killing a fly with a baseball bat, *over-kill*.

Marge, in good humor, mildly put down her husband, John, for a corny joke, in the middle of a party. Since John's parents ridiculed him as stupid all his life, he now hears Marge doing the same thing. He reacts with violent rage that shocks and embarrasses everyone. Ninety per cent of the anger is directed at John's parents and was totally inappropriate to the situation. When chronic anger has been properly dealt with (by going to the original source and facing it out), one is released to acute or situational anger that is no longer tied to the past.

Unresolved parental conflict can cause many marital and parent-child difficulties. We tend to use our spouse and children more than any others as the scapegoats for our past, demanding from them the unconditional love we never received from our parents, and inflicting on them the anger we could never resolve with our parents. Compounding this is the tendency to marry someone like the parent we "haven't finished with" because we subconsciously desire to improve that relationship.

Situational anger is only a reaction to *that* situation and is appropriate in intensity and feeling to the immediate moment. Once expressed and responded to, that anger is gone: there is no more reason for it.

"It irritates me when you kill my spontaneous feelings by calling my humor corny."

Or in John's case, sensing and feeling the warmth in Marge's kidding and, therefore, not being irritated because he feels loved anyway.

11. Anger Is: Confrontation And Building A Foundation

Confrontation is used as a bridge in the relationship providing an arc of communication. It is reaching out, instead of waiting to be reached for. It is a message of trust and support for the other as well.

"It is O.K. for me to take my needs seriously and confront you with my feelings. I trust that I won't do it destructively or with vindictiveness. I trust you are strong enouh to handle my feelings and care enough to want to. I support our relationship with this sharing of myself. It is too important *not* to share. I'm thereby creating an opportunity to share and relate, offering—yes, expecting—the same in return."

The larger the base of trust, confidence and knowledge, the more anger and confrontation or intensity can be sustained. There must be some awareness of who you are and if you can be trusted. "Are you setting me up for a fall?" We build this solid base by expressing feelings and getting feed-back.

Intensity needs a solid base to come back to or it can be destructive. Going out too far on a limb requires the firm foundation of a solid tree. The foundation is the relationship.

12. Anger Is: A Rhythm Process

Each of us seems to be born with a rhythm that is natural and comfortable to ourself, but so many environmental factors have distorted this rhythm that we find it difficult to identify it.

Learning a new skill may help you identify your rhythm process. Is it fast, slow, start-stop, an hour and then a break, all day or whatever? If you can be aware enough to pick up the maximum speed and pace that is successful for you, without pushing your limits, or being lazy, and then fit in the *pattern* of learning as well, you will maximize your abilities and success possibilities.

Incompatible rhythms are often seen as power struggles. "If you don't keep my pace, do it my way (which is more efficient, of course) and have my energy level, it is an affront to me and a deliberate irritation."

This may sound like a minor issue, but it is one of the most subtle but common complaints we hear from couples, who almost always take it personally and feel their spouse is acting that way to annoy them. Are you are aware of your own "best times" and personal rhythms?

Examples are numerous. One person needs 10 hours sleep and the other five. One wakes up at 6 am spouting, "Good morning, God." The other falls out of bed at 9:30 am, groaning, "Good God, it's morning." At midnight, however, the latter is just getting a second wind, and wants to dance all night, while the early morning spouse went to sleep in the middle of the movie.

One races across a parking lot while the other falls behind mumbling about not being loved or noticed. There are different ways of doing dishes, making beds, or raising kids, and separate tolerance levels to noise and stress. In all this, there is always a right way to do things (mine) and a wrong way (yours). Sounds petty and it is, but once taken personally, the issues run deep and hurt deeply.

Once we have recognized a rhythm pattern that is comfortable for me and different for you, it is easier to tolerate the differences. When you keep demanding a person change and do something your way, and they don't it is easy to interpret that response as a passive-aggressive way of telling you to get lost. Both parties need to see differences for what they are. After that we will be free to solve our mutual problems the best way we can, without the added tension of questioning our partner's motives. It is possible the differences in temperament, athletic ability, rhythm and interests create too large a gap to overcome. Even then, a divorce will be much less emotional and ugly since we now understand the differences are not hostile and deliberate or anyone's "fault."

13. Anger Is: Healing

Healing is also a rhythm process. How long does it take *you* to heal? The experience ends at the point you can re-engage and relate again. Healing is the final piece in any angry confrontation. You can't be close again until healing takes place. When you go against your natural rhythm, your body rebels. On the other hand, some people enjoy open wounds; they refuse to heal in order to maintain guilt and continue to blame the other.

We owe an obligation to be true to ourselves and not to manipulate others.

Anger heals me as I express it. Anger heals you as your understand and respond to it. Anger heals US as it cleans out the toxic resentments between us.

When the true motivation is to reveal myself in a vulnerable way, reaching out to you, anger becomes the contact that promotes healing, through intimacy and caring.

XIV. The Abuses Of Anger

In a very true sense, destructive anger is really a *distortion* of anger, not a real and direct expression of self, and has two basic purposes in the relationship, control and distancing.

If you will stop and consider your own anger and the motives involved, it should not be difficult to recognize your own need for control and distance in any specific situation. We are trying to control: 1. our self image ("I don't want to appear as weak, vulnerable, hurt, embarrassed, etc."); 2. the other person ("If I can control your behavior, I am safe from whatever you are doing or may do that frightens me"); 3. *and* what happens, the eventual outcome of our disagreement ("If I get my own way, I win, or I keep from losing").

In the process of this self protection, of course, we distance each other and hence feel safer for the moment, at least. Because the closeness and intimacy of the relationship itself often creates a factor of fear, we may even create an incident in order to provide distance. Also, the fear of a fight, or of rejection or losing or whatever, may have created the need for distance and for time to recover.

Many of us need, desire and desperatively *strive* for intimacy and love, yet are at the same time terribly *afraid* of this closeness and find it difficult to sustain for any appreciable length of time. Rather than admit this paradox to ourselves and try to work through to a solution, we often subconsciously create an "excuse" for a fight to justify the distancing and thereby avoid the real problem: I need to be close, but I am afraid of being close.

The following is a list of ten ways we use anger to distort, control and distance. There are undoubtedly others you can add to the list and many of these have overlapping qualities.

How Relationships Become Derailed: The Abuses Of Anger

1. "It's All Your Fault"—The Blamer

These are the "right-wrong", "good-bad" and "win-lose" people. This is probably the most difficult couple to work with in therapy and we've had our share. There is absolutely no contact in the exchange and it is definitely used for the purpose of creating more distance. Nothing works better for this purpose. Neither partner takes responsibility for his own actions nor those of the other.

"My actions and your actions are all *your* fault. I would always act in a proper manner if not for you. *You* set me up. I have to defend myself. You're wrong and you never will admit it. You will never see my point of view. You don't listen."

This is in reality a survival defense. Both parties have to win to survive: losing is *death*, admitting you are wrong, stupid and a total failure. Because of the seriousness of the consequences, neither party will ever concede, so it's usually a stand-off in each individual situation, although each will claim "you hurt me more than I hurt you."

A noted athlete in counseling with his wife admitted his whole theory of competition, relationships and life is to "avoid losing." Here is a man who drives himself incessantly, has an extremely destructive temper, excels even beyond his ability, and rarely loses. But, he's not a "winner." Every victory is just one more day of avoiding the inevitable loss. He cannot really savor the satisfaction of victory, and hundreds of victories do not improve his self image or self esteem. A loss (of a game or argument) simply reveals to the rest of the world what he feels every day, "I'm a loser, a failure, a person of little worth." That's too high a price to pay, so he "wins."

The final word about the blamer is that he *never* reveals his own feelings or what's going on inside. He talks about you—your motives, your feelings, your badness—but never about his hurt.

The real issue breaks down to this. One party (Susan) says, "You hurt me." (It would be nice if the statement came out so direct and matter of fact; that message is usually buried in accusing moralizing of the other's motives and lack of character. The underlying issue is: "You hurt me.") Sam responds: "I am not a bad guy." (This is also disguised beneath hostile attacks and lethal accusations.)

Since neither one has heard or understood the other's message, they continue to debate two different subjects with no possible solution. Sam *hears* Susan tell him that he *is* a bad guy, has always *been* a bad guy, and always *will* be. Furthermore, everything he does will be influenced by that fact. Perhaps Susan *is* saying that because it is safer to talk about Sam's badness than to admit Susan's hurt. Regardless of how she expresses it, the bottom line remains, "You hurt me" or, at least, "I got hurt in that exchange." She is fighting to have him apologize and be sorry that she got hurt. Only then would Susan feel loved and cared about.

But if Sam apologizes and expresses genuine sorrow that she was hurt, in his mind he is admitting that he *is* a bad guy, he *was* wrong, she *is* right. "She *wins*, I *lose, and* she'll never let me forget it." So, Sam must talk her out of that need. "You shouldn't feel that way because . . ."

If this sounds foreign to you, you're not a blamer, and perhaps it is impossible for you to believe people can take situational feelings to such a life and death extreme, but they can and do.

How do you break this pattern? First, by revealing what the *real* issues are: Susan is hurt; Sam doesn't want to be thought of as a bad guy. Once this is expressed and made clear, Sam is free to respond to Susan's hurt ("I'm sorry you feel that way; I didn't mean to hurt you.") and Susan loses her need to attack Sam since he has responded to her *feelings* rather than to her words.

When we are no longer adversaries, defending and attacking characters, we can sit down to discuss and solve "our mutual problem." We are trying to understand and change *behavior* that bothers us and at the same time doing so in such a way that both can feel listened to, understood and loved. When you feel your "life" is at stake, it is impossible to listen to or care about someone else.

The solution sounds easy and it is. The difficult part is getting a frightened person to listen long enough to *hear* the solution.

2. "Why Did You Do That?"—The Questioner

Interestingly enough, this person asks questions that cannot really be answered. He is not looking for information and understanding but actually putting you down in a subtle, indirect fashion.

George spills his drink all over the dinner and onto Mary's dress and she screams at him "Why did you do that?" It is difficult to put a question mark there because it is more of an accusation than a question. What she is saying is: "Why are you so stupid?" "Why are you consistently clumsy?" "Why are you thoughtless?" The insinuation is that you are deliberately choosing to be hostile and hurtful and did it because you *wanted* to. "Why did you want to spill your drink on me at this moment in time?"

The laughable part is that George finds himself trying to provide an *intelligent* answer to that question. He can't come up with one that will satisfy Mary ("I don't know if I was born that way or if it took years of practice.") so he blames it on *her* to get himself off the hook. "You confused me." "You asked for the butter and I was trying to pass it." "If you weren't always yelling at the kids, I could relax at the dinner table." "You never liked that dress anyway."

Interrogators are dishonest because no answer will satisfy them. They love to debate facts, demand justifications, explanations and reasons which are *never* good enough or accepted. They never have to reveal their own feelings and they totally control the conversation by placing others on the defensive.

The solution: Don't try to give an intelligent answer to a stupid question. Deal with the issue, not the question. George could simply say:

"I'm sorry I spilled my drink on your dress."

"I know my clumsiness upsets you; I wish I had better control of it."

"You really see me as a hostile person who manages to work you over, don't you?"

"Are you saying I did it deliberately?"

Any of these responses deal more closely with what really happened and what her reaction implies. What if she stays on the attack? George needs to stay with the *issue* and refuse to be dragged into a name-calling contest.

3. "I'm Only Trying To Help!"—The Critic

If you criticize from a place of love and caring, people generally will not be deeply hurt. Criticism is most hurtful coming from one who is threatened and has his *ego* at stake. It is also most hurtful *to* this person.

People who criticize can rarely take criticism. They know subconsciously what an effective weapon of control criticism is because of the devastating effect it has on them. Since the best defense is a good offense, they go for the first punch with a killer instinct. Mostly, they are not aware of following this double standard.

In a therapy session that included a married daughter and her parents, the mother consistently started sentences with the intimidating phrase—"You already *know* . . .

. . . I love you . . .

. . . that's immoral . . .

. . . You shouldn't have done that . . ."

When the therapist pointed out to the mother that those statements were judgmental and critical, she became flustered and upset. "I don't mean to be critical and make her feel stupid. She *has to understand* that it is a habit of mine. That's just the way I talk."

Before the sentence was hardly finished, her tone of voice and mannerism turned abruptly from embarrassed apology to anger and bitterness:

"My husband always says that to *me*—'you already know'—and I *always* feel he is calling me *stupid* and I *deeply* resent it. I have tried for years to get him to stop that, but he doesn't care about my feelings at all."

Until it was pointed out by the therapist, she *never* got the connection between what her husband said to her and what she said to her daughter. It never occurred to her that the daughter felt stupid (or that she was calling her daughter stupid) or how her husband could be so dumb as to not recognize her feelings. The hostility in the husband toward the wife (whether he would admit that or not) was being expressed also by mother to daughter.

Criticism and anger are best expressed directly and openly, not with indirectness, sarcasm and ridicule that can later be denied.

There *is* a place for warm, gentle humor—a kidding of the human condition—"Yes, I notice your clumsiness and forgetfulness and it is mildly irritating, but if I can kid you about it, I can live with it most of the time."

4. "When I Get Through With You . . ."—The Vicious

This can be defined as a "deliberate attempt to hurt someone *in the area* you know is vulnerable." It is designed primarily to achieve distance and it *works*. Viciousness creates deep feelings of being wounded and hurt. Adjectives provide good weapons here. Calling someone a "creep" hurts, but a "fat" or "ugly" or "religious" or "bucktoothed" creep personalizes it and that hurts even more.

Surprisingly, the vicious attack often occurs after a long period of warmth, closeness and intimacy. This makes it more effective because of the element of surprise and the lack of warning. It is used as a homeostatic process for those who cannot sustain long periods of intimacy. They need to balance the intimacy with space because the closeness can no longer be tolerated but they do not know how to simply ask for space, time and privacy. Therefore, the distance must be justified by hard feelings and a vicious interchange accomplishes that.

Needy people, who go for "instant intimacy" (often found as groupies at psychological marathons and workshops that feature instant touching and feeling intimacy), often find themselves using viciousness to provide relief from intensive, overwhelming romantic episodes. They do not "ebb and flow" with a relationship and are so dependent they cling 24 hours per day till they reach a saturation point. Since they do not understand the concepts of space and privacy in a relationship and are afraid of being misunderstood or rejected if they asked for it, they find the solution in a good fight.

Awareness of the problem within yourself or the partner involved is a good first step to change this behavior. Total possessiveness is the most obvious sign of insecurity and dependency. All of us need to develop our own sense of inner peace and security through time alone and inner awareness. Togetherness is more nourishing and appreciated when there are spaces and time to rest.

5. "I Don't Get Mad, I Get Even"—The Avenger

Tit for tat, getting even, king of the mountain, got 'cha last, up the ante, and escalation are various ways of describing this process of destructive anger which can also be vicious if necessary to accomplish the goals.

"You hurt me, so I'll hurt you worse, or show you I don't care." This is the most common excuse for sexual acting out, alcohol or drug abuse.

"My spouse and I had a big fight so I went out and got drunk, or laid, or whatever."

Sometimes we *want* them to know we got even, often we do not. It is sometimes satisfaction enough that we did it, if they find out, now we are open to receive more retaliation.

This is not a simple disagreement but a nose to nose, ego inflated power struggle, that involves winning at any cost. There is a constant escalation. The source of a power struggle is insecurity and survival of the ego. If I admit I am wrong—that is proof I am *all* wrong.

6. "The End Justifies The Means"—The Manipulator

This is winning by intimidation, being angry for the purpose of producing an effect, *not* because you feel it. A *very* effective method in dealing with those who are afraid of yelling and fighting. Raise your voice and get your way quickly and without bloodshed, also without sharing your real feelings.

Those who resist any new approach to intimacy with the reaction "What's the use of trying, it won't work?" only see anger as manipulation, not as a true expression of self. "No matter what I do or how I behave, I can't manipulate you to give me what I want. If I can't get what I want, why waste my time expressing myself?"

This person is only concerned about results (controlling the other) rather than integrity expressing the self.

A healthy person says what he feels and behaves constructively because it meets his own needs, and it makes him feel good about himself. Of course, he also has hopes of receiving an appropriate, similar response. The success of this venture lies in his own behavior (for which he is responsible) rather than the *responses* (for which he is *not*).

An interesting point: when you feel a need to "protect" a relationship by being less than candid and manipulating in an indirect fashion, the results are usually negative. When you get angry enough that you "don't care" about the reaction, you feel an obligation to express your true feelings and let the chips fly even if it costs you the relationship, you usually get *heard*, and get the results you wanted.

We are not saying "don't care" about the other person and trying to see how destructively you can hurt them, but you don't care about *controlling the results*.

7. "Who Me?"—The Innocent

This is one of the most frustrating and effective means of destructive behavior simply because even the perpetrator himself is able to stay deceived. This varies from cunningly planned covert activity to totally subconscious reaction. The passive-aggressive person frequently denies the intent behind the act and seems totally innocent of wrong doing.

This behavior is characterized by what the people "omit" or "forget" rather than what they *do*, and generally infuriates the victim, who is then made to feel petty for complaining.

Symptoms are: forgetting, accidently breaking things, always being late, "nice guy syndrome," innocent questions, not understanding, complimenting beyond reality.

In a 12-hour couples' marathon, the authors took 15 minutes to carefully explain some general rules and expectancies for the day. The first three hours were exceptionally exciting, with many breakthroughs of insight and feelings. During a quiet and thoughtful lull in the activity, a rather angry and hostile woman participant asked in a very innocent and confused "little girl" voice: "What are we supposed to be doing here? I really don't understand what we are here for . . ."

The *real* reasons for the act are kept out of awareness and denied. The key is not in what they *give*, but what they withhold in the process of giving.

8. "Sock It To Me"—The Victim

Violence is a direct result of suppressing *assertion*. Assertion is comfortably taking your needs seriously—in a direct manner. Violence is assertion gone sour.

When a person does not feel the right to take his needs seriously, when he holds them inside, tension builds until he blows. Building assertion avoids violence.

A large, powerful and angry husband once asked in a couples' group what he could do with his anger. "You won't let me hit her anymore, so I try repressing it. Then it builds for several weeks till I blow up and scream and holler and *that's* not acceptable. What can I do?" He had no concept of quietly, firmly and expectantly asserting his needs and feelings *and being heard!*

The other side of the coin is this: *the victim* (in family violence) *will never let go of the factors that create violence.*

Almost without exception the victim is a totally cooperative participant. Usually the victim has the same amount of anger and knows how to *provoke* the sadist, who expresses it for both of them.

In every lecture series we get notes from the audience describing a terrible series of abuses by one spouse to the other for 15 or 20 years, a kind of "Can you top this?"

Our response is simple: What are you still doing there 15 or 20 years later? What does that say about *you—the victim?* Can you be any less destructive and sick than your spouse?

Violence is a method of contact and homeostasis, though not a very satisfying one. Sadism is the flip side of helplessness. Sadists were usually the objects of sadism as children. All child abusers were abused. To be a sadist requires a helpless object. Since you were once the victim, you choose now to be the winner for a change.

Punitiveness comes from a need to control others. In the case of parents, we can see this as a very clear need. It comes from a fear of *not* having control. We are not talking about appropriate punishment toward the children. When a person experiences inner chaos, he feels a powerful need to control his outer environment, often through fear and punishment. When there is inner peace and tranquility, he can tolerate fewer controls and more chaos in the outer environment.

Punitiveness generally produces three reactions in the recipient: 1. It creates resentment and hostility. 2. It does *not* work, except temporarily. 3. It blocks generosity. Obligation and fear will produce the minimum response one can get away with to avoid further punishment, no more, no less. When punishment is removed, people are much more generous by free choice.

Two favorite expressions in est are: "Get off it" and "Release it." What they boil down to is this: we can't let a situation go because our ego is involved and we put ourselves in a win or lose, life or death situation. The child (or spouse) picks up the challenge and now he can't let go either. It is not a matter of no longer caring what the other does, but of *letting go* of the manipulation and power struggle. *Tell* the other person how you feel and what you need and expect. You are leaving him an implied choice of consent and acknowledging you can't totally dominate his life. When respected in this manner, the person usually gives you the behavior you wanted.

9. "Get Out Of My Way"—The Aggressive Intruder

Aggressive behavior that intrudes into another person's psychic space is characterized by a negative, selfish, uncaring attitude, the opposite of assertion. Assertion is taking care of *me* in an appropriate manner, while aggression is attacking *you* in a hostile manner. Aggression produces resentment because it treats people as objects. It is used by needy, desperate people "taking" what they really don't deserve, or could get any other way. It is assaultive violating behavior, justified by the extent of the *need.*

"I was angry."

"I was drunk."

"I was hungry."

Or blaming *you—*

"You shouldn't have done that."

"You dared me."

"You made me mad."

This "I want what I want when I want it" mentality is often expressed as loud, intimidating *noise*. Constructive anger, in contrast, is not noise, it has *feeling* behind it. Noise is without feeling, just volume, contrived. Although we call it anger, a temper tantrum is totally self-indulgent and has no contact with anger. It is a catharsis, a blaming with no vulnerability. Actually the person is having a good time.

Some people feel assertion is no match for aggression because assertion is bound by the rules of courtesy and appropriateness, while aggression is not. We admit there is no changing another person who refuses to be reasonable; however, each owes it to himself to assertively stand his ground, share his feelings and meet his own needs, regardless of the irresponsible behavior of others.

10. "Let's Laugh At Him"—The Joker Is Wild

This is the practical joker, the Don Rickles of your social set. Great sense of humor, makes everyone laugh, especially those who are the butt of the joke. All the better to cover up your hurt.

Sarcasm is almost always a cover for hostility, a method of indirectly releasing anger and feeling superior. It is backed by a strong sense of denial. If you complain or get offended, "you have no sense of humor" or "I was just kidding." Oh, *yeah*.

Sarcasm is a release valve to keep from blowing up. Take away a person's sarcasm and *pure* anger generally follows. Since ridicule is used a lot to keep children in line, most of us feel like children again when we receive it. It is very difficult to penetrate the defense mechanisms of the person with this behavior trait, making it doubly hard to deal with the *real* issues of feeling involved. The victim is made to feel foolish for being so "sensitive" and easily hurt.

How many of these ten points can you identify with? When was the last time you used such behavior? Can you see new possibilities for changing that in the future?

For those of you who couldn't identify with these points because you rarely get angry, the next chapter is for you.

XV. The Withholding Of Anger

We have discussed in detail the abuses of anger and, certainly, all of us can see ourselves in each of those illustrations and give concrete examples of how we have been on both the giving and receiving end of destructive anger.

So can all of us go out right now and be experts in spotting and eliminating the negative, plus accentuating and using the positive? Fat chance!

What our intellect has consumed, our emotions must yet integrate and learn to express. This takes time, effort and desire. It does not come easily or without a price to pay. Also, there are blocks we must first remove before we can *use* anger in actually improving relationships and getting needs properly met.

While some of us find it almost impossible *not* to express anger, even when the consequences are harmful to ourselves and our loved ones, there are others who find it equally painful and discomforting *to express* anger, hurt, fear or any other intense emotion. It's too naked, vulnerable and dangerous to put oneself on the line, presenting the other person with material that could later be used against you, and risking the reality of rejection—all because your feelings and needs were unacceptable.

Interestingly enough, many of these folks are, therefore, experienced as and labeled by others as: unfeeling, cold, unaffectionate and emotionless. Part of the game, then, becomes a challenge to get them to *feel*, experience, be alive, even if we must hurt them to do it. Otherwise, we have no idea how they feel about us or if we have impact on their lives. We laugh about the engineer stereotype who fits this pattern, a person more comfortable with machines and projects than people, yet they often are.

The truth is, they may not be comfortable with people because they are *too* emotional, *too* volatile, and *too* vulnerable to allow their emotions to come to the surface. Some carry these emotions quite close to the surface and are in a constant inner sense of turmoil and unrest.

Others have become so practiced at this way of life, their emotions are buried deeply and not easily reached. For these, some deep, life-shaking trauma (like the possibility of a divorce) is needed to plumb the depths beneath which these emotions have been buried.

Surely, all three persons reside in *most* of us, with varying percentages, of course. By discussing the options more openly, perhaps, we can turn the percentages more to our favor. Let's look at the blocks to anger.

Blocks To Anger

Anger Block #1: Lack Of Knowledge Or Information

Some people just don't know they have the *right* to get angry. They've never been given permission and don't know how to give it to themselves.

"She didn't mean it."

"He had a good reason to be hurtful."

"They were drunk."

"I want to be seen as an understanding person."

"He's too old; he wouldn't understand."

They can give dozens of reasons, excuses, whatever, to justify the other person's hurtfulness and the fact that they should not be hurt or angry in return.

There are two kinds of ignorance, really. The first is just not knowing that anger has any potential for positive benefits and, therefore, *can* bring improvement to a relationship. For this person, a simple matter of education may open an entirely new experience with a minimum of time and effort.

The second is more difficult: the person is so out of touch with feelings that there is no conscious awareness of being hurt or angry. This person needs an extended period, usually with professional help, of asking the question, "What am I feeling right now?" until the response is automatic. Discover your feelings, explore them without judgment and share them with others.

Anger Block #2: The "You Owe Me" Syndrome—Or— The Overwhelming Power Of Guilt

"How can I possibly get angry at her when she's done so much for me and sacrificed so much for me all my life?"

It *must* be Mother. Who else is so pure and unselfish? And reminded you of it just yesterday?

"He's such a *nice guy*—I come out the heavy—or look like a fool."

Could that be dear old Dad?

"I must be terribly ungrateful and selfish to be mad at him/her. He's so good to me, and I don't seem to appreciate it."

Where do these feelings of guilt come from? Much of the time they are programmed into our subconscious by the incessant grocery list recited by our parents over and over all our lives.

Debt comes from obligation; they often *want* us to feel obligated so we can more easily be controlled and manipulated to love them or at least do their bidding. If this sounds like the beginning of a blanket condemnation of parents, and wholesale blaming of the parents to get neurotic adult children off the hook, it is not meant to be. Where the shoes fits, we hope to add enough pinch of pain to help both sides break a destructive pattern, and find a new and more exciting way to relate—with *love*—not with guilt and obligation.

There is neurotic guilt and there is normal guilt—a world of difference not always easily discerned, even within ourselves.

Normal guilt comes when the person has violated his own integrity, broken his own values and deliberately struck out to injure or destroy another (either from fear, vindictiveness or whatever). *Not* to have guilt under these circumstances would be pathological (what we call a sociopath or psychopath—a person without social or personal conscience). *Neurotic guilt can be defined as that which is inappropriate to the situation.* This occurs when a person is conditioned and trained to feel guilt under certain circumstances because of someone else's value systems, even when they know they've done the right thing at the right time.

Example: Bob invites his parents over for Sunday dinner for Dad's birthday. A last minute opportunity arises for Bob to take an all-expenses-paid trip to Hawaii that weekend and he cancels or postpones the birthday dinner. Both parents are deeply hurt and feel rejected and Bob feels guilty. Why? He was programmed to believe that if someone gets hurt because of something he does, he's responsible, regardless of his motives or the circumstances. That's neurotic guilt and should be rejected as such.

Whether or not we "we hurt someone" depends on our motivation and reasons. "Getting hurt" depends on your interpretation of the reasons and motives, plus secondary needs for control and power.

"If I hurt you, I'm sorry I hurt you! If you felt hurt as a result of my taking my needs seriously and acting in a manner I felt best served my interests (after taking *your* needs and feelings into due consideration), then I'm sorry you got hurt. But I didn't mean to hurt you." Motive makes the difference.

Why do parents give their children love? Is it an overflow of expression that comes naturally from a confirmation of self love, couple love and unconditional positive regard for these individuals to whom they gave birth? Or is it for the purpose of *being* loved by the children?

Some people give an abundance of "love" that is actually designed primarily as a means of obligation, control and getting even more love in return. That is exploitation.

One of the most potent examples of this kind of parent-child conflict and confrontation was seen in the movie, *Guess Who's Coming to Dinner*, where Sidney Poitier portrayed a black man planning to marry a white woman. There was a very emotional scene between Sidney and his parents where his father listed all the sacrifices they had made over the years to see to it their son had all the advantages they never had and would not face the handicaps they had to face. In In a very dramatic conclusion the father blurted out that they did not want their son to "pay them back" by marrying a white woman. The father was demanding obedience to this request on the basis of "You Owe Us!"

The equally impassioned response (paraphrased here) was, "I don't owe you *anything*. Either you gave it freely out of love or the whole relationship was a hoax. There are no strings on love. I owe *my* son—my children—what I was *freely given* but I don't *owe* for love."

We don't totally agree a child owes *nothing* to his parents, but the principle is correct, love has no price tag and obligations are not love.

What then, do we owe our parents? The same we owe ourselves and the rest of the world, to be the "Best Me Possible", to love as we are loved, to give generously and openly of ourselves.

If our methods of doing so and our values of "best" differ from those of our parents, that may make both of us sad at the differences; and the parents certainly have the right to disagree with us in these areas. Ideally, they will believe enough in us to believe we are honestly being the "best me" possible and go on loving us unconditionally, regardless of their reactions regarding our behavior.

Carl Rogers, the highly respected creator of Client-Centered therapy once remarked that his most difficult personal task was allowing his wife, children and co-workers to have different beliefs, values and ideas than his own, without taking it as a personal rejection of himself and his beliefs.

There is the issue: parents usually over-react because they take these differences personally. They see such differences as a rejection of themselves, rather than as an honest expression of the child.

Guilt also comes because most of us find it difficult to admit angry or hateful feelings towards our parents, or anyone we love. Gratitude and anger may easily co-exist. Love and hate are not necessarily opposites, *indifference* would be opposite to love.

You are often angry *because* you love them, *because* they are important to you, *because* they have the most power to hurt you.

We're not claiming even the exploitive parents are totally insincere with their gifts, *but* the gift *does* have a double edge, "How can you be mad at me, when I'm so good to you?"

"I'm not mad at you because of the goodness, but because of something you did that hurt me."

The over-giver has a strong need to be loved and appreciated, *plus* a strong fear he's *not* lovable. His behavior says, "If I *don't* give, I won't be loved. No one could love me for just being me. The relationship will end. He or she will leave me if I don't continue to please." So this kind of love is contaminated by fear of abandonment.

Another variation of this theme is the weakness or martyr syndrome. "He's so weak he can't handle my feelings, especially anger."

If the parents or spouse can get you to believe that about them, that they are too weak to be confronted, they have accomplished total control over the relationship. You have been rendered helpless, left to deal with your feelings alone, as you can, however you can. *Beware of the weak, helpless martyrs of life—they never lose!*

The core of this problem for the person trying to relate to a martyr or who finds himself being exploited is that he is consistently defining his responses and sense of worth around another person's reactions and values, rather than his own. He tries to "guess" what is expected of him and what will bring the most favorable response, thereby surrendering his power to the other.

He is also assuming that the other is always "correct" in these responses and knows best in any situation. Or that it doesn't matter what's right or best, as long as he gets the favorable response he wants or avoids the unpleasant one he doesn't want. "Peace at any cost" is generally more expensive than any of us can afford.

All this is different than being "sensitive" to another's emotional state. We do not advocate reckless selfishness, or taking what you want regardless of how it affects others. Doing what is truly the "best for me" in any particular situation (which we strongly advocate) has to take into prior consideration all those who are important to us and will subsequently be affected by our decisions.

Even though it is unrealistic to assume our feelings and needs will always be in complete harmony and agreement, taking the other person into consideration in our decision making will generally make it possible to incorporate both our needs at little (or less) cost to either. *Considering* someone is different from being *controlled* by someone.

Do what's best for you. It's the best you have to work with.

Anger Block #3: A Strong Moral Judgment That Only Sees Anger As A Negative Force And Therefore Not To Be Expressed

This type of attitude and value system could be produced by two quite contrasting backgrounds: A violent home, where screaming and hitting were commonplace and terrifying, or a cold, unfeeling home, where anger was not tolerated.

If a person has had no prior experience with a healthy expression of anger, where people confront each other directly and intently, *and come out of the situation with resolution and feelings of closeness and love, it is difficult for them to imagine that this can and does take place.*

Anger as such has no moral value, the motive determines whether it is destructive or constructive.

In a violent home, children cannot handle violence. They do not understand the limits and have no natural defense of their own. This includes both verbal and physical violence; to watch it or receive it can be traumatic in devastating fashion. If you did go through this in your childhood, the guided daydream approach is by far the most effective relief we know.

Children *do* need to experience and share intense feelings, disagreements, expressed anger.

And they need to experience that no one got hurt, that people still love each other, that nothing of the good is lost, no harm, no foul.

The child must also be given the right to *his* feelings of anger, as well as protection from his own tendency to violence.

Modeling behavior for your child, explanation of limits (what is *accepted* behavior and what is *not*), and firm consistency of discipline —these, coupled with love, affection, and freedom to grow and experiment, are all necessary ingredients for teaching a child to deal with emotions.

"I don't throw tantrums, and you can't."

"I'm not rude, and you are not to be rude."

"I don't break things, and you can't"

"I don't call names, and you can't"

"I don't hit, and you can't hit."

Spanking, by the way, is not hitting. It is a punishment designed to fit the crime (not an angry release of tension for the parents with the child as scapegoat).

The more outlets for anger you can allow the child, the better. If he is not allowed to cry, talk back, disagree or express displeasure, what will he do with the anger?

"The same thing I had to do as a kid: hold it in or get my head knocked off." Yes, and how loved did that make *you* feel?

Give the child some outlets that *are* acceptable, or he'll find his own that are *not* acceptable, eventually. You can count on it.

"You *can*: yell, cuss, disagree, beat up your punching bag, tell me you hate me, tell me what you'd like to do if you could!"—whatever the parent can tolerate in his own comfort zone.

"You *cannot* do anything that would be hurtful to *me*, you or the relationship between us." A good line to draw.

But what about violence through intimidation, insults, character assasination and humiliation, with *no* recourse for the child.

Two male students now in their 20's related to a Marriage and Family Life class the details of being reared in that type of home, one by a step-father and the other by his natural father.

Both went away to the service and grew into powerful men. One came home and provoked a situation where he totally beat up his father. The other came home and the step-father woke up at 2 am with the step-son holding a large knife to his throat. There were no words, no movement, no change for the next three to four hours. Then tired of the game and feeling he had made his point, the son left and never saw the step-father again.

You might feel like, "Wow, what satisfaction they both must have felt to get even in ways most of us could never do."

Neither one expressed much satisfaction or seemed to feel that good about it.

The experience was rougher on them than the fathers; both sought therapy for these and other problems.

Perhaps a more helpful method would be direct verbal confrontation, where the adult is able to verbally express what the child was not allowed to.

Anger Block #4: The Need To Impress Others And Fool Oneself—The Perfectionist Syndrome

"I don't want others to see me out of control."

"I don't want to look and feel foolish."

"You win if I let you upset me."

The idealized self goes further and deeper. "I must act the way a *perfect* person *should* act, regardless of how I feel or I destroy my image of myself." A need for perfection is a tough act to overcome. These perfect responses are learned in childhood, practiced in the teens, and perfected in later years.

Only positive feelings are accepted without guilt. A strong, rigid religious upbringing where "niceness" is constantly demanded may reinforce this to an extreme.

An Army chaplin once commented to us that "Ministers are the world's angriest men, because they are not allowed to feel or express anger." Perhaps that is the reason they ride herd on "principles" and hate "sin" with such a passion; it's their only legitimate outlet.

For years the culture has conditioned women to believe it is unfeminine to express anger. In some settings it is actually considered attractive for a man to be crude, violent, vulgar and hostile but for a woman, *no!*

Actually, a "nice guy" has the same problem. Don't blow your image by expressing angry feelings.

It is overtime for the double standard to fall. *Be what you are*, express what you *feel*, not impulsively or out of context. but appropriately, according to your integrity.

Anger Block #5: Fear Of "Going Crazy" Or Out Of Control

These are people who have suppressed their feelings for so long, it has left them feeling like a string of firecrackers, once they start blowing, they might not be able to stop. Add to this a history of violence, where they actually *did* hurt someone badly or went temporarily out of control, and the problem is multiplied.

This is a *real* danger and cannot be minimized. There are scores of people fitting this description, who are potentially dangerous. Some of them are almost milktoast in appearance to compensate for this fear, others give off volcanic rumblings from time to time that warn you not to tread too close.

What steps can be taken? Here are several steps to consider:

a. Respect the fear *and* the violence. It is not therapeutic or catharic for people to get hurt.

As therapists, we would first look for the origins of the anger. *Who are you really mad at, and why?* Prior events that traumatized you and brought on these feelings of hate, must be brought to awareness, re-experienced, understood and faced. *Then* they can be released.

b. Violence comes from suppression, not *expression*. Holding feelings inside builds a pressure that eventually requires release. We must find a constructive way to be heard. A violent person (or one who tends to violence and violent feelings) does not *expect* to be heard and has already programmed himself so that he will not be heard. The history is that he probably hasn't been, so the expectancy is certainly based on prior reality. Many children learn early in life their parents don't listen to them or take them seriously.

Because of this emotional set, however, he is often not aware when he *is* heard. His expectancy is so conditioned that whenever a new confrontation takes place, an automatic defense system goes into effect and he seems unable to wait, listen or react appropriately to this individual situation. He perceives a threat and reacts rashly to protect himself.

c. One method or providing a safe environment for experiencing trauma, anger and fear is through guided daydreams, as we have discussed previously. In this relaxed state, it is possible to experience rage, maim, kill, go berserk or out of control without danger to self or others because it is all in fantasy. Also, there is a "guide" or therapist to protect, reassure and comfort you through the experience so that you are not alone. Perhaps it is difficult to understand how fantasy can be so effective. It is not the same as an idle daydream where you imagine beating up someone you dislike and feel better for a few minutes. Guided daydreams reach deep into the subconscious and allow the client to deeply and meaningfully "live and experience" emotions, not just think about them.

As we've mentioned before, most people eventually get to the "monster within them" and learn to love and tame *this* monster, rather than destroy it. Accepting the shadow and negative side of ourselves as a legitimate need being poorly expressed helps us to be less angry at others around us as well.

d. How can I protect myself from my own angry outburts? Until you have some measure of physical control, you will have to avoid situations that trigger you off. *Walk away* from potential violence. Some husbands have done that for years, but the wife doesn't know it. All she knows is that he walked away from her and discounted or rejected her feelings. So she generally provokes *more* to get a response, creating more potential danger.

If the husband can tell his wife he is walking away to avoid violence *but* wants to find a way to listen to and respond to her feelings, he'd get a better reaction.

Find a substitute release. One man's solution was to roll his window up in the car, turn on the radio and *yell*, curse and swear. Physical release is also helpful. Pound a pillow, or the bed, imagining you are hitting the person you hate at that moment. It may sound childish and you may feel foolish at first, but *it works!* One therapist I know suggests all his clients buy or create their own punching bag (out of a burlap bag and old clothes and rags), hang it in the garage and have a 15 minute "hostility discharge" twice a day, before going to work and after coming home. What you have accomplished, is a release of tension and toxic buildup in your muscles *and* a subsequent energy and emotional release as well.

Since anger transforms itself to tension in the muscles and nervous systems, a weekly visit to a chiropractor or massage can often accomplish the same thing, particularly for those who do not exercise. A 10 to 15 minute treatment can totally relax the body, requiring several days to build the tension back to its previous peak.

Of course a regular exercise program that includes sports, (tennis, golf, handball, softball, etc.) jogging, or working out can help keep the tension released *and* give you an emotional release for anger as well.

e. Learn to take your needs seriously. Anger buildup is often the result of an inability to say "yes" to yourself or "no" to others.

You have the right and obligation to do what's best for you, without explanation or justification. We are not talking about extreme selfishness that does not take others into consideration, but the everyday choices of life where you can choose to do something because you want to; without feeling it will automatically take something away from your loved ones, or say "no" for the same general reasons. If we can't do this without feeling guilt, then the resentment and anger begins to build. *Then* we justify it with the anger.

f. Don't push yourself. *Take* your time. You are struggling with an extreme and potentially explosive problem. Be patient. *Ask* your family for patience, understanding and help. If they see you are trying and working to find new solutions with the goal of getting closer to them, patience comes more easily. If they see your request for patience as just another method of buying time and keeping them at a distance, they will be resentful. We must learn to share our struggles and growth so they can feel a part of it and have something to work and hope for.

g. Learn to accept and develop *all* your emotions. Violent people are generally afraid of *all* emotions and experience them all as anger. Emotions such as tenderness, warmth, vulnerability, fear or anxiety are the most frightening of all because they make the person feel weak and unable to protect himself. The anger becomes a fortress of protection that is needed to survive.

Whether aware of it or not, these emotions are there and available in all of us. Gradually allow each a place in your area of experience, like easing yourself into a hot jacuzzi or the cold ocean.

Take a small step, relax, experience, and then take another. As you live through these experiences, you become less frightened until you can be comfortable with many intense emotions, both pleasant and unpleasant.

Anger Block #6: Fear Of Getting Hurt—Retaliation

When you're a 98-pound weakling in a world of giants, this is very real. In an interview for *Playboy* magazine, Robert Blake (Baretta of television fame) was quoted as saying, "Yea, though I walk through the valley of the shadow of death, I will fear no evil, for I'm the meanest S.O.B. of them all." That may be a great credo to live by if you are Robert Blake, but most of us can't pass the physical.

When you've gone through life being intimidated by bullies, you learn indirect methods of maintaining your sanity and expressing your hostility. Retaliation can take many forms:

a. Silence or withdrawal. The dirtiest of all in some respects, there is no defense against silence. It is a total denial of the other's personhood; a crazy-maker in that it leaves the other person trying to guess what's going on inside you.

b. Physical violence toward a smaller person, a scapegoat you can beat up on.

c. Acting-out behavior: vindictive, getting even, flirting, stealing, sexual acting-out, etc. Safer than direct conflict and effective in bringing pain to the other person.

d. The close-off. Ending the relationship, or constantly threatening to do so. This is particularly effective with a dependent, frightened spouse, until they get tired of it and call your bluff. Then the bluffer falls apart and reveals *his* dependency and fear.

e. Ridicule. Striking out at the person's self esteem.

All of these were discussed earlier but are repeated here in the context of fear of direct violence and anger.

Anger Block #7: The Final Block—The Hidden Agenda

This is more of a mechanism of control than a block. I am capable of anger but choose *not* to express it, because if I do:

"There won't be any sex tonight."

"It will ruin the concert, vacation, party or trip . . ."

"My spouse won't listen anyway."

"It won't do any good so why bother to experience the stress and pain."

or

"Look how great I am. I should have been angry and wasn't."

There's nothing wrong with picking your issues ("Is it worth it?"), your time and the place ("Being appropriate).

Having an intense fight in public might not be appropriate. What's important is your *real* motive: is your motive appropriateness or avoidance because you don't expect the expression of your feelings to bring a positive result?

How Do We Remove The Blocks?

Here are seven suggestions for releasing blocks and opening yourself to intimacy and love:

1. Explore the blocks: where did they originate? What feelings are being experienced? What are you really afraid of? What is the worst thing that could happen? Could you handle it? What are the basic issues?

There must be *no* judgment of your feelings at this point or you can't be free to explore them. You are looking for personal information and understanding.

2. Listen to the blocks: They are trying to give you messages about yourself. Just as thirst, fever and pain give us messages of truth from within our bodies that must be responded to, so are the blocks to anger. For every block there are multiple reasons, information, examples of who you are and how you became that way, as well as new options for change.

3. Validate your feelings: own them and admit them as your own. Give yourself permission to experience even the most irresponsible or undesirable feelings, *without* judgment. Don't scare them off.

4. Be aware of the cost: What do these blocks protect you from? What do they *keep* and *prevent* you from? They protect you from immediate pain and discomfort. They also prevent you from achieving intimacy, happiness, better sex, a successful marriage, a good self-image, as well as physical and emotional well-being.

Is it worth that cost to achieve the temporary relief, to momentarily relieve your anxiety?

5. Experiment and learn new ways to express your feelings:

Discover the feeling underlying the anger, your real need. Anger is almost always a secondary and protective reaction, rather than a primary feeling. It is a *reaction* to feelings of hurt, embarrassment, humiliation or fear.

Then, respond to your own feelings and need *directly*. Once aware of the true primary feeling, express it in a straightforward, honest manner. Anger is generally indirect, rather like a game of charades: "I'll act out my feelings and you guess what they are." That is bad enough. It gets worse when we give the wrong clues. "I am angry and yelling at you because I want you to love me," may be the truth but it will rarely get the results you want. Showing how hurt you are for not being loved might be more effective.

6. Take the risk and discover that you *can* handle pain. You are not going to be overwhelmed by the first sign of discomfort and anxiety. Stand your ground, experience your strength; prove you can take it without being destroyed.

7. Explore alternatives: Remember you *can* walk away. If you have tried to be reasonable and honest, but your partner insists on attacking and insulting you viciously, you can always choose to leave the situation. You aren't obligated to be anyone's scapegoat.

You *can* reject the insults. Just because someone deliberately sets out to hurt you, doesn't mean you have to accept the hurt. You don't have to *believe* the insults and you don't even have to believe your partner actually means them. All you really know is, at the moment, your partner is angry and wants to hurt you.

You *can* express yourself firmly. Regardless of your partner's attitude or approach or motives, you can be what *you* choose to be in any situation. Express who you are, how you feel, how you are being affected by this conversation and relationship *and* how you wish to change it. You are only responsible for *you*, but you are responsible for you.

You can ask for what you want and not settle for less. "But he won't give it. It won't do any good." That's beside the point. Take responsibility for meeting your own needs, with or without the cooperation of others. When we express ourselves without defensiveness or attacking others, we are generally heard and responded to. Even if we don't, we still feel good about ourselves and will set out to find another way of getting our needs met.

8. Be willing to let go—release control.

> Give what you *are* . . .
> Say what you *feel* . . .
> Respond to what you *receive* . . .

Then, let the situation *be*. Accept the reality of the results. Know when to stop pushing, trying or controlling. "This is who I am; I can do no other." There is no argument against integrity.

Hopefully, these chapters will have clarified and more fully identified the destructive uses of anger and the reasons for withholding it. As you more easily understand your own motives you can "catch yourself in the act" of defeating the purposes of getting your needs met. Being able to identify and clarify the angry feelings is a major step toward minimizing destructive tendencies, and opening new areas of possibility in the *positive* use of anger. There *are* methods of expressing anger which minimize pain and draw people closer rather than pushing them further apart. As a result, both partners have better opportunity for getting needs met, feeling heard and cared about, as well as feeling cleansed of the hurtful emotions previously bottled up inside them.

Part IV

The Final Product

You cannot separate individual well-being from marital success. Marital growth is based on personal growth, and the problems reflected in a relationship are those found within each individual. Your love for others is based on love of self; the healthier you are, the healthier your relationships will be. The struggle to be me with you is what A Fresh Start for a New Age Relationship is all about.

XVI. Love

Love can only be experienced . . . and can never be truly defined.

The love of a person does not imply possession of that person, but affirmation of him as a human being. It means sharing gladly in the full right of his unique humanness. If one truly loves a person, it is impossible to seek to enslave, control, or manipulate him—either by the rules of law, the weakness of neurotic dependence, or the jealousies of possession.

Whenever we experience genuine love, we are transformed by this moving experience toward greater capacity for good will toward the other.

Love is the passionate and compelling desire of two or more people to produce together an atmosphere or environment within which each can be, to spontaneously act out and express his deepest real self, to produce together an intellectual soil and an emotional climate in which each cannot only grow, but flourish to a greater extent than either could achieve alone.

> Love is the substance that life is made of,
>   the evidence that life's worthwhile,
> For by it, two people unite as one,
> Through love we understand the integration
>   of diverse personalities, so that the final
>   end is greater than the separate two.
> By love, one person offers to another
>   the sacrifice of a giving spirit,
>   the complement of respect and admiration,
>   the fulfillment of his innermost self.
> By love we thrill daily to the exploration
>   of the other's mind.
> Therefore, through this inter-stimulation and
>   emotional exchange
> **We have the knowledge that we have pleased our mate.**
> **Without love it is impossible to please him.**
> **He that loveth must first believe in himself,**
>   **and then give of himself to his partner.**

—CDL

What is love? A teenage girl once said, "It is that itchy feeling down inside you can't scratch."

Webster defines it as, "A feeling of strong personal attachment induced by sympathetic understanding."

Fromm defines mature love as, "Union under the condition of preserving one's own integrity, one's individuality. Love is an active power in man—breaking through the walls that separate man from his fellowmen—which unites him with others . . . Love makes him overcome a sense of isolation and separateness—yet permits him to be himself, to retain his integrity. In love the paradox occurs that two beings become one and yet remain two!"

This is a paradox that many people find difficult to comprehend. In love one and one make three. Both people are unique and complete within themselves with the full ability to be productive human beings on their own. Put together, the wholes are greater than the separate parts because love brings together emotional, intellectual, and physical potential. The combination of two people who are complete within themselves, but who contribute so powerfully to complement each other's lives, results in their being even better people combined than they could ever be separately. Therefore, one and one really do add up to three in a mature union.

Cooley calls this the "looking-glass self," wherein we get ourself-opinion as a protection of what others think of us. Harry Stack Sullivan refers to the self-dynamism as being made up of the reflected appraisals from the child's experience. Another Sullivanian term that fits into this picture is "consensual validation"—the agreement of others that confirms our own feelings and beliefs.

From the time of infancy to adulthood, whether it be from parent, friend, or sweetheart, every one of us craves to be admired and appreciated and needs to be. As one matures, he also receives a sense of self-worth from his own accomplishments.

Love Is Revealing

Perhaps the most difficult and yet the most necessary act of love is revelation. True intimacy cannot come without knowing the other person deeply. Possibly, the largest barrier to sharing ourselves intimately with others is our own fear of knowing what's inside. How many of us do not want to know ourselves too well because deep inside we are secretly afraid that there lurks a very sick or sinister person?

People often avoid a therapy encounter simply because they suspect that they are corrupt inside. To have a professional validate this for them and tell them that it's hopeless would be beyond their ability to accept.

As therapists, it is extremely exciting to be "the first to know" some deeply fearful truth about a client, never revealed to anyone else; and to be able to respond with compassion and understanding rather than criticism or repulsion. Peggy could not maintain eye contact when revealing she was molested by her father over a period of months as a child and felt dirty, guilty and scarred for life. Frank was equally panicky to reveal he had explored the genitals of the family dog as a small child and was quite sure this was proof there was something terribly wrong with him for his abnormal act.

The look of relief to be able to "let go" of this information and no longer have to carry it alone is unbelievable. To also receive reassurance of their "OKness" and the therapists' love and compassion can be similar to a conversion or healing experience.

Deep within every person is the best "you" possible. The deeper you go, the more you will like yourself. It is similar to having a well in your backyard that has some of the freshest and best tasting water available anywhere in the world, but this water has not been used for many years and is very deep within the earth. For many years people have been throwing trash and refuse on top of the water in the well. The water is now so polluted that to try to drink it is extremely distasteful. If all the refuse and waste could be removed from the top, underneath still flows the fresh, cool, and clear-tasting water. The waste and refuse in this case would be our own fears and defenses which have caused us to do things against our own integrity, which are destructive of our well being.

Experience reveals that it is impossible to love someone without knowing them and it should be impossible to *know* someone without loving them.

To be truly intimate with someone is to know them deeply. To know not only what they do, but why they do it . . . the deeper level motivations of protection from fear, inadequacy or rejection. To know someone on that level brings feelings of closeness and affection, along with deep love.

All of us have rationalized reasons we give ourselves and others for what we do, but there are also the heavier, deeper and more important reasons that would reveal our weaknesses, pettiness and the like if known.

We see this consistently in group therapy sessions where one person struggles to admit to the other members some negative truth about himself that seemed horribly humiliating to reveal; only to discover the group was not shocked or dismayed, no one rejected him or pulled away and other members admitted similar features within themselves. At this point there is sometimes an overwhelming feeling of warmth and mutual affection. We all feel better understood, accepted and cared about, with no judgment or condemnation.

Paradoxically and ironically, the reason that we do not let people get intimate and close to us is because we are afraid that they will not like us and will thereby use this information against us and hurt us. When you like yourself and expect others to like you, you find it very easy to share yourself with others and to let others share themselves with you.

Fortunately there are limitations to this as no one can know another completely . . . probably no one can ever know himself completely. Part of the beauty of love is that there is always a mystery involved and there is always more to be learned about ourselves and the other in the relationship.

Love Is Giving

Do you respond to that statement, "Well, that might very well be true, but receiving is good enough for me."? Some people see giving in a relationship as "giving up" or sacrificing needs or feelings or desires for the needs, feelings, and desires of another. For the person who already feels deprived, it is difficult, if not impossible, to see love as primarily giving. The deprived person, like the infant child, sees life basically as the process of *being* loved and *receiving* from others.

For the person whose basic needs have been met and is not a deprived child, giving becomes the highest expression of his potency. In the act of giving, the productive person experiences his strength, his wealth, and his power. To be fully human and to love maturely is to give of what's alive in you. To give the best that you can; your joy, interest, understanding, knowledge, humor, sadness, or whatever you are experiencing at any given moment. Giving is in itself exquisite joy—giving is its own reward.

If I give a dime's worth of love in order to receive a quarter's worth in return, that would be *exploitation*. If I give a quarter's worth of love to get a quarter's worth in return, that's *bargaining*. If I give a quarter's worth of love and ask for nothing in return, that's *love*.

Love Is Receiving

There is another side to the coin. *Love is receiving.* Giving implies making the other person a giver as well. They both share in the joy of what they have brought to life. Love is a creative quality that produces love; impotence is the inability to produce love.

If my love is a mature, productive love that comes out of a person who cares for himself and has no need to exploit others, it will be returned. This is not to say that one hundred per cent of all people will love me in kind, for that would be impossible and unnecessary. Love comes in many intensities and versions.

Love Is Caring

Care can be defined as the active concern for the life and the growth of that which you love. Caring is a concern that the other should grow and unfold *as he is* and not as I might neurotically need him to be to suit my own purposes. It implies that I have no need to exploit or use him but can allow him the full freedom to be himself.

It also implies no jealousy on my part. Jealousy actually has no part in love and is in no way a sign of loving or being loved. Many people interpret the jealousy of their girlfriend or boyfriend as a sign that they really care, but actually this is not so. Jealousy has very little to do with the other person, but is actually saying, "I don't feel very good about myself, and, therefore, any other person can take my mate away from me." This implies that almost any other person is better equipped to love and care about my spouse than I. I am jealous of someone else's success—this implies that I don't feel that I deserve that success; therefore, I don't want to feel that they do either. In spite of the fact that I do not deserve it, I covet it, and want it for myself and feel resentful that I didn't receive the same "luck" of my friend.

Caring wants the other person to be happy, in his own way, and on his own terms. Caring says I am happy that you are happy. I believe in and support your judgment, decisions and directions. I am buoyed by your success, cry with your hurt, laugh at the expression of your humor, experience your anxiety and hurt with your doubts!

I can let you be you—even if that is expressed by different means and in divergent ways from mine. I will not see these differences as threats to our relationship but as expressions of your uniqueness. *What* you do or *how* you do it will not be as important as *what you are.*

Love Is Admiring

Admiration is that which excites pleased approval and appreciation of the worth of the other human being involved. We all need to be loved, appreciated, and respected. We want folks to admire us and have confidence in us. Where do we receive our own self respect? From what source comes confidence in our own abilities and talents? If you felt from age zero that no one in the world had confidence in you, could you have confidence in yourself? Of course not!

Love Is Trusting

The reason most often expressed for one's inability to give himself freely in a love relationship is the lack of trust in another human being. Someone who has been hurt and deprived all his life finds it very difficult to trust.

The real issue involved is the inability to be able to trust myself, my judgment, and my ability to protect myself. If I truly love myself and care about myself and believe in my needs and feelings, and am able to trust my judgment concerning these, there is no one who can destroy me. Some people give and are exploited as a result. Others give and are loved in return. The difference is self-love.

If I love myself, I do not wish to be exploited. I give myself freely to this other person and find it easy to trust that he will accept, receive, and return this gift. If he does not, but tends to exploit and use or abuse this love, I withdraw it. I trust enough in my own strength that I am not afraid of being destroyed by the pain or discomfort of being betrayed in a love relationship. I know that I can handle this kind of pain and disappointment without being emotionally destroyed. This makes it much easier for me to risk in a relationship.

I have no need to be naive and expect all other people to be trustworthy, but by the same token, I do not wish to be cynical and negative in my feelings about people. The person who approaches life with cynicism is rarely disappointed by the results.

If, after a suitable period of time, I see that I am being exploited, I simply withdraw the love and give it to someone else. The trust actually is in myself—in the deepest sense—and that's why I am able to trust others.

Love Is Freedom

Some people see love as a jailhouse. This is often true of marriage today. It is sad that more people do not actually feel free in a love-relationship, especially one that includes marriage.

In order to avoid this feeling of entrapment, some couples are simply living together without the legal sanction of marriage vows. They do this not so much as a put-down of marriage but as an alternate marital lifestyle which gives the illusion of more freedom of movement. Since each person feels that he or she can leave with less residual entanglement and responsibility, the daily choice of staying is more comfortable, and love seems to retain its form more easily.

These people fear that they cannot maintain this feeling of personal freedom in a marriage relationship.

For a love relationship to be mature (whether marital or not) both people must ideally bring freedom to the relationship and maintain it within the relationship. I cannot give my spouse freedom, nor can I take it away; by the same token, my spouse cannot give mine to me or take it away.

Freedom, again, is the power of choice. I choose to be in love or to be married to this particular person and I maintain this daily emotional choosing in the light of the fact that I can always choose not to be. If I cannot choose *not* to love, then I cannot *choose* to love. There must always be alternate choices.

This freedom, which sounds so risk-taking and risk-producing, is actually the producer of more inner security and peace of mind than we can receive any other way. When our security depends on legal ties and restrictions, we are using compulsion, obligation, and guilt as a false or phony security that replaces the personal freedom of our unique personhood.

What many people forget or misunderstand is that there is no freedom without personal self-discipline and responsibility. Freedom is not the right to be irresponsible or inconsiderate but the right to *know* who I am and to truly *be* who I am.

The person who refuses to call and say "I'll be late for dinner" or says "I'll be home at 7 pm" and arrives at 4 am is not exercising freedom, but rebelling against "parental" authority.

In order to be truly free, one must be responsible to his own needs and those of others; considerate and appropriate in behavior. Sartre said, "There is no freedom without responsibility."

A person who is driven by every whim or finds it impossible to say no or deprive himself of momentary pleasure—or relief from anxiety and pain—is not free; but on the contrary, is a slave to whatever circumstances within which he finds himself.

A person who is free can weigh values and judgments against his own integrity and come up with answers that are both satisfying for the moment and productive for the future.

When a person is openly given freedom and comes home refreshed and alive, the spouse gets the benefit and appreciation. When they come home to you, it's because they have chosen to, not because they had to.

In summary, love is that mysterious chemistry of physical and emotional intangibles that cannot be explained or described. At the same time it is a fragile and changeable emotion, greatly affected by our behavior and attitudes. We have tried to describe some of the ingredients that can enhance the love experience and provide a proper environment for growth. Probably they are not enough to *create* love (friendship perhaps) but we find it difficult conceiving of love existing for long without these ingredients.

The depth of love and the intensity of the relationship is very personal to each of us. May *you* be able to find and maintain the love bond that most completely satisfies and fulfills the innermost self.

XVII. Intimacy

How To Make Any Relationship Work—Even Yours

Everybody talks about intimacy . . . but sex is as close as most people get.

Everybody wants intimacy . . . but no one seems to know what it is.

People avoid intimacy . . . for fear of losing something they don't really have . . . themselves.

True intimacy is sharing my deepest, most real self with another human being . . . and having the other do the same with me.

Intimacy is loving, but I must first love myself.

Intimacy is trusting, but I must first trust myself.

Intimacy is revealing, but I must first reveal to myself.

There are seven vital aspects which help create intimacy in a relationship and should be discussed briefly. They are:

1. Feelings—Yours and Mine
2. Self-revelation
3. Honesty—a Caress or Club?
4. Trust
5. Openness to Life
6. Listening
7. Acceptance

1. Feelings—Yours And Mine

Every feeling you have is important and has meaning for you. Dorothy is constantly revealing deep and insightful feelings in the process of her therapy and then lightly dismissing the subject with the casual, "Isn't that silly?" Because the feeling is in apparent contradiction to her conscious motivations, life-style, and general way of thinking, she dismisses this contrary feeling as being silly.

If feelings did not have a cause, they would not be there in the first place. So, even the most irrational feelings must have a legitimate source that is meaningful and important. Feelings will reveal a lot about the person if we can dig down deep enough to find the source and understand it.

Every feeling you have is either trying to *reveal* something to you or to *hide* something from you.

The only reason we don't want to reveal our true feelings (to ourselves or someone else) is fear . . . the fear of destroying, or being destroyed, of hurting, or being hurt.

Betty is thirty years of age, single, aggressive, and independent. Highly intelligent, she is something of a rebel and sees herself as a very strong and dominating woman. Strangely enough, the only area in which she feels competent as a person is sexually in bed with a man, and she is rarely able to relate to them well on any other basis. She has no close women friends and finds it very difficult to be open and friendly with women.

Betty's mother is fifty, attractive, and divorced. She is a very successful business woman with her own career, and very well known in charity and social circles.

Within thirty minutes after the start of an all-day marathon in group therapy, Betty was feeling extreme anger and hatred toward her mother, describing her as weak, inadequate, stupid and totally incapable of being a mother. Even Betty seemd rather surprised and overwhelmed by the intensity of her angry outburst. She seemed sincerely surprised to find that she had been harboring such intense hatred regarding her mother. When asked if she had ever talked with her mother about these feelings, she replied with disgust and contempt, "If I told Mother how I really felt about her, she'd have a heart attack and die."

As the issue was discussed further, it became more obvious her deeper fear was that if she confronted Mother with this hatred and hostility and told her how Mother had failed to meet Betty's needs, Mother might simply reply, "That's tough, and you can go straight to hell."

Betty really expected that Mother would draw into a shell, become defensive and unhearing, and, therefore, reject her without being touched deeply by Betty's feelings at all. Then Betty would be left with the problem of not having a mother. She was very frightened that her mother's rejection would destroy *her*.

For most of us that's where it is—fear is the barrier which keeps us from being intimate—fear of destroying and more probably and most often, fear of being destroyed.

This is due to an inner anxiety that says to us "You can't handle that particular situation. You do not have the inner strengths to survive that potential hurt, so don't venture out and take the risk. The pain will be unbearable." Or, in contrast, the message may be: "Your spouse (friend, parent, etc.) will not be capable of handling your feelings and will suffer a nervous breakdown or at least insufferable pain and you will be stuck with the guilt of that as a burden the rest of your life."

All of us have different levels of tolerance to emotional and physical pain but it is the *fear* of pain that controls our lives . . . not the pain itself. If we believe we can handle the pain and do not fear it, we succeed quite well. In fearing the loss of love or relationship with the other person we are making them more important than we are. If I lose the love of my friend over a disagreement, that will be a loss; I will experience that loss and not minimize it *but* with the awareness that I can and will survive without that person. I hope we can work it out, but if we can't I don't want a phony relationship anyway.

It is true that the other person can retaliate by punishing you with guilt, by playing "destroyed" or making it look as if you have destroyed him by getting sick or having a heart attack or going into a deep depression or even committing suicide . . . that is their right and their choice, and you have no power or control over that person's response.

You do not have to accept this guilt or believe yourself a bad person just because someone else lays that trip on you. Your feelings are either trying to reveal something to you or to hide something from you. We often watch what people *do* in order to find clues of what they are feeling, but sometimes it is better to watch what they *don't* do for even deeper information.

If you are an extremist, the opposite extreme is usually what you most fear. People who cry easily, as an example, may be very angry on the inside and most afraid of this anger. People who are easily angry, carrying a constant chip on their shoulders and exploding in very irrational and often inappropriate ways, are most afraid of being hurt.

The solution to the dilemma of extreme feelings is to allow yourself the luxury of experiencing whatever emotion you fear the most, whether hurt or anger, and thereby convince yourself that it will not be destructive to you and will not be painful beyond your ability to endure. Once convinced enough to let the anger or hurt come to the surface, a person is able to experience the deep satisfaction of his real feelings and the surprising and new reaction received from others.

It may seem rather strange in a chapter on intimacy to spend so much time on knowing one's own feelings and being honest and direct with one's own feelings rather than talking about the feelings of other's. However, one complements the other.

That's the key: when we are deeply in touch with our own feelings and what's going on inside our own emotions, we are very, very much in tune and in touch with the other. Whenever we can be open to all our feelings, whether negative or positive, we can then be open and receptive to others. When we can allow ourselves to feel the full range of our own emotions: anger, hurt, confusion, happiness, pride, disgust, etc.—we can be open and available to these feelings in our friends.

2. Self-Revelation

You have a responsibility to be real ... this responsibility is primarily to yourself and secondarily, to others. You have no responsibility, control or ability to predict what type of response you will get from others when you are truly real with your feelings.

All phoniness, defensiveness, game-playing or whatever else keeps us from being real with our feelings is protection against our innermost fear. All fear, as stated before, really goes back to the fear of being destroyed or destroying another. Probably the most basic fear is that of *being destroyed* and that is precisely the reason why I must begin with myself in any type of therapeutic growth and intimacy with others.

The first thing I have to do is know myself. There is no way I can reveal myself or be intimate with others until first I reveal myself and am intimate with me. Some of us are past experts at kidding ourselves about almost everything. We are very good at deceiving ourselves on a conscious level from knowing what's really going in deep inside. This process can be reversed, but it is hard work, and you really have to want to do it.

It sounds overly simple, but you can start by asking yourself a basic question over and over and over again until your subconscious hears it and believes it: "How do I really feel right now? What is really going on inside me? What do I really want to do? Why am I reacting the way I am reacting?" If you really want to know and will take time to stop, ask, and then listen, you'll get the answer.

It may take weeks or even months, but eventually you'll get to the place where this will happen more or less automatically and on a subconscious level so that you have a pretty good idea of what you are feeling and why. The important point here is not that you are totally aware at all times consciously of what's happening on a feeling level, but that you are *open* to this information at all times. If you are constantly open, the information will come to the surface whenever it is necessary for you to know it. If you are constantly closed, the information will never surface except under extreme pressure or because you consciously want it to.

Surprisingly, this may be the most difficult step of all—the step of self-revelation. Most of us do not want to know our true feelings or to be familiar with what's really going on inside us because we are afraid we will not be able to live with this information. If we *do* anything with the information, we are afraid of being hurt. If we *don't* do anything with the information, we are afraid of being frustrated . . . therefore, we'd rather leave it buried.

The problem, of course, is that even though the information is buried, it goes on affecting our lives and relationships, but because it is operating on an unconscious level, we have little or no control over the behavior connected with it. When we bring the information to the level of awareness, then, and only then, do we have the choice of what to do with it and conscious control of the behavior connected with it. Once I know what I'm feeling, I have the choice of how to handle this information and whether or not to pass it on to others and, if so, in what manner.

3.   Honesty—A Caress Or A Club?

Honesty can be used as a club to hurt or as a caress to heal. Motivation plays a very important part here. If you are deliberately revealing your deep, honest, and real feelings to the other person for the express purpose of punishing, hurting, destroying or with any other kind of malicious intent, then perhaps your guilt is legitimate. Even so, while all of us have the power to hurt other human beings, particularly those who are important to us and to whom we are important, we still don't have the power to destroy even if we want to. The other person can either protect himself, retaliate in turn, or simply walk away from your life. While it may be hurtful to lose, they won't be destroyed by it. So, even if we wanted to destroy another human being, each person has the power to protect himself against you and cannot be destroyed unless he chooses to let you do so.

On the other hand, honesty for the purpose of revealing who I am, where I am and why, for healing or improving relationships is not destructive and does not deserve the resulting guilt. Any guilt connected with this type of motivation and approach is neurotic guilt, thrown on you by the other person who does not want to hear your feelings.

Honesty is not telling everything you know. It is telling what is important to you, to the other person, to the relationship. Many therapists and theorists insist on total honesty . . . complete vomiting of all feelings, thoughts, past deeds and activities, etc. Possibly this is because most of us are very good at deceiving ourselves. If you vomit all, you don't have to be responsible or worry about choosing . . . it's all on the table for the other person to see and experience. We believe this can either be helpful or very hurtful.

A person has an affair and comes home to confess to their spouse and clears their conscience. In confessing, they feel relieved and forgiven . . . cleared and clean. Now, what is the spouse going to do with this information? What are they going to do with their own guilt and bad feelings? They are not supposed to use it against the confessor because they have confessed, and yet, the spouse holds inner feelings of self-doubt, rejection and hurt that surely accompany that type of confession. Clearing your conscience at the expense of someone else is unfair.

If there is an affair and in the process something important is learned about the marriage (pro or con), it makes sense that the learning partner share that new understanding with the spouse in order to improve the relationship. For example, people in such a situation learn that there is more love in the marriage than they were aware of, that the relationship has lost its courtship or fun or spontaneity; that anger or resentment or fear has driven them apart, etc. It is this kind of feeling information that should be shared . . . either for the purpose of improving the relationship or at least revealing what is wrong or bad about it. The fact that there *was* an affair and the information came as a result of that affair is not necessarily to be revealed.

We are not suggesting, condoning or criticizing affairs. It is evident that a lot of people don't have the courage to confront issues and needs in their marriages on any kind of consistent level and so allow resentments and subsequent distance to build up. Then they often create a crisis, such as an affair, or a bitter violent fight to bring things to the surface. This is usually done at a subconscious level of motivation. Rather than condemn or judge people for their counter-productive behavior we prefer to help them learn from it by pointing out why they needed it, what was learned or accomplished and what their options are now. Many people require a crisis before they are able to even ask for the help of therapy. Unfortunately they accumulate many handicaps to success through this delay. A day-by-day honesty that tries to improve the marriage before it gets out of control is the best kind.

Being able to discriminate between what is legitimately private information and what is important to be shared is not easy. Often when we "protect" the other person from the truth, we are insulting their capacity for being real or strong.

In a family with five daughters, the father was constantly treated as the outsider. The favorite expressions went something like this: "Don't tell Daddy; he wouldn't understand . . . Don't tell Daddy; he'll get angry . . . Don't tell Daddy; he'll be hurt . . . Don't tell Daddy; but don't let him know he's not being told." In their desire to protect him, they were insulting him, rejecting him, and leaving him out, assuming he was too weak to handle it. What could be more castrating than not being included in one's own family circle? Instead of showing unconditional positive regard for their father's strength and potency as a man, their protecting him "for his own good" was simply a statement of his inadequacy.

One daughter, in the process of her therapy, decided to be honest with her father and, as might be expected, he was very defensive, and it was difficult for him to respond. The daughter's predictions were all correct—he got angry, he didn't understand, he was hurt, and he did not know how to respond.

With strong feeling, the son-in-law proclaimed to this father that his wife was the only daughter who was treating him like a father . . . that they were tired of treating him like a baby, protecting him, and making him as an outsider in the family. For the first time in his life, he was going to be included by someone. They believed in his masculinity, in his ability to be a father, and his ability to respond to feeling . . . and intended to relate to his strengths and not his weaknesses. They refused to relate to him as a weak and inadequate man and expected him to respond with strength and feelings.

It took almost a year . . . but with the help of his wife, and the love and patience of his daughter, the father was finally able to respond. At this writing he is a better father to all of his daughters because of this confrontation but has a very special and unique relationship with the one daughter and her husband who were able to relate to him in strength and expect strength in return.

4. Trust

Another problem in intimacy is that of trust. Many of us do not want to be intimate in sharing our deeper feelings of anxiety, fear, inadequacy, or desire because we cannot trust the other person with the use of this information. We are afraid they will take this information and gossip about it or use it against us to hurt us in some way at their pleasure or discretion.

My protection at this point is my ability to trust myself. It is much easier to trust others, even strangers, if I have a deep sense of trust in my own judgment and in my feelings regarding myself. If I have true self-love as discussed earlier, I will not let myself be destroyed. If I have trust and confidence in my own strengths, in my ability to withstand pain and to handle crisis situations, and know what my own limitations are, then I can take risks I could not otherwise afford.

If I am acquainted with the healing benefits of grief, suffering and pain and am not afraid of feeling these, I can allow myself to be intimate and thereby vulnerable to the possibility of hurt. I trust my judgment that once I discover the other person is being vicious or malicious or deliberately punitive and hurtful and destructive to the relationship, I have the ability to stop them or to withdraw from the situation, thereby not allowing myself to be unduly hurt or eventually destroyed. Once confident that I can either handle or avoid destructive situations, I am more comfortable in being intimate and revealing myself or sharing myself with others.

If I love myself, trust myself, and am revealing of my true feelings to myself, I am ready to be intimate with others.

5. Openness To Life

To be totally open to all the realities of life . . . internally and externally . . . emotionally and intellectualy . . . is to be a truly healthy person. To experience these various emotions and realities with little need to defend, deny, or distort, is to be fully human.

A healthy person is open to the totality of human experience—both good and bad. All human experience is available to him, and he has little or no need to defend against the knowledge of its existence.

He knows the healing benefits of true pain and grief and has little need to ever defend against these, because he knows them to be beneficial to his growth and not destructive of his person.

He is very much in touch with his full strength potential—both physically and emotionally—and therefore can take whatever risks are necessary to his continued well-being.

The process of stripping away these layers can be any method that helps a person to experience emotional pain, fear or discomfort in a supportive environment. He experiences what is there and comes out of this trauma without being destroyed as he had feared would happen. This leaves him in a state of relaxation, calmness and experienced personal strength.

As he successfully works through these layers, the person becomes less fearful, more confident of his own strength and more in touch with his deep inner self-hood. Obviously growth never ends, but all of us can certainly reach a level of openness at which we can continue the growth process without a helping agent.

Once you've accomplished what was just described, regarding contact with one's deep feelings and emotions, being aware of them and expressing them to others, the next step is to be able to give the same to others.

6. Listening

We need to be able to listen at a deep level to the other person's needs. This entails forgetting for the moment your need to defend yourself against the other because you are no longer afraid of him and know that he cannot wipe you out.

The other's needs must be important to you and it is important that he know this. Our defense usually is to weigh the other's need or requests through our own value system and judge their legitimacy. If we feel it is illegitimate or we are incapable of fulfilling this need regardless of its legitimacy, then we tend to *deny* the legitimacy of the need. In the process of rejecting the need, we are really rejecting the other person.

A common example of this might be a husband who has to work nights and weekends in order to make ends meet and whose wife is constantly complaining and nagging him regarding this. His wife's arguments sound very legitimate: he doesn't spend enough time with her or the children, they never go anywhere, she spends lonely hours doing nothing and feeling rejected, he comes home too tired to meet her sexual needs, etc. . . .

Her husband's reasons also seem legitimate: he is working overtime for more money, he is trying to take financial care of his family, jobs like this are not plentiful, he is not qualified to do other work, this is the price he has to pay for advancement, etc. . . .

We seem to have an insoluble situation—the man can't quit his job, and the wife feels lonely and rejected. When she constantly nags her husband about this situation, he becomes defensive and guilty. He knows she is lonely and her nagging has validity. He feels guilty everytime he goes to work because of what he is doing to his wife, and he feels guilty if he doesn't or if he leaves the job because of what he would be doing to himself.

He resents her for putting him in this conflict, and his answer is that she has no right to bother him about this when she knows he cannot change the situation and is doing it partly for her. He can't do anything to change the situation and so she has no "right" to be hurt, or to feel badly, or to nag him about it. In rejecting the legitimacy of her need, he is telling her that she has no right to her feelings.

What his wife may really be asking with all of her nagging and bitching about the job is whether or not her husband really loves her, is aware that she is alone and hurting, whether he cares that this is a very difficult situation for her, whether he recognizes that she is sacrificing for the family as well as he. Does her husband appreciate her sacrifices and the fact she has to take care of the kids alone and has to do without her husband a great deal of the time?

Perhaps if the husband were able to let his wife feel and express her hurt, loneliness and disappointment and accepted the legitimacy of her feelings, he could respond to her needs. If he could tell her sincerely that he cared for her and wished he could change the situation and didn't like it any better than she, she might be able to relax and stop nagging. The deepest need of the wife is to be heard and understood, and for her feelings to be accepted as natural, normal, and legitimate. If the husband can do this, then usually he does not even have to solve the problem. (That means both their feelings are not wrong or bad but have a legitimate reason for their existence. Their real issue is acceptance of these feelings.)

7. Acceptance

First, we accept the legitimacy of the other's feelings. Second, we express our caring about these feelings (they are important to us); third, we say we're sorry that we cannot change it (if we can't); and last, we both are able to accept the reality of the situation and to live with it much more easily. Unfortunately, our tendency is to feel that admitting a person's feeling are legitimate is saying that we have to supply a solution to the problem. Many times we cannot change a hurtful situation, but we can still accept the feelings connected with it.

Usually for most of us, this is all we really need or want from the other . . . whether it be a parent or a spouse or a friend. If you can sincerely and positively respond to a person's feelings first, this will leave you all the time necessary to try to work out a solution to any and all problems.

Looking again at the husband who's working nights and weekends, if he can meet his wife's needs by sympathizing and caring about her loneliness and hurt and she is, therefore, able to feel loved and comforted and to relax and quit nagging in return, a strange thing often happens. Before you know it, he finds he can spend more time at home because he has been using this legitimate excuse to get away from the strain and the stress of his relationship with his wife and his children. At this point, he needs to express his needs and to honestly tell his wife why he hasn't spent more time at home, and what his problems are with her. It is now his wife's turn to be non-defensive in listening to him and in an honest exchange of real feelings and caring for each other.

When it comes right down to it, in spite of what we may insist on from other people, most of us don't really need anyone to judge us, correct us, interpret us, explain us, deny us, argue with us, encourage us, or even reassure us. We all need someone to care about our feelings and try to understand how we feel. The happy truth is that we can cure ourselves and make our own decisions when we are given this type of atmosphere of acceptance, caring and love.

You can be happy, successful, enriched, fulfilled, and find meaningful life-purpose and direction . . . and share all this with the important others in your life.

XVIII. The New Language Is For You, I Really Care

When two non-integrated, rather dependent people meet, they immediately set out to impress each other and put their "best" foot forward to this end. The fear is that if you really knew my faults, weaknesses, inadequacies, and frailties, you wouldn't like me. If I can impres you first with my strengths, perhaps you can tolerate or ignore or even not notice my faults. Underlying this attitude, of course, is a basic dislike for one's own self. "If I told the truth, I don't really like me all that much, so how can I expect you to?"

When two independent, self-sufficient and actualizing people meet, they automatically and immediately begin the process of expressing who they are. Language is the communication of "who I am and how I feel" to another human being. "I want you to see, know, experience, and understand me in my entirety. I wish to share with you, the actions and motivations of my being." The underlying concept here is an expectancy that, "the more you know about me, the more you'll like me because I like me."

"If by some chance you don't like me, that's O.K. too because I am being real and assume you are too, so if we don't connect at least we gave it our best opportunity. Neither one of us has reason for guilt or to feel critical of ourselves or each other because you can't ask more than genuineness from anyone. We can appreciate what we did share with each other without being upset that it wasn't more."

On the other side, if two people hit it off by putting only their best parts on display, they never know if the other really does like them or has been deceived by the "phony front" presented. So you never know under those circumstances if you are liked or not and the suspicion remains: "If they really knew me . . ."

The person who shares the real and total self always knows where he stands. Since his actions are primarily based on his own feelings and needs and not from trying to guess how he can best impress the other, even dishonesty on the part of the other has a minimal effect.

Acknowledging the fact that each person's primary responsibility is to his own needs, expressing and fulfilling these, an important consideration in doing this, is the need to pleasure and share with you. Meeting my own needs cannot truly be separated from meeting and responding to yours.

True love is born out of the loins of a loving individual, who is expressing his own need to love, not his need to *be* loved.

However, that love requires an individual to desire it and receive it, or to some extent the love is incomplete.

Love is a power that produces love, and there is no sadness so complete as a truly loving person with no one to validate and revel in that love. We might add here that we do not believe that condition can exist long. A loving individual will draw to himself someone with whom to share that love.

The most loving gift one person can bestow on another is the compliment of sharing real feelings in a non-defensive way.

No Demand Revealing

From sex therapists Masters and Johnson comes the phrase "no demand sex." "I would like to pleasure you for the enjoyment I can receive for giving it and you can receive by accepting and experiencing it. My only desire from you is to allow me the pleasuring and for you to experience it to your best advantage. You are not under obligation to respond in a certain manner, become sexually aroused to make me feel adequate as a lover or even to reciprocate. I am giving it because I *want* to give it, not in order to get something from you."

We would like to expand that concept to *no demand revealing*. "I would like the opportunity of sharing and revealing myself with you because that will bring me pleasure. I want you to know who I am and how I feel, how I am receiving and perceiving you. I wish to share this with you and my only desire from you is that you listen and understand; that it pleases you to have me reveal and share. There is *no demand* for a prescribed manner of responding and no attempt to manipulate your behavior."

Under the pressure of stress situations, most people tend to attack the other's motivation and character, rather than revealing their own feelings. It's like a game of charades. "I will tell you how bad a person you are and you interpret from my statements about your character that I must be angry with you or hurt by you. The charade is covering *my* feelings which have not been directly revealed." Character assassination generally starts with the word YOU and goes like this:

You: are bad, vicious . . .

      deliberately hurt me . . .

>enjoy seeing me suffer . . .
>do not want to change . . .
>don't know how to love . . .
>have a memory for my faults like an elephant . . .
>always criticize me . . .

In group therapy one night, a woman took off quite bitterly, raking her husband over the hot coals of the previous type statements. She was asked to restate her words in such a way as to talk about *her* feelings rather than an interpretation of her husband's behavior. "Make it an 'I feel' statement."

She replied quickly and easily to her husband, "Sure, I feel you're vicious." (Rather than "I *feel* sad and attacked when you behave that way. It looks and feel vicious.")

She just couldn't get in touch with her own feelings. It was less frightening to attack him and too vulnerable to let herself or her husband feel her hurt underneath the angry attack.

I feel: hurt, embarrassed, defensive, confused, tied up in knots, etc., tells the other person exactly what kind of impact their behavior is having on you at that moment.

What often keeps us from sharing this simple information is that we don't want to give our spouses the satisfaction of knowing they hurt us. The ultimate vindictive put down is "You're not important enough to have the power to hurt me."

Other reasons for not sharing might be:

"I can't accept weakness or fear in myself."

"Admitting to weakness leaves me too vulnerable to further attack."

"Now that you know you've penetrated my defenses, you'll take advantage of that and finish me off."

Or, the one we hear the most often: "It won't do any good." Translated loosely, that means "It won't do any good for me to show my true, tender, private feelings to you because *you won't change your behavior.*"

This comes from the value system entitled "you have to change so I can be healthy and since you won't change, I can't be healthy and it's all your fault."

When your behavior is primarily based on how you can manipulate and change the other for your satisfaction, you're both in trouble.

"I want to reveal my feelings because I need to share who I am, not because you need to change who you are."

If your goal is to change *anyone*, it must be to change yourself.

When you act in a healthy, non-defensive and revealing manner, the relationship cannot remain disturbed and destructive. It is very difficult to treat someone in a negative fashion if they refuse to cooperate.

"I have to change because it is in my best interests to be as healthy as I am capable of being. I hope that inspires you in the same direction and provides a safe enough environment for you to take the same kind of risks with me. But, even if you don't change, I still have to be me."

When we ask others to change first, we are giving them God-like power and responsibility over our lives. When our well-being is more important than staying in a destructive way of relating, we will act appropriately and accept whatever the consequences may be. "I have no power over you or the results of my behavior toward you. I only have responsibility for my behavior. What you do with my behavior is your choice. I certainly hope you will respond in a positive way, but if not, I can only accept that."

Many times change is not even necessary once real motives have been revealed. For example; a child grows up feeling unloved because he was emotionally beaten and put down constantly and the parent reveals that the *real reason* for the abuse was the parent's own fear of inadequacy and frustration over not knowing how to be a good parent. Now, with this awareness, the child is *freed*. He no longer needs to take the behavior personally feeling, "He treated me that way because I'm bad or hated or unloved; it's my fault, etc." Now he knows the truth. "It is my parent's problem not mine. I didn't cause that vicious behavior; I'm just a scapegoat."

Someone may say, "That doesn't help much. The abuse was still there; I'd be just as mad at being a scapegoat." The miracle comes from the revealing. Often, when the parent or spouse can take the responsibility of his own actions and admit his own faults, you understand him, feel warm and close to him and can even forgive him.

When you know the *truth* about yourself or the other in your life, it *does* "set you free" from self-condemnation and persecution.

Truth about oneself entails admitting factors that are often embarrassing, uncomfortable, and even frightening. Therefore, a major tendency is to talk ourselves or our loved ones out of such feelings. "I shouldn't (or you shouldn't) feel that way because . . ." "It's immoral . . . it's bad . . . won't do any good . . . makes me feel guilty." "I can't accept that part of myself . . . It doesn't exist in God's kingdom," etc.

How can one change the things he doesn't like if he can't admit they even exist? Denying their existence does not prevent these feelings from affecting one's life. It only keeps them largely out of our awareness, where they can affect us on a subconscious level of motivation.

Every thought and feeling is a message from within, trying to tell us something about ourselves. To the extent we are willing to listen for the purpose of sympathetic understanding, we will be able to go to the source of the feeling, meet the real need involved, and correct the situation. Negative feelings dissipate when real need has been met.

All of us have a right to the full range of emotions and feelings, even those we've been taught to disapprove of. Once this has been accepted by ourselves and shared with our loved one, intimacy occurs.

Not only can we share the negative feelings we have about each other, but the fears, needs, desires, anxieties, and doubts we have regarding ourselves.

The result is the same as "no demand sex." Once pressure for performance or change is removed and replaced by a sharing of information, so we can better understand ourselves and each other, this natural sharing of "what is" will allow nature to take its course.

No Solution Response

No change has been demanded—no change required. Someone shares an intimate fear, anxiety, or doubt and immediately we are overwhelmed with the desire to take it away from them; solve it and reassure them or talk them out of the feelings.

"You're being anxious makes me anxious. I must calm you down so I can calm down." For a quiet person stuck with a hysterical spouse, this is almost an impossible situation. They see no solution except to somehow stop the hysteria—by any means possible.

Wait!—Don't perform, solve, give suggestions or judge right or wrong. There is no need to and it probably will make it worse. And don't run away. This is another often resorted to tactic by the "big, strong competent person" who is terrified of hysteria or interprets all deep emotional feelings as hysteria.

Running away generally causes an increase in the emotional level to try harder to get your attention. (We will go into this further on in the chapter.)

What Do I Do?

1. *Listen* to the message.
2. *Feel* the emotion expressed by the other party. "If I were expressing that, how would I feel?"
3. Now, *feedback* how *you* feel.
Listen, feel, feedback.
You might get upset, you might even cry, but you won't die. Like it or not, the *key* is *feeling the pain yourself.* We don't want to listen

and certainly can't give appropriate feedback if we are *afraid* of the pain. Many, if not most, of our unemotional, stoic-type individuals are grossly overcompensating for an intense fear of feelings. They are so overwhelmed by the fear of pain or losing control of emotions, they will not allow feelings to come to the surface, but are constantly fighting against them.

What is your spouse trying to say to you? Regardless of the circumstance, the number one message is "I hurt" . . . What does a hurting person need most? *Comfort.*

Not the kind of comfort that comes from someone solving your problem or talking you out of your feelings. The comfort that comes from not being alone . . . Having someone share your pain. "Someone knows at this moment what it is like to be me. Someone wants to share my burdens. Someone wants to love me through my hurt." *That's enough.* For some of you, you'll never believe that till you try it.

"What can I say when someone overwhelms me with their feelings and emotions and I desperately want to bring relief to both of us?"

There is a beautiful, healing phrase for people who cry out in anguish. "I feel so hurt, angry, embarrassed, upset, suicidal, frustrated," or whatever.

"I know you do," shared quiety, reverently, with deep feeling and compassion. It comes as a refreshing breeze in the desert sun, an intimate caress of love and understanding, and often brings tears to the recipient.

"You do?" is the inner feeling of surprise, although it's rarely expressed out loud. "I thought no one knew or cared how I felt and this is why I was so upset."

"I know you do" acknowledges the right to feel, however, you feel, and says your message has come through loud and clear. "I am in touch with your emotions and very aware of how they are distressing you. I feel the deep pain that you must be experiencing. You are no longer alone. I may not be able to solve your problem or change the circumstances, but I can promise you won't have to bear it alone. For whatever it's worth, I'll be here with you."

And almost always, *that is enough* to comfort the person who is hurting, to give them the courage and strength to survive the problem.

Remember that *words* are only tools to communicate inner feelings. If "I know you do" isn't honest or sounds sarcastic or hostile, don't expect the results we mentioned. If you *feel* love, compassion, and a genuine desire to help, then we can give you some key phrases that express that desire very well. If you don't feel anything but disgust, frustration, fear and anxiety when your spouse is upset, then *you* need some help in understanding your own reaction.

If you just can't accept or respect a person's right to feel inner pain and express that pain to someone they love, it's possible your value system has been deeply warped by a childhood environment that denied *you* that opportunity and convinced you it was bad, weak, effeminate, or whatever.

The first step needs to be an examination of these values, probably with a good professional counselor, to work through to your *own* right to feel and experience the complete range of emotions, so that you won't be frightened by either yours or someone else's.

Healing Phrases

Other key healing phrases that can be utilized to comfort and draw out someone's feelings are:

I understand . . .

That must be very frightening . . .

I feel your anger, frustration, disappointment, etc. . .

Tell me more about that . . .

Go on—I really want to understand your feelings . . .

Talk about that . . .

Also, you can repeat their statements or re-phrase them to show you are listening and understand.

Ask questions to clarify, to make sure you are understanding correctly. *Not* in order to challenge. Many questions tend to make people feel put down and come out "How could you be so dumb or childish?" That only creates defensiveness.

"I knew you wouldn't understand."

"Then, why did you bother?"

"Because I was stupid enough to give you a *chance* to be a person."

Sound familiar? Both trying to hurt the other more than "you hurt me."

Good questions *really* want to know the answers. Ask "why" without using the word. "Why" inevitably seems to irritate and rarely brings the proper response. The most common answer it provokes is, "I don't know."

"What was going on in your head when I expressed my anger?"

"What feeling do you think caused the reaction you expressed?"

"What do you think my motive was when I turned quiet at the party?" (In response to my getting bawled out for being quiet.)

"You told me about your anger, but I'm still not sure how you interpreted my behavior toward you. Can you explain that more fully?"

"What were you afraid might happen if you had not defended yourself?"

More healing phrases:

"Let me see if I heard you correctly or if I really understand . . ."

"I'm really sorry you had to go through this . . ."

"Now I understand why you reacted the way you did . . ."

Many of you may be saying, "Yeah, but they don't know my spouse. That sounds great in a book but *no one* talks that way in real life and besides, it wouldn't work." (Translation: "My spouse wouldn't change or be comforted or act any differently if I tried that. I'd make a fool of myself trying and get laughed at.")

It's true there aren't many who talk that way and that's why there aren't many happily married couples. That's why we need a new language. And it *does* work.

It's not easy to overcome defensiveness and fear to present a vulnerable side of yourself to another, but what a payoff. It changes *you* regardless of your spouse's reaction. *You* feel good about yourself and that you didn't get sucked into another vindictive go around, or another excuse to get drunk.

It changes your spouse. 95 per cent *will* change, will respond differently. They can no longer stay the same. It takes two to play the game you've created between you. If one changes the rules, the other can no longer control the situation in a destructive way.

A word of caution . . . don't hit and run.

One of the biggest handicaps to learning this new approach is that the spouse (or parent, child, friend, etc.) is not expecting it and is often caught in their own habit pattern of response. They may continue to respond *as though* you had been defensive because that was what they expected.

Surprise could also work in your favor. Because it *is* unexpected, the shock value may have a tremendous, positive effect and usually will on a person not too defensive.

If you are locked into a pattern of relating with an extremely frightened and defensive person, you might not get a positive response at first. *Try again!*

Fred: I'm mad enough to get a divorce right now.

Mary: I know you are.

Fred: Well, that's good because when I get through with you, you'll be sorry we ever met.

(He didn't hear her concern or didn't care at that point. Perhaps he wasn't ready to give up his anger that quickly. Many people will quit here with the thought "see it didn't work" and jump into the fight with both vindictive feet. If Mary really cares about herself and Fred, she won't.)

Mary: You must really feel I've hurt you deliberately to be so angry, Fred.

Fred: You're Goddam right. You bitch. You've been emasculat-
ing me from the beginning. I can't stand the sight of you.

(Now she's been directly attacked and the temptation becomes strong to fight back, call names, hurt him as bad as he's hurt her. If she can concentrate on *Fred's* hurt and understand that as the cause of his unreasonable attack, she won't have to defend herself. The more she is afraid that his criticism of her is *true*, the more she'll want to deny it.)

Mary: I'm truly sorry I've made you feel that way. I guess I haven't
found a very good way of sharing my feelings with you if I've
hurt you that badly.

Fred: What textbook did you get that out of? Did your therapist
tell you to say that so I'd apologize?

(He knows she's trying hard not to be defensive and it's making him uncomfortable and guilty. He feels safe with destructive anger, he is not safe with tender or vulnerable feelings and may even be afraid he'll cry, so he went to the heart with that sarcasm and accused her words of being phony, contrived, and manipulating, and not even hers but the therapist's. It's also an indirect slap at the therapist, since her relationship with the therapist is perceived as a threat to Fred.)

Mary: I'm trying to respond to your feelings, Fred, but apparently
you don't want me to. Perhaps you're just too angry or maybe it is too late and you do need to see an attorney. I don't
feel like being attacked any longer and the conversation
seems to be deteriorating, so I'm going to quit. Perhaps later
we can talk about it more clearly.

Fred never responded properly but Mary refused to "hit and run." She never did get sucked into a name calling contest that would jus-tify Fred's anger to himself. Now he has to justify his own anger. At least she gave him no new reason today and he has to deal with his own guilt for being unreasonable.

Mary can feel good about herself for several reasons: She was able to really listen and hear Fred's hurt beneath the anger, inspite of his negative attack; she didn't respond to his attack with one of her own; she felt no need to defend her character and was, therefore, able to apologize for whatever behavior caused his anger; although she didn't defend herself, she didn't get destroyed; since she wasn't afraid of being destroyed, she stayed relatively calm; when she had enough, she simply walked away instead of getting nasty or withdrawing into a sullen silence.

You can win either way. Most of the time, if you don't hit and run, you'll get a positive response out of it. Even if you don't get that response, you'll feel good about yourself and that's the real purpose.

And it's even a good bet that when defensive old Fred has time to calm down and realize what happened, he will feel differently about Mary.   Even if he's too defensive to admit he's wrong, he'll probably show her in some manner that he appreciated and respected her behavior, by doing something positive later that day. A man with courage would go to her later and apologize for his unreasonable attack and try to talk feelings more calmly.

One of you (both is better) needs to *model* to the other that you really do mean what you say about wanting true intimacy and communication.

If we can provide an atmosphere of safety, protection, acceptance, love, caring, concern, and good feedback, we'll have to give very little advice, solve few problems, take little responsibility for the results.

And . . . our spouses will see us as psychic geniuses who read minds (no one ever listened to or understood them before) and give us all the credit for solving their problems and bring them happiness.

A client in therapy once described a year of grief, woe, and distress for 30 minutes. The therapist's response: "You must have felt like the whole world was closing in, and out to get you."

His eyes widened and he almost recoiled, "How did you know that —I've never told anyone that—not even my wife."

"Because I put myself in your shoes and that's how *I* felt." This is what we call *intimacy* . . . when a person feels understood, cared about, important, no longer alone, loved (even accepted when I didn't deserve it) . . .

And . . .

feels like giving all the above to you.

There is a warmth and satisfaction of closeness that cannot be described or replaced.

XIX. New Age Qualities—
What Can We Expect?

Speaking to a group of marriage counselors in Southern California recently, Dr. William Glasser, the psychiatrist who wrote *Reality Therapy*, declared that marriage was a "survival institution" in an "identity society."

"As we move to an identity society (which began after World War II) marriage is not an answer. What is? I don't know."

Dr. Glasser defined the "identity society" as one in which a desire for a sense of identity is more important than the need for security. In the identity society, people are saying, "I want to be recognized in this world as a human being with potential. I want to do something with my life that makes sense to me and I want to be cared for."

The authors of *Open Marriage* tried to take marriage to the place of "personal freedom leading to personal growth and resulting in synergy or couple growth."

Since then, a plethora of magazine articles have appeared proclaiming the returning benefits of traditional marriage, as more people discover that "open sex" didn't work.

In one such article by Joan Barthel in *Ladies Home Journal* entitled "Old Fashioned Marriage is Back in Style," she admits "the O'Neils weren't referring only or even primarily to sexual freedom as the synonym for open marriage. Still the term is nearly always interpreted that way."

This admonition came near the end of the article that centered on tearing down the whole concept of Open Marriage and promoting traditional marriage because "open sex doesn't work."

This is a classic example of people using a value system to protect against an anxiety reaction. When the choice is between growth and security (or the illusion of security), most people will opt for security because of the anxiety involved in risk taking for growth.

In their book *Love and Addiction*, Peele and Brodsky argue that security is highly desirable and should be preferred over sexual and romantic satisfaction. "The divorce rate will level off as more people become aware of the basic psychological reason for marriage: to give a person a sense of belonging. Perhaps people will have to learn to measure marriage not in terms of what gives them the greatest pleasure, but in terms of what gives them the least pain... it may mean developing a higher tolerance for emotional pain and sexual frustration in order to gain the deeper satisfactions of loyalty and unequivical belonging."

They seem to be saying that the need to belong to someone and to be safe in that protective environment is primary over all other needs, particularly sexual needs. They make the further point that it was sexual attraction that brought all of us together, but this should be relinquished for a more spiritual love.

We are not prepared to agree that only sexual attraction brought every couple together. While people can enjoy sexuality without love, we cannot forget that a deep, spiritual love can heighten one's sexual awareness and desire. We would be suspicious of a spiritual love that did not include romantic passion for husband and wife.

For too long we have accepted the pious cultural concept that sensual passion or desire and spiritual love are mutually exclusive. Why should we have to choose between them, and if we do, who is to say which one takes priority for any one couple?

Even Dr. Glasser seemed very troubled and uncomfortable with this identity society (which after all is not new if it began after W. W. II.) and lamented the stress this puts on the "survival institution of marriage," which is apparently more concerned with security than growth. He expressed sorrow that divorce teaches children that marriage doesn't go on forever and told the marriage counselors they had an obligation to try to keep marriage together when children are involved.

So, as you can see, there are many conflicting viewpoints regarding marriage and its ultimate function and purpose in our lives.

What is possible to be achieved in marriage? What can two reasonably healthy people create out of their intimate relationship? Instead of looking fearfully at the risks, can we expectantly examine the possibilities?

Using Glasser's terms, it is exciting to believe in the concept of an identity society where people want to be recognized as human beings with potential and want to do something meaningful with their lives that makes sense to them.

If marriage is out of step with that goal because it is a "survival in-stituion," one can only say that the growth of marriage is 30 years behind the growth of individuals and there's a need to catch up in a hurry.

Survival is our most basic and primitive need. To the extent we have not grown beyond the need to simply survive, our growth has been truly stunted, and it is no wonder people are more readily giving up marriages that are out of sync with their basis life value system.

Marriages whose primary purpose is to help the individual survive in a lonely, cold, hostile and disappointing world, which function to shield people from the stark reality of their personal emptiness and lack of creativity, which provide an illusion of comfort and stability to help us "make it through the night," are marriages doomed to bore-dom and resentment, restrictive of the persons involved and bring-ing little or no fulfillment.

Society seems more concerned with the survival of marriage as an institution than the survival, and growth of the persons involved in marriage.

We do our children no favor by teaching them that marriage has to survive, even if it is at their own expense.

We need an identity marriage for an identity society, a marriage with growth potential that brings meaning to the lives of the partici-pants.

Qualities Of The New Age Relationship

With this in mind, let's look t the ultimate New Age couple and some of the ways they might relate to each other. Keep in mind these are not necessarily super-people, idealistic to the point of mysticism. The New Age Relationship is readily available to each of us. For most it will certainly require effort—a stretching, growing, risk-taking ad-vance that passes through corridors of fear and uncertainty, dis-appointment and failure—but an effort that refuses to be discouraged until the goal is accomplished.

This is a goal of comfortable expectancy, secure in what we have, looking forward to the mutual challenge of the future, basking in the pleasures of the past, a New Age Relationship based on the following personal qualities:

1. *A lack of defensiveness that allows each to perceive circum-stances as they really are; not "as I need them to be."*

Our individual perceptions must either complement each other or be seen by each in the same general context. People who approach life from very different frames of reference can both be "right" but totally miss the point of each other's reality. Even more common is when husband and wife each share what happened in their argument last night and the stories come out so differently from each other that it sounds like two different families.

    Jane: We got in a bitter dispute over who was going to do the dishes.

    Bob: (interrupting with obvious irritation) It was *before* the dinner and it was over your mother. The dishes never came up.

When we can't agree about simple facts, how can communication begin or issues be readily identified? This is not an uncommon experience and can only mean that one or both are so frightened of being blamed, wrong or bad, that they cannot look at any situation in search of truth. Instead they find ways of distorting the issues in order to protect self and make the other the culprit.

When one is not threatened by someone's judgment, it is possible to perceive others as they really are, and interpret their behavior as it was really intended.

A New Age couple consists of two people with good judgment who see things as they really are and don't play games. They have enough ego strength to protect their individual self worth, so that defensiveness between them is minimized.

Without this need to protect oneself from blame and accusation, both are free to perceive life situations with a minimum of distortion and a maximum of desire for understanding and truth. Problems between them are therefore more easily understood and resolved.

This kind of couple can tolerate uncertainty and ambiguity more easily than others do because of their own inner peace. They do not lead the rigid, structured life style that some people do as an armored protection against the uncertainty of not knowing. Not being constantly overwhelmed by anxiety regarding themselves or their relationship, they are not forced to press issues to premature conclusions or to make impulsive and inflammatory accusations.

Tolerating uncertainty and not always needing immediate gratifications gives them room for flexible searching and the patience to allow events to naturally unfold.

2. *Strong, positive feelings of self-love and acceptance, combined with a non-possessive love for others.*

Emotionally crippled people create emotionally crippled relationships. It takes two individuals who bring a sense of self-worth, love and pride to the relationship to make it special and enhancing.

Honesty with oneself about what is done and why it is done creates feelings of self-worth, leaving little need for guilt, shame or anxiety. One can freely give and receive this type of sharing and believe in the essential inner goodness of the individuals and the couple relationship itself.

This couple can separate individual and isolated behavior situations from the basic character of what each person *is*. "I may not always agree with or approve of what you *do* but I love, appreciate and believe in what you *are*."

Some people have difficulty with this concept of separating behavior from character, insisting that the behavior is *always* a direct reflection of the character. If one judges the behavior bad, the character must be bad as well. Two factors are involved here. Who is to judge the "goodness" or "badness" of the behavior? This often falls into controversial areas of value judgment and what person has the right to impose his or her value judgment over that of the spouse?

Areas of religious faith, war versus pacifism, sexual conduct, economic policies and habits such as drinking and smoking are just a few of the examples where value judgments may be violently opposed.

Since none of us is perfect nor should need to be or act in a perfect fashion, there must be room for imperfect or negative behavior without that person's character being permanently defamed by it. We can tell a lie without being a confirmed liar or commit a vindictive or hurtful act without being forevermore a vindictive and hurtful person. When one can believe in what the other party *is* and their essential goodness as a human being, their positive motivation to be appropriate, it is fairly easy to forgive, to be tolerant of and even understand behavior which disagrees with or seems in conflict with their character.

The structure of the relationship—open or closed, permissive or demanding, set roles or household sharing—does not determine its success or failure; but the key to succes is the ability of the two persons to choose, define and flexibly flow with a life-style that consistently reflects their values, encourages their growth and meets their needs.

This combination of self love and non-possessive love creates such an environment.

3. *An openness to the totality of human experience, both inner and outer, positive and negative.*

A New Age couple welcomes each day and experience with an expectation of OKness rather than a sense of dread or concern. They are not necessarily "high" or in a hyper state of ecstacy, that would be unreal on a continous basis, but with solid feelings of comfort and goodwill. "I can handle it, learn from it, flow with it, do whatever is appropriate. My backlog of responses is sufficient to the day and I'm glad to be alive, in a world I experience as generally friendly and reasonable. I will not be overwhelmed by the extremes of life, either positive or negative. Because I am reasonably in touch with my feelings, I can truly be spontaneous in life and feel certain my reactions will be appropriate and not just impulsive."

Having a spouse to share in this confidence and strength certainly provides an additional safe environment or increment of strength to add to this reassurance of sufficiency.

We might add that spontaneity differs from impulsiveness in that it is always appropriate to the reality of the moment. Impulsive behavior may or may not hit the target. If it does, it's pure coincidence. Spontaneity comes from being in touch with one's integrity—operating from the inner core of one's being. When this is true, perceptions are correct, feelings are appropriate, and behavior fits the occasion.

The spontaneous couple is one that provides a consistent spark of electricity that flows between them. Each one has the potential to "turn on the other one" and is consistently "turned on" by the wit, warmth, and individuality of the other. "Your love of life inspires me and makes me glad to be alive. You bring a sparkle to my eye and a spring to my feet." There is a constant energy flow that continually recharges each other as though they have found the secret to total and unending source of supply, a real perpetual motion.

At the same time, each has his own source of supply and is not totally dependent on the other. That's where the spontaneity comes in—an extra spark that motivates, but not great depression or anger if it is missing.

For these people, familiarity does not breed contempt but they can see value in and be inspired by the basic, everyday experiences of life.

Perhaps this explains why some marriages seem to breed boredom and discontent, while others are always new, exciting, and stimulating. People who primarily look to others to supply most of their excitement and reason for living are bored with themselves and are more often than not, boring people. So they must constantly search for change, diversion, or escape.

Those who primarily look to their own inner being for stimulation and excitement, who like to grow and learn from life, are exiting to be around. When two such people are married, they stimulate each other to new heights and do not tire of each other's company. Since they also have privacy and right of movement within the community, there is no claustrophobia or need to run away. They are busy, active people who keep a proper place for escape and nurturing the child within them, but not to excess.

4. *Problem-centered—rather than ego-centered.*

"The meat is tough" brings a reaction from the cook that causes one to wonder if it was cut from his or her own leg. "Your breath is bad" is not a comment on your character, but on what smells.

The ego-centered person cannot separate his ego from whatever the problem may be. He keeps feeling, "Why don't you like me." and responds with, "I am *too* a nice guy."

A teacher writes a test for her class and feels it is an excellent sampling of the material covered. Her class claims that the test is tricky, irrelevant and unfair. If the teacher is ego-centered, her reaction will be: "Why don't you like me? How can you hurt me like that? How can you call me a bad person and teacher (without socially redeeming features) when I work so hard for you and try so hard to be liked?" Those are her inner feelings, which will probably never be revealed to the class. What the class will probably hear is an angry, defensive, impassioned dissertation designed to prove that they have no right to feel that way, the test is a good one and they have poor judgment. Why the violent reaction to criticism of a simple test? Because the teacher cannot separate her ego from the test. She is on trial, her integrity, intelligence, character and self-worth and *that* is what she is defending.

A problem-centered person might feel disappointed or surprised at the class's reaction but would not tend to take it personally. "If I am a good person and a good teacher, I can afford to blow a test now and then without loss of personal worth." She would respond to the class by asking for clarification of their feelings and share her own personal views regarding a solution to "their mutual problem and concern." That would bring about a reasonable compromise for all involved. All of this has nothing to do with whether the class "likes" the teacher or the teacher "likes" the class members. They simply share a mutual problem to be solved.

Put that principle into a couple relationship and the emotions become even more intense as the stakes become higher and the egos more on the line. Mention that the food doesn't taste good or that the sex was not overly exciting last night or that there won't be enough money to pay the bills this month and your spouse may immediately jump to the conclusion that your comment is an indirect but vicious attempt at character assassination. They respond by fighting for their lives. Sometimes it *is* indirect character assassination and sometimes an innocent comment or mild complaint without critical intent. The ego-centered person will be offended regardless, the problem-centered person will not.

A problem-centered couple is one that can look at a situation regardless of how personal it may be, and say, "We have a problem to solve between us, let's go to work on it." No judgment, just looking at what is and how it affects us and why, and how we might modify the situation to affect us differently.

If you judge my behavior or approach as inappropriate to your needs or feelings, that does not necessarily determine that *I* have, therefore, been judged bad as well. The judgment ego response is so common it seems "natural," a part of our inborn nature, but to be defensive is undoubtedly *nurtural*, part of our cultural nurturing.

When a person really likes himself, he expects others to feel the same, so he is more objective about his work or behavior and others' acceptance or rejection of it. This is especially true in a relationship where there is abundant evidence of love and feelings of well-being for the other.

Remember, we are now talking about attitudes and motivations. One can appear to have a mission life and be a service to others for purely selfish reasons—to "buy love" or look like a generous person when he just wants to feed his ego or pocket book.

The problem-centered couple has their relationship in overdrive and it requires only minimal attention. At the beginning they may have concentred all their energy to solving problems between them, learning a new language, discovering new methods of pleasing each other and making the relationship a functioning one. Once learned, maintenance may require little effort.

Because this couple is not wasting energy being defensive or protecting themselves from the constant fear of attack they are often generously involved in solving problems "outside themselves"— community projects, charity events, public affairs.

A loving couple finds it necessary to share elements of this love in the same manner a loving person finds it necessary to have someone with whom to share his or her love.

5. *A need for physical and psychological space, as individuals, as a couple and as a family.*

These people not only do not mind solitude, but actually seek it. This detachment is expressed in their ability to be objective in their viewpoints about others. It is not that they do not like people, for they do. They also like themselves and do not mind being alone with themselves. What we are saying is that they really don't need people as a crutch but can enjoy them for what they are when together. Those who cannot stand to be by themselves and are constantly seeking out others to fill a void or a vacuum in their lives, can't really like or love people, because they need them too badly. If you need someone for a crutch, you don't really respect that person for *being* your crutch, and you feel hostile towards him because he reminds you of your own need dependency.

This couple need can be expressed in a variety of options. Each of the individuals has a need for and takes the opportunity to be alone with himself—to retreat for his own recharging process—without having to fight his spouse for it, or feel guilty for needing and taking this time; *and* can freely give it to the spouse. People who freely give and receive privacy, do not have a need to *withdraw* from the other as an escape from responsibility or confrontation.

Privacy should not be confused with withdrawal. The couple will often have a need for privacy as a couple—apart from family, children, friends, or outside commitments. This is a time to be alone with and totally experience each other. Another time may require an aloneness that includes the children—a family intimacy.

Privacy may call for time away from your spouse to explore other worlds or people as opposed to being alone by yourself. This is the area that frightened a lot of people in reading *Open Marriage*. "If my spouse is allowed time alone with others, it is *inevitable* this will lead to sexual involvement."

It stands to reason, many of us don't want most of our time away from the other or why would we want to be married? It is also clear that no one person can meet *all* the needs of another and that is too much to ask. Freedom to explore our world, to meet and enjoy others without the restriction of possessive jealousy is an important quality of growth. If self-actualizing people need and have this detachment, the actualized couple must have this freedom as well.

In most cases when a person expects sexual involvement to result from every friendship between the sexes he is really speaking for his own needs and feeling. "That's what *I* want or would be tempted to do in that situation, so everyone else does too."

Jealousy is not based on love, but fear. The irony is that the most possessive people generally enjoy a double standard that allows and excuses their own infidelity while condemning and controlling the spouse.

"Perhaps I'm not person enough, good looking enough, successful or loving enough to keep my spouse. And someone out there may meet my spouse's needs better than I can. So, I better keep a tight reign on my spouse so he or she will not have the opportunity of finding that person. It is better to keep a person by a destructive method than to lose them by a good method of relating and wind up being alone and rejected."

Is that really true? Is your survival as a person that tied to someone else? Keeping a spouse under lock and key brings feelings of claustrophobia and actually pushes them to try to escape.

Possessiveness of mate always leaves a lingering doubt of whether they remain out of love and loyalty or because you successfully maintained control.

Allowing space or freedom in a relationship does not mean you don't care what the other person does. Freedom is not an invitation to infidelity. But why does fidelity have to be demanded or controlled? Fidelity can only be a gift of love—whether it is emotional or physical. It cannot be demanded or controlled.

This issue here has nothing to do with sex outside marriage. That subject will not be covered in this book. What we are talking about is freedom for each spouse to explore his world without restriction by the other. "If your behavior frightens, confuses or upsets me, I want the right to share that with you and resolve it with mutual concern for each other's feelings. As a result, you may choose to modify your behavior or I might better understand, but I do not wish to control your freedom to be you."

The best protection against breaking a trust is the trust itself. We would like to share with you what that trust means to us.

A couple's creed of trust.

"I trust you. I trust what you are. I trust your good judgment. I trust your love for me. I trust you would not deliberately hurt me. I trust if a mistake is made, we can work it out between us.

"I trust me. I trust that I can live through any grief or disappointment that occurs. I trust in my own ability to survive.

"I trust us. I believe in what we have and give to each other as individuals and as a couple. I trust that we are real with each other and each is bringing to the relationship his most authentic self.

"Since I can trust, it is the very best of myself, the most genuine aspects of myself that I share. If that is not enough for you, I must accept that, even though the disappointment will be great. I can only give what I am. You can only give what you are. I believe that will be enough."

6. *I AMNESS—a sense of personal authority and independence that transcends the relationship and the mutual environment.*

We're not talking about defensive rebellion or selfish commital, "but what's really *best* for me, for my integrity, is really best for the important others in my environment." These are self-starting, self-sufficient, and creative people.

Many times when the issue of ultimate authority is raised, we hear the question "What if *both* feel 'this is best for me' and have opposite viewpoints? Doesn't there have to be an ultimate decision? Who will make it?"

Our society has always given that legal right to the men. A couple lived in California and he's offered a job opportunity in New York that he cannot pass up, so he takes the job. The wife says she won't leave California and refuses to go with him. In the past, he could sue for divorce on the grounds of abandonment and she might not get much in the settlement because it was "her fault." A wife was required to follow her husband. With the new California divorce laws, either one can file for "irreconcilable differences" and since there is "no fault," property settlement is not affected.

Does a husband really have the right to *impose* his will on the wife? Does the wife really have the right to impose her will on the husband? The situation described above is being more and more reversed. Wives are getting opportunities for jobs that call for moving to a new community, pulling up roots, and forcing the husband to find a new position. Why not?

If it is that important to the one who wants to move, it is difficult to imagine a loving spouse standing in the way of the move, even though there would be inconveniences. But, and this is a *big but*, if both decided this was an *integrity* decision (one to go and one to stay) and could not compromise it, then each would be obligated to his own integrity. A spouse cannot ask another spouse to go against his/her own integrity, even if the law gives them that right.

We feel this is a rare occurrence. Most situations can be compromised and whoever feels strongest about his particular opportunity or desire will generally win, which is fine if they are equally matched —not so fine if one is overwhelmingly dominant.

Loving individuals are looking for ways and means to meet both their needs and are equally interested in both needs being met, so they work hard to understand each other and not let this impasse happen to them. People who want "masculine rule" seem to feel this is one of their strongest issues—someone has to break the tie vote. When either the man or woman takes that role of "ultimate authority," the integrity of the other is violated (providing both are standing on integrity at this point). If their integrity needs are that incompatible, perhaps the marriage should not survive. People come before marriage. This is more theory than concern because the issue of integrity conflict is rare, especially between those who truly love and understand each other. For those who don't, the difference might be a test of power or contest for authority, somewhat of a "king of the mountain" game, and that's manipulation, not integrity.

For something to be truly "best for me" we must consider the feelings and needs of the important others in our life to come to that conclusion. They won't always agree and it is our responsibility to be true to ourself and not lie to ourself if we want to claim that decision. If we're kidding ourself, all involved lose.

As for the New Age couple's relationship to their world, they get along with their culture but are somewhat detached from it. They do not allow themselves to be "squeezed into a mold." They are not particularly rebellious nor do they agree completely with the culture.

Each can tolerate differences of feelings, needs, and ways of expression or life style in both their spouse and the world outside and enjoy finding ways to encompass the differences without a great deal of stress or discomfort. Where we agree and share, this is no problem. Where there are differences, we find a way. What we achieve as individuals heightens tremendously in the couple unity.

7. *A generous and affectionate concern for humanity.*

Even though they are aware of, and troubled by, the many shortcomings of humanity, including their own, the New Age couple is happy to be part of the human race and happy to be involved in this race.

It is precisely because of this point that couples can be open, tolerant, non-judgmental, and forgiving of each other; rather than gossipy, suspicious, and accusing. They can be aware of negative reality, without being carried away by it.

Some people try to handle this with a "power of positive thinking" approach. "Let's try to pretend that the negative does not exist or didn't happen." That is an escape from reality that doesn't work. You don't have to deny or distort reality to avoid negative consequences. Seeing things as they really are makes it easier to relate to them with an appropriate response.

Since these folks can tolerate their own imperfections, they find it fairly easy to tolerate those of their spouse. They are free to point them out and discuss them, but generally without rancor or defensiveness.

8. *A deep capacity and need for intimacy at many levels.*

Intimacy can be defined as the act of revealing and sharing private aspects of oneself which are not generally on display to most people. Intimacy also provides an atmosphere of warmth, safety, and caring wherein another person experiences the desire to do the same with you. Many people are good at one without the unifying balance of the other, causing a distortion of the relationship. How sad it is to be able to provide a safe environment where others are free to be themselves with you, but where you are not free to share yourself with them.

Intimacy is not only revealing facts or secrets but having an attitude of closeness that is often difficult to define. It comes in varying shades of depth and openness, depending on the current circumstances and the persons involved. There is everything from the casual intimacy of getting to know a new friend to the deepest sharing of lovers.

Some people go through life and have rarely or never experienced this on any level. Others seem frightened by it and deny the necessity for closeness. They seem to fear the vulnerability involved that leaves one open to pain, disappointment, loss, humiliation or exposure. It is safe to say the more one likes himself, the easier and more desirous it is to *share* that self. The less one likes himself, the more he feels the need to hide this negative information from the world.

The relations of a New Age couple are deep and profound but with a few, rather than many other people. The couple probably has many acquaintances and social contacts but their deep and profound relationships are restricted to a few. They are able to take other individuals and couples into their intimacy and sharing, thereby extending their "family circle" and increasing the love power involved. This brings nourishment, support, and involvement into the couple relationship from outside and strengthens the bond between them.

The number one relationship would, of course, be with each other. These people are experienced at achieving a depth of intimacy and bring this to the marriage. This takes an ability to be open to sharing of oneself at an important level.

Any hostility they have is situational and not chronic. They will respond with anger when anger is appropriate to a particular situation and time and are not the kind of people who carry "chips on their shoulders" looking for an excuse to blow their tops or inappropriately over-react.

Because their anger is situational and not chronic, they don't tend to "gunnysack" grievances and carry silent resentments that drain off love and closeness. Each can understand and handle the other's anger because it is directed at the situation and is appropriate to the moment. There is less need to feel attacked or to take things personally.

This is where an intrapersonal relationship within ourself is so valuable, as we mentioned in previous chapters; the need to understand the various subpersonalities within our nature. The integration and harmony within must evidence itself in the outer experience. Our inner growth and the quality of friends we find ourselves relating to are reflective of each other.

9. *Dominant people, without a need to dominate or compete with others.*

We have previously defined a dominant person as one who takes complete responsibility for his own life; a "take charge" individual who sees what needs to be done and does it: independent, strong, capable and assured. This has no connection with a need to dominate or control others, which is generally associated with insecurity, jealousy, fear and lack of self esteem. Both persons may appear strong and be successful but their inner selves are worlds apart.

When two healthily dominant people join forces, they make quite a team.

They can respect people, learn from them and relate to them regardless of race, creed, culture, position, etc.

This kind of person (or couple) does not feel a need to prove himself superior, compete to make a point, or put someone down in order to feel his own sense of authority. In a couple relationship, this is extremely important. Each is not only comfortable with his own sense of authority, competence, and accomplishment, but is also highly aware of and proud of those of the spouse.

There is no struggle to be boss, no hassling for position, no fear of being put down or discounted. Rather than jealousy for one spouse's success, there is a deep feeling of pride that includes both as part of that success.

In a couple therapy situation, the wife was proudly stating she had changed and matured over the past three years. Her husband sarcastically pointed out that he felt some part in that and would like a little credit but didn't expect to get any. She very quickly blurted out that he got none of the credit, "it was all my doing."

When asked why, she replied, "If I give him any credit, that would leave me worthless."

What a tragedy! She could not conceive of giving him any credit without "going in the hole" herself. Not only would it *take away* from her credit, but worse yet, leave her with no credit at all . . . worthless. Ironic in one who was proud of how much she had changed and matured.

On another occasion, where the husband worked and the wife reared five children during a 20-year marriage, the husband admitted the major reason he did not get a divorce was that he did not want to share his community property with his wife. It was *his* job, *his* success, *his* money, investments, etc. She did nothing to earn it and had nothing to do with his success, and he resented sharing one dime of it with her, regardless of the law. How sad.

Where both partners have sufficient ego strength and feelings of self worth, they can share in the whole spectrum of each other's growth and success, both being fortified and neither being deprived. A person who cannot learn from anyone, give another credit for accomplishment, or who even feels threatened or put down by the success of others, is truly a deprived person.

As a deprived person, he feels so empty inside that most of his energy goes to trying to fill that bottonless pit of emptiness.

10. *A highly tuned sense of priorites.*

For many people, "the end justifies the means" but not for the New Age couple. It is more important to them "how they live" (their character values) than whether or not they attain their goals, even though their goals are very important to them. They also seem to enjoy the means to an end more than the average person.

This is one of the areas that keeps the marriage stimulating, exciting, and growing. It fights boredom and stimulates response. Not only are they learning from yesterday and building for tomorrow, but they are especially enjoying the wonders of today.

"Here and now" living incorporates all these values. Some folks live in the past and never see the fresh opportunities of today. They either glory in the past accomplishments because they now feel past their ability to produce, or use the "bad luck" of the past to excuse the failures of the present.

Others tend to build for tomorrow—saving, hoarding, looking forward to that someday when they will "arrive" at security or fun or whatever. But tomorrow never comes. It is always today, and a future that doesn't include today isn't much of a future.

The self-actualizing couple enjoys the planning and preparation for tomorrow, enjoys the event planned for when they are experiencing it, and comes home with a suitcase of happy memories when they return.

Many people set goals of success such as "President of my own corporation," "a million dollars net worth," "lead singer in a band," "married and parent of a child." They say, "Then I'll be happy," only to discover that the outside accomplishment didn't bring the happiness they expected, and they had to set a new and higher goal.

Actualizing people set goals to provide stimulation and structure in their lives and are pleased and proud to accomplish these goals. They feel satisfaction in their achievements and living up to value standards. However, their happiness comes from *within*. They enjoy living and even if they miss their goals or change them in mid-stream, the fun was in trying, in doing one's best, in purposeful and meaningful living, rather than keeping score. They tend to live in the here and now.

11. *A warmly compassionate sense of humor.*

Their humor tends to be philosophical and non-hostile, much in the manner of a Bill Cosby or Flip Wilson. It's laughing at the human condition without putting anyone down. The opposite of this, of course, is humor at someone's expense and humiliation.

Comedians who specialize in hostile put downs have their role in making us laugh, sometimes out of embarrassment or shock, but have probably found an indirect method of releasing their own chronic anger or resentment, without having to face it directly, and are being well paid in the process.

There is no better saving grace in marriage than humor. Those who can poke warm, loving fun at themselves and their partners can save many a bad situation from becoming explosive.

Sarcastic humor that humiliates one's spouse in front of others will eventually destroy love and the marriage.

Couples without a warm sense of humor take themselves, life, and situations too seriously and tend to get hurt feelings more easily. The ability to see humor in unusual or unexpected situations, such as spilling coffee in a restaurant or cigarette ashes burning through a new suit of clothes, can ease tension, relax others and soften disappointment. The alternative to this is often anger and finding someone to blame. When you don't have to be perfect and you can feel warm, humorous feelings of affection for your own faults and failings, you can more readily accept responsibility (rather than blame) and not over-exaggerate the consequences.

12. *Positive, creative energy flow.*

All of us seem to have a certain amount of creativy that varies in degree. Creative people do not waste their energy potential defending or explaining or being anxious, and so this energy is free to be used for creative activity. For most of us, then, the healthier we are, the more creative we can be; and the more tense and bogged down with problems, the more our creative energy is drained off.

It is easy to see how this principle can be applied to couples. Creative people have creative marriages. They are not boring people but are busily pursuing life and sharing that excitement and energy flow with each other. When things go wrong, they are busy seeking solutions rather than defending against accusations or doing jury duty to determine the degree of guilt and term of sentence.

They have a lot of positive energy to invest in life and each other, and each tends to supply or supplement the other rather than being depressing or draining. It is very difficult to live with persons who experience constant energy leaks of depression, guilt, shame, anxiety, and defensiveness. On the other hand, a positive creative energy flow can be exhilarating and expansive to both partners.

This is what the self-actualizing, self-sufficient, and satisfied New Age couple would be like. Again, we emphasize these are not super-people or perfect ones by any means. You will notice we said little about roles but tried to emphasize feelings and attitudes.

If roles or ways of relating are chosen by the individuals and are comfortable within the couple framework, it doesn't matter if they are traditional or contemporary. If they are imposed by "shoulds, guilts, outside pressure or cultural expectancies" then, unnatural stress is placed on the relationship, and the individual and couple needs of the persons involved are not being listened to or met.

New Age Precepts

In summary,

Each person is of equal importance in and to the relationship.

Each trusts in the essential goodness of the other and so looks for no insidious desire to inflict pain.

Each is a person of deep integrity and expects the same of the spouse.

Each takes responsibility for his own success and happiness as a human being and expects the same of his spouse.

Each is committed to the relationship and to creatively helping it to grow.

Each is committed to providing an environment of safety and support within which both can grow.

Each is committed to genuiness and authenticity with each other.

These are not empty words or foolish promises. They do not seek to control an unforseeable future. They are not looking for loopholes and escape clauses. These are the meaningful commitments of reasonable people.

"I'll love you forever or till death do us part" is not ours to commit. We cannot predict the circumstances of tomorrow or control the consequences of today.

We *can* commit to give the best that we have.

When two growing, actualizing people find each other and share each other in the ways described *it will be enough.*

Did you test your marriage against the above points? How did you do?

Throughout this book we have maintained that you cannot separate individual well-being from marital success, that marital growth is based on personal growth, that problems reflected in a relationship are those found within each individual, that love for others is based on love of self, that the healthier the individuals, the healthier the marriage. This is the struggle to be me with you, what *A Fresh Start for a New Age Relationship* is all about.

XX. A Final Word

Life can readily be defined as a series of relationships. It is important to all of us that these relationships be productive and meaningful—that we love and be loved—like and be liked—respect and be respected. So often we are taught that this entails being "nice;" being sensitive to the desires of others so we can "please" them; and we try to become skilled manipulators so others will think well of us. To this end we become more concerned with how we "ought to feel" and what we "should do." We weigh the "rightness" and "wrongness" of our own personal feelings and needs in the light of the expectations of others.

For us the basis for all productive and meaningful relationships is honesty and love. But before one can be honest in his relationship with others, he must be honest with himself. Before he can love others, he must first properly love himself so that he is a person with love to give. Before he can respect others, he must respect himself.

Possibly the most difficult chore for many of us is simply knowing what we really feel and why. We get so caught up with the rightness or wrongness of our feelings—personal guilt—and how we should feel, that we don't really know what we do feel.

Our emphasis has been less concerned with the goodness or badness of our feelings than with simply exploring and examing how we do feel. As we discover what we really feel and learn to live on a conscious level of feelings and needs, we discover why we feel as we do about ourselves, our parents, friends, and acquaintances. Knowing why helps us to understand and accept our feelings as legitimate and rational. This in turn gives us complete freedom of choice in acting on our feelings. We are free to be angry or not—to be sad or happy—to withdraw or communicate—to overlook or confront. Until we know and understand our feelings and needs, we cannot be free in choosing our relationships but are shaped by circumstances and entrapped by unconscious motivations over which we have little or no control.

Self-awareness then leads to self-acceptance and unconditional self-love. (I love myself and believe I have self-worth and value because I exist and need no other reason.) Once we can be comfortable with ourselves, we have a real freedom and little or no guilt because we no longer have to be dishonest with ourselves and others.

This in turn makes it easier to see and understand the real needs and feelings of others—to know what they "really mean" underneath the fear or hostility. Living on a level of self-awareness we can relate to people on the basis of their needs and feelings, honestly giving them our interest, care and concern.

Self-awareness then becomes the key to living by one's own integrity, doing what is constructive and best. This, in turn, should also be best and most constructive for the important "others" in one's relationships.

By knowing and understanding our own feelings and needs we honestly relate to the feelings and needs of others. The productive and meaningful relationships we achieve give meaning to life itself. We hope this book will help in making relationships, and lives, more meaningful.

Life Is For Living

Life is for living
for stretching and growing,
an adventure in time and space.

Life is for living, producing
and learning
with each breath of sunshine too precious
to waste.

Life is for loving
romancing and courtship
with wonder and awe to unfold

Life is for loving
through struggles and hardships
learning and growing
to have and to hold.

Life is for caring
and intimate sharing
revealing the difficult fears;

Life is for caring
through seeing and knowing
and laughing through passionate tears.

Life is for living and loving and caring
and you are the one who
must share

Life is for living and loving and caring
. . . make it a must
for this year.

—CDL

References

Quotations from some of the following works with the permission of the authors are gratefully acknowledged:

Assagioli, Roberto. "A higher view of the man-woman problem," by Roberto Assagioli and Claude Servan-Schreiber in *Synthesis* 1, pp. 116-123.
———.*The act of will.* Viking Press, 1973; Pengquin, 1974.
——— .*Psychosynthesis.* Penguin, 1976.
Bach, George R. and Wyden, Peter. *Intimate enemy: how to fight fair in love and marriage.* Morrow, 1969.
———. and Deutsch, Ronald M. *Pairing.* Avon, 1975.
Berne, Eric. *Transactional analysis in psychotherapy.* Grove Press, 1961.
Biddle, Earl. *Integration of religion and psychiatry.* Collier Books, 1962.
Campbell, Joseph. *Myths to live by.* Viking Press, 1972; Bantam, 1973.
Cooley, Charles H. *Social organization: a study of the larger mind.* Norwood, 1916; Schocken, 1962.
Desoille, Robert. *The directed daydream* (translated by F. Haronion, Ph.D.). Psychosynthesis Research F(undation, 1966.
Ellis, Albert. *Humanistic psychotherapy: the rational-emotive approach.* Julian Press, 1973; McGraw-Hill, 1974.
Erickson, Erik H. *Childhood and society.* Rev. ed. Norton, 1964.
Faraday, Ann. *Dream power.* Berkley Medallion Books, 1973.
Fromm, Erich. *The forgotten language.* Holt, Rinehart & Winston, 1951, 1970.
———.*The art of loving.* Harper, Row 1956, 1974.
Ginott, H. G. *Between parent and child.* Macmillan, 1965.
Glasser, William. *Reality therapy.* Harper, Row, 1965.
Greenwald, Harold. *Direct decision therapy.* Knapp, 1973.
Harlow, Harry F. "The heterosexual affectional system in monkeys," *American Psychologist.* 17: 1-9. 51.
Harris, Thomas A. *I'm ok—you're ok.* Harper, Row, 1967.
Holmes, T. H. and Rahe, R. H. "The social adjustment rating scale." *Research,* 1967.
Jung, Carl G. *Man and his symbols.* Dell, 1968.
Jung, Emma. *Animus and anima.* Spring Publications, 1969.
Katchadourian, Herant. *Human sexuality, sense and nonsense.* W. H. Freeman, 1974.
Kempler, Walter. *Principles of Gestalt family therapy.* Kempler Institute.
Maslow, Abraham. *Toward a psychology of being.* 2nd ed. Van Nostrand, Reinhold, 1968.
Masters, W. H. and Johnson, V. E. *Human sexual response.* Little, Brown, 1966.
May, Rollo. *Love and will.* Norton, 1969; Dell, 1973, 1974.
———.*Man's search for himself.* Norton, 1953; Dell, 1973.
Mead, Margaret. *Blackberry winter: my earlier years.* Morrow, 1972.
Missildine, Hugh W. *Your inner child of the past.* Simon and Schuster, 1963.
Morgan, Marabel. *The total woman.* Revell, 1973.
O'Neill, Nena. *Open marriage, a new life style for couples.* M. Evans, 1972; Avon, 1973.
Peele, Stanton and Brodsky, Archie. *Love and addiction.* Taplinger, 1975.
Perls, Fritz. *The Gestalt approach eye witness to therapy.* Science and Behavior Books, 1973.
———., Hefferline, R. and Goodman, P. *Gestalt therapy.* Dell, 1951.
Rogers, Carl. *Client-centered therapy.* Houghton Mifflin, 1951.
Sartre, Jean-Paul. *Being and nothingness.* Washington Square Press, 1943.
Shostrum, Everett. *Man the manipulator.* Bantam, 1968.
Singer, Jerome L. *Imagery and daydream methods in psychotherapy and behavior modification.* Academic Press, 1974.
Skinner, B. F. *Science and human behavior.* Macmillan, 1953.
Sullivan, H.S. *The interpersonal theory of psychiatry.* Norton, 1953.
Vargui, James G. "Subpersonalities," "Reprinted with permission from Synthesis 1, *The Realization of the Self,* © 1974, 1977, by the Psychosynthesis Institute of the Synthesis Graduate School for the Study of Man, 3352 Sacramento St., San Francisco, CA 94118."